MIKE ARNOLD, DAVID GARDNER

FINISHING MACHINE

ROAD RAGE MURDER OR SELF-DEFENSE?
A TRAINED KILLER'S FIGHT FOR JUSTICE

Versus
Publishing

Eugene, Ore.

Published by
Versus Publishing
401 East 10th Ave, Suite 400, Eugene, Oregon 97401
Phone: (541) 525-9117
www.facebook.com/versuspublishing
twitter.com/versusbooks
www.versuspublishing.com

Title: Finishing Machine: Was it Road Rage Murder or Self-Defense? A Trained Killer's Fight for Justice

Authors: Mike Arnold and Emilia Gardner

Cover/Book Design and Production by Damonza.com
Editing by Ellen Wojahn

First Edition, 2017
Paperback book ISBN: 978-0-9978484-9-6

Disclaimer: This book is a work of creative nonfiction, which Lee Gutkind, the godfather of the genre, defines as "nonfiction that employs techniques like scene, dialogue, description, while allowing personal point of view and voice (reflection) rather than maintaining the sham of objectivity." The authors do not claim to be objective, and whenever we determined it was necessary, we have changed names, details, and determining characteristics of people.

This book is intended for enjoyment purposes only. The authors of this book are licensed to practice law in Oregon. Nothing in this book makes the reader a client of the authors or of the authors' law firm and this book is not intended as legal advice. If the reader has questions of a legal nature or needs legal advice, the reader should contact and consult with a licensed attorney in the appropriate jurisdiction. If the reader believes he or she is a client of the authors just by reading this book, the reader should contact and consult with a licensed psychological professional.

To Gerald Strebendt. While we went about the business of living our normal lives, Gerald went about the business of surviving the hours, minutes, and seconds of a life interrupted. Watching him handle himself with grace and dignity in the face of hardship cannot help but inspire us. Gerald, we are so glad that you chose us to represent you. We are proud of you, and we can't wait for you to come home.

There are two things I can't stand: liars and bullies. If our government is doing both, we will scorch that bully with the cleansing power of sunlight and truth.

— MIKE ARNOLD

CONTENTS

ABOUT THE AUTHORS

(Photo: Summer 2008; Husum Falls, White Salmon River, Husum, Wash. Mike guiding Emilia off a waterfall three weeks before Emilia's first day at Arnold Law. Their first and only real waterfall together but the first of many metaphorical plunges. Photo credit: Andrew Coit.)

Mike Arnold is a trial attorney in Eugene, Oregon. He grew up in Parkville, Missouri, and moved to Oregon to attend law school. He tells stories for a living, delivering a narrative through facts and evidence to juries around the state. Often, these courtroom stories end with a **jury's two-word verdict**. Mike also enjoys telling stories to his daughter. These tend to be more complicated tales that reveal, to Abigail's dismay, that someone in the family is actually an alien or a robot.

Mike gained notoriety as an attorney when he stood on the courthouse steps as **Ammon Bundy's attorney** and told the remaining occupiers of the

Malheur Wildlife Refuge to «please stand down.» In the aftermath of the standoff he was credited with assisting in the negotiation of a **peaceful resolution** for the four remaining holdouts of the Oregon occupation.

Another of Mike's murder cases was featured on a **CBS "48 Hours" episode** entitled «Trail of Tears.»

Mike is also the host of a legal podcast called "Law Is War with Mike Arnold," which includes episodes with analysis of the Ammon Bundy (Oregon Standoff) verdict, murder of Nancy Cooper, trial objections, jury selection, jury nullification, etc.

Ep. 6: Was He Framed For Murder?
The True Crime Story of Nancy Cooper

Emilia Gardner is an Oregon attorney. Reading was her first love, and there were no bounds to what genre of book she could and would curl up with and enjoy. A love of writing soon followed, but it would never take the place of consuming the words on the page written by others. Emilia is a straightforward woman and attorney, and her communication style is evident in her writing: simple, to the point, and effective.

OTHER BOOKS BY THE AUTHORS:

ACKNOWLEDGMENTS

THIS BOOK WOULD not have been possible without the patience and support of our families and office colleagues. In particular, we offer a special and heartfelt thank you to Mike's wife and law partner Jacy Arnold, who supported us unflaggingly, despite us having come off of a marathon sprint of cases that culminated in 2016 with the Ammon Bundy case.

Words alone cannot express our thanks to our editor Ellen Wojahn who helped us take a series of ideas and stories and make them into something more. Her professionalism and advice were vital for our first full-length book.

Thank you to our legal assistant Meagan Greely who worked tirelessly on Gerald's case with us, often the silent partner in the background. Thank you to Lissa Casey, our colleague at Arnold Law, for her creativity and advice throughout our representation of this client. Thank you to Ashleigh Dougill for her late night pro-bono edits and comments in the early stages of drafting.

Thank you to Joanna Martinez from the Crofut family for speaking to us about her father and this case. We reached out to many of the key characters of this book for comment, including the family of the decedent, judges, district attorney, and detectives. Only Joanna chose to comment.

Finally, thank you to all of the experts and investigators named and unnamed in this book. If there is such thing as a justice system, it is because you all are part of it.

PUBLISHER'S NOTE

Thank you for your interest in Gerald "The Finishing Machine" Strebendt and his attorneys' story. **Please email comments, typos, and errors to:**

books@versuspublishing.com.

PREDATOR OR PREY?

T he evening was cool and a haze hung low over a dark, rural road where only a truck's headlights provided illumination. It was January in Springfield, Oregon, so a low fog was not unexpected. But as the evening deepened, the clouds suddenly gave way to a brief, un-fore-casted downpour.

One man, trained as a Marine sniper, found himself standing alone. Moments before, he and another man – a stranger – had been in a confrontation. Then came the rain. And now there was only a lingering mist, back-lit by the headlights.

He had been trained by the military for exactly this: a coolly evaluated threat, followed by a split-second decision to take action. But he wasn't on the gun range, not tonight. He hadn't calculated his move through the lens of a scope, and he hadn't picked off his target from a safe and detached distance. There were no instructions from afar. This was different. It was up close and personal. The cloudburst had not been rain, and the mist was not made up of water. It was bits of blood, brain, skin and skull.

The shooter lowered his gun, and raised his cell phone to his ear. He needed an ambulance. A man lay shattered on the pavement, his life ebbing away as cars continued to flow past the scene. All around, an audience of dark homes, fences and trees stood as silent witnesses to what had occurred.

A woman, having left the safety of her vehicle to investigate the sounds she had heard, screamed at the sight of the long black gun and the violence it had wrought.

Was there any doubt who was the predator, and who was the prey?

(Photo: Dramatization of the final moments.)

A POTENTIAL CASE?

I was at home on my small farm outside Creswell, Oregon, on the night of the shooting. Having put my four-year-old daughter to sleep by reading Dr. Seuss' "The Pale Green Pants" a couple of times front to back, I had returned to the living room to relax. The house was quiet, the lights dimmed. The wood stove was stoked with Douglas fir rounds that I had bucked from a fallen tree from the wooded part of our property the previous year. While enjoying the warmth of the fire, I alternated between reading a case file and online news stories. I noticed a story of gun violence pop up online. Curious, I began reviewing the sparse but gripping details on the small screen of my iPhone.

My name is Mike Arnold and I am a criminal defense attorney who specializes in complex cases. I am the managing partner of an eight-attorney firm located in Eugene, Oregon, almost two hours south of Portland... and just across the Willamette River from Springfield, where the shooting I was reading about had occurred.

The criminal defense section of my firm was built on the bread and butter of low-level crime, cases involving domestic violence, driving under the influence, sexual assault, etc. I had consulted on several murder cases, but never defended one on my own. This largely owed to the fact that violent crime isn't that common in this part of the Willamette Valley. Any gun crime that occurs catches people's attention in a big way, and that is especially true for members of the local bar. Defense attorneys like me know that we'll receive an inquiry call on at least half of the cases that our community considers "high profile." That's why I pay close attention to crimes when they are reported. It helps me be ready when someone in trouble (or the family member) makes that initial phone call.

On their websites, the local newspaper and all three television stations provided breaking details of the Springfield shooting: there had been a motor-vehicle collision, the parties had argued, an assault rifle had been brandished, and an unnamed man was shot dead. Road rage, police speculated.

Road rage by whom?

While most people confronted with these preliminary details would assume that the shooter was the hothead, it was instinctive for me to consider the opposite possibility, that the decedent himself was the bad actor. That's just how defense attorneys are; we tend to take a 360-degree view of every set of facts we encounter. We know from experience that things are not always as they seem.

After refreshing the screen a few times and checking some other news outlets for the additional details I was hungry for, I found myself going into criminal defense mode. In my head I worked through the various scenarios by which a roadside shooting could be considered legally justifiable, mentally plotting out how I would handle each one in a pleading or a courtroom argument. Thinking three steps ahead – or 30 – is an occupational hazard in my business. But I knew that most of my speculation would be fruitless until more was known about the incident. For the man with the gun, the facts, when established, would make the difference between a self-defense-based exoneration on all charges, or life in prison on a murder conviction.

Toggling between the online briefs, I found myself wondering how badly the vehicles had been damaged, because it would tell me something about the speed of the vehicles at impact. But the photos and videos that had been posted were too dark to tell me anything, and it frustrated me. Don't news photographers and TV cameramen carry spotlights?

More questions popped to mind. How far was the decedent from the crash when he was shot? Did the shooter fire from inside his vehicle, or from the road? I noticed that one TV reporter had captured footage showing a small canopy erected over what was presumably the dead man's body.

C'mon, somebody give me an estimate of distance! Report on something other than what the police tell you!

My curiosity, you should know, was not entirely professional. As a concealed firearm carrier, I am always interested in the circumstances of shooting deaths. I try to put myself in the shoes of both sides like a jury does, trying to figure out what happened and how it could have ended differently. I want to understand the details so I can learn from them, and not just as an attorney. I don't want to be the victim of a shooting, and I don't want to shoot anything other than blacktail deer and other four-legged prey. The two-legged type? Only in the pixelated video games of my youth.

Courtesy of a subsequent news update, I learned that the shooter was claiming self-defense and had been released after questioning. Police said that charges, if any, would be lodged after an investigation was complete.

This didn't surprise me. That's how these cases usually go at the beginning. But now the story had me completely hooked.

This was a case I could personally relate to and feel morally confident in defending. My work as an attorney had made me an ardent believer in, and strong advocate of, the Second Amendment to the Constitution. As an American citizen, I have the right to bear arms, and a right to use them to defend myself and my family. As the holder of a concealed carry permit, I often have a handgun tucked under my shirt or suit jacket. I don't enjoy carrying a firearm; in fact, I'm more comfortable leaving it at home. But I see my gun as a necessary tool for the job of living. I'd rather have it and not need it, than need it and not have it.

To me, a gun is not much different than an ax or a pen knife or anything else I use to complete my work around the farm. But there is an important distinction. If I forget to carry a knife to break open the hay bales to feed the livestock, I might have to walk back to the shop to retrieve it (or I might use the ax, if it's nearby, to break the bailing twine). But delay and improvisation are all but impossible when you're in a situation that requires a firearm. What are you going to do, say "Just a minute, I'll be right back," and turn your back on the threat to go get a gun? Of course not. To me, carrying a firearm is like carrying insurance. Maybe you'll never use it, but it's there just in case. As the saying goes, "I carry a gun because a cop is too heavy."

One of the reasons I carry a weapon owes to the particulars of our law practice. My wife and law partner, Jacy, is an excellent divorce lawyer who specializes in complex, high-asset (read: high-stress) cases. Violent behavior and threats go with the territory. I keep a shotgun in the office "just in case." I also carry on my person, and my attorneys and staff are authorized to do the same. Each of us has taken time to plan how to respond and escape in the event of an active-shooter scenario.

Thankfully, I have only had to "use" my firearm twice, and the situations were remarkably similar. On both occasions, domestic-violence victims who were getting restraining orders with the help of our law firm were tailed by their abusers to their appointments with us. Both times the guys aggressively entered the office and angrily demanded to see their wives, terrifying my receptionist. Both times these abusers failed to take no for an answer and threatened to search the office for "their" women. When I appeared and politely asked these men to leave, both times I saw their eyes stray to the Glock 21 visible on my right hip. I don't know if their true intent was violent or if they just wanted to scare our clients (who were well within earshot of both confrontations and were indeed frightened). But I do know that the men quickly apologized for any inconvenience and left. Maybe it was the sight of me, a 220-pound, 6-foot-plus guy…or maybe it was the silent presence of a device made by Gaston Glock.

It shouldn't be surprising then, that I believe the right to bear firearms goes hand in hand with a person's natural right to self-defense. If the shooting I was now learning about online was going to hinge on whether the shooter felt his life was threatened, then I fairly salivated to be part of his defense. The right to use lethal force in response to a threat is a very complicated legal concept, one that offers lawyers plenty of room to plan, argue and maneuver.

The right to self-defense isn't found in the U.S. Constitution. It's an innate right that is a creature of statute, so it varies from state to state. In Oregon, people have the right to use the degree of force they reasonably believe is necessary to stop or prevent the imminent unlawful force of another. When talking to jurors or clients about the right to use force in self-defense, I'm often asked how someone can know when a shot or punch is justified. My answer: If you have time to consider what the police or jury would think if you pulled the trigger or threw the punch, then the threat probably isn't imminent and there's time to remove yourself from the situation. But if you are too preoccupied with surviving the next few seconds to consider the consequences of your actions, that's a different story. You may be found to be legally authorized to defend yourself. That is, unless you're the unfortunate "unreasonable" person who "overreacted" in the eyes of a jury. But it's better to be judged by 12 than carried by six, they say, and that's another phrase I appreciate.

Eventually one of the media sources I was following identified the shooter as 34-year-old Gerald Strebendt, the owner of Northwest Training Center, a mixed martial arts gym in Springfield.

Wait a second. Isn't that where Adam trains?

Adam Shelton, a young associate attorney with our firm, had begun training at Northwest Training Center after relocating from Portland. Not only had he told me about it, I saw the evidence to prove it. Adam sometimes came into the office looking like he had crashed his motorcycle: bruised everywhere and sometimes missing some skin on his legs, arms, elbows or face. Damaging workouts aside, Adam had never failed to speak highly of his training, his gym mates, and yes, his coach. Now I stood looking out an east window at a shadowy stand of oak trees, wondering if Adam had heard yet that his martial arts coach was the shooter. It also made me wonder if Adam's association with the shooter could increase the odds that we would receive a call requesting legal advice. While lots of cases cross our desks, as I've said, the majority of my clients have always come through personal connections with past or present clients, friends, or colleagues.

This put a new and interesting slant on my nighttime news reading. Might this crime and Adam's association with the shooter give me my first real murder case to defend? The experience would greatly enhance my own skills. But the benefits of defending a case such as this would extend beyond me to the associates working for me, up-and-coming young lawyers who were doing criminal defense, family law, and other civil cases. This case could benefit the firm and everyone in it. And, undoubtedly, it would give me the chance to participate in a community discussion about an issue I cared a lot about: the constitutional right to bear arms. Hell, even if the case got nowhere near me or my firm, it was going to be fascinating. For legal voyeurs like me and my associates, just being in the same county with the case was going to be a learning experience.

(Photo: Adam Shelton with Brazilian Ju-Jitsu blue belt in hand and Coach Gerald beside him. 08/09/2013)

Since 2001, when I became a lawyer, the complexity of the criminal defense cases I took on increased pretty slowly – until the last few years. In 2011, I helped get a false rape charge against an Oregon State University student dismissed just days before trial. In the summer of 2013, I successfully defended a first-degree manslaughter charge lodged against my client, who was acquitted in the motorcycle wreck death of his girlfriend. In recent months, I had been very busy with some cases that were significant for a firm our size – a trade secrets case involving the outdoor clothier Columbia Sportswear, a breach-of-contract lawsuit against FedEx, and various criminal cases from around the state.

Could 2014 be the year I would get to apply my practice philosophy to a murder case? Given my age (37), experience, and the short tenure of our firm, it would be a coup to land such a case, given the number of high-quality and experienced criminal defense lawyers in Oregon who would also make anyone's short list.

It wasn't long before the social media comments started rolling in online. Many commenters claimed to have personal knowledge of the Springfield shooting. One asserted that one car rammed the other. Another said that one of the men had been chased from his vehicle by a gun-wielding maniac before he was killed. Others swore that the dead man had been pulled from his vehicle and shot in the back of his head while kneeling in the street. They proclaimed, practically in unison, that the killing was not justified. Some said that Gerald should be executed, just as he had executed his victim. The whole story struck me as sad – horrible, really – and legally messy.

The next wave of incoming information pushed my already strong interest in the case up several more notches, as people began buzzing about the background of the killer. Gerald Strebendt, it turned out, was a minor martial arts celebrity on the national/international scene. He fought at a major Ultimate Fighting Championship (UFC) event more than a decade earlier. He volunteered to coach the University of Oregon's Jiu-Jitsu team, which traveled all over the Northwest to compete. He trained several successful amateur and professional fighters. His mixed martial arts gym seemed to have been built on his two minutes and 45 seconds of UFC fame, his years of competitive professional fighting and training of fighters, and some connections to MMA celebrity Eddie Bravo.

Interestingly, when I googled Gerald Strebendt's name, I found some evidence of local civic involvement to balance the man's profile. He had been a part of the Community Development Advocacy Committee for the City of Springfield. The committee included six at-large community representatives – including Gerald – and had advised the council on housing and community development matters. Still, it took only a look back at the comments below the online articles to see that if I got this case, I'd have my work cut out for me. Posts had begun appearing from people who claimed that Gerald was hot-tempered and had a history of driving aggressively. I continued scouring the internet, knowing that if Adam's connection to the shooter resulted in a consultation, I was going to have to know more about this incident than even Gerald did.

It took an "Are you coming to bed soon?" from my wife to bring me back to some semblance of practicality. My practice was thriving, but I had been struggling for some time with how to balance my work with family life. I had recently set a personal goal to slow down a bit, help more at home, get more done around the farm, and take a more consistent approach to management of the office. I could already tell that those resolutions were in some jeopardy, just judging by how quickly and completely this case caught my attention.

I forced myself back to task – preparing for an existing client's hearing on a 50-plus count indictment. Whenever my thoughts strayed back to this new potential case, I told myself that even if this shooter decided to call Arnold Law, neither I nor the firm were really in a good position to take it on. I was really, really busy and didn't need a new case.

What's more, my right-hand senior associate attorney, Emilia Gardner, had just delivered her second baby. That left the firm seriously short-handed, because if I'm the firm's field marshal, its ideas guy, Emilia is our logistics general, the one who pulls together the troops and gathers the supplies to make things happen. She often gives me a sour look when I crash into her office with some new and overly ambitious plan of action, but if it's in the realm of possibility, Emilia is the one who will make it happen. I knew that if this case did come through the door, it would be nearly impossible to take it on without her as my second chair.

I couldn't resist. I set down my case file and sent a quick text to Emilia, including a link to one of the news stories on the shooting. She'd probably be up with the baby, I figured. Then I emphasized the first text by sending a follow-up: "New case?" Then, not getting an immediate response, I began trying to wrap up my work to get to bed.

Emilia responded within the hour. "Looks bad for shooter," she said. "Brother says he knows him. Sounds guilty. Near my mom's place."

Emilia's mother, Lupe, lived south of Springfield on a country road. "How far away does your mom live?" I wrote.

"About half a mile. It's on the new road that punched the highway through. Used to be a field."

"Could your mom have seen or heard anything?"

"Nah, she's on the other side of the hill."

Then I posed the important question. "Could we handle it?"

"Who is we?" she responded quickly and brusquely. "This baby is my current job. You are on your own."

I had to laugh. If we landed the case, I knew I could talk her into working on it, maybe luring her back to the excitement of a big case with some flexible working hours. But I responded: "We'll talk more tomorrow, when you are more sleep-deprived and malleable."

I knew that Emilia was possible to convince because I had done it before. That big trade-secrets case, the one involving Columbia Sportswear, landed in my lap not long after her first child was born. I was working every minute of the day and sleeping on the floor in my office some nights, really struggling to get up to speed on the hundreds of thousands of pages of documents. Emilia took pity on me, bringing her newborn son to the office to help out until the new case was under control. By that time, however, little Jacob had grown very comfortable with nursing and sleeping in his mama's arms while she reviewed discovery or drafted pleadings. Emilia ended up staying on the case, and Jacob came to work with her until he learned to walk.

(Photo: A very pregnant Emilia with Jacob in hand a few months earlier.)

I hope he calls, I thought. Then I went to bed.

Day dawned surprisingly quickly. I cut short my usual farm chores to get in my truck and drive into town earlier than usual. I wanted to touch base with Adam, my associate. Did he know yet that the guy he trains with was involved in a road-rage shooting?

Adam had indeed heard the news. Fellow martial arts students had spread the word, asserting that Gerald Strebendt was innocent of any crime, and that the incident had left him distraught.

"Reach out to him, be a friend," I suggested to Adam. "Make sure he doesn't talk to the police except to say, 'I want a lawyer.' And tell him not to tell his version of what happened to anybody, not even his friends or family."

By then I knew that Gerald Strebendt was in a load of trouble. The morning's newspaper had identified the shooting victim as an unarmed man in his fifties, significantly older than Gerald, and that Gerald had shot him at close range. Whether it was going to be our firm or somebody else's, this guy needed legal representation in a hurry. I was especially concerned that he not submit to police questioning or interrogation without the presence of counsel because, generally, law enforcement investigators are looking for evidence of guilt, not innocence. They are case-provers, not truth-seekers. I didn't know if Gerald was guilty or innocent, but I have seen clients make their cases much, much worse by talking to law enforcement.

Nor did I want a man in Gerald's position to tell his story to anyone else outside of law enforcement. The inevitable stress-induced glitches in his memory would only hinder his case if the stories he told were inconsistent. Should a friend be subpoenaed to testify, the discrepancies alone could be enough to convict him.

To me, though, it wasn't just a matter of protecting the man's rights and preparing for a potential trial. I also knew from my extensive research into police shootings that when someone takes a life, there's a need for quick psychological and emotional intervention to prevent the development of post-traumatic stress disorder. A good lawyer would assist Gerald in finding that help.

After listening to me ramble on about some of this, Adam raised an ethical concern, and it was an appropriate one. He had only been practicing law for a couple of years, and he worried that contacting his Jiu-Jitsu teacher would represent a violation of Oregon's Rules of Professional Conduct prohibiting the solicitation of clients.

I felt confident, based on my ethics consultations over the years, that Adam could call Gerald to offer some basic and free legal advice. The state actually encouraged it as a matter of public policy. Still, I suggested that Adam review the Oregon RPC for himself. Then he could decide whether his relationship with Gerald – whom he considered a friend – would qualify as an exception to the rule.

It was after noon when Adam flagged me down in the hall. "I tried calling Gerald, but it went straight to voicemail."

"Damn. Oh well. His phone was probably seized as evidence. That's not a good sign for him."

Adam continued. "I sent him a message on Facebook with my cell and work numbers, though. I'll let you know if he calls."

At the end of the day, as I was headed out the door to meet my family for supper, Adam caught me again. "I talked to Gerald," he said.

I stopped and put down my briefcase to give Adam my full attention. "What did he say?"

"He was glad I reached out to him. He doesn't have a phone. As you suspected, SPD took his cell last night."

The phone was probably tucked away in an evidence locker, I knew, either dead by now or buzzing continually.

"How's he doing? Is he okay?"

"Not really. He's pretty freaked out, and he has a lot of questions."

"Did you help him out?"

"I talked to him a little about his rights."

"Just tell me you told him to shut up and not talk to anyone."

"Yeah, of course, and he agreed. He says he's been getting a lot of crazies sending him messages on Facebook about how he's going to jail for the rest of his life. Death threats, too. He had to shut down his account. He asked if you'd meet with him."

"Did you tell him I would?"

"Absolutely. He was relieved to hear it."

"So when's he coming in?"

"Tomorrow, mid-morning. His fiancée, Kristin, is going to bring him."

I got out my phone to check my morning.

Adam waved away my phone. "Don't worry, I already talked to Meagan. She says your calendar's clear."

Together Adam and I walked out the doors of our fourth-floor office onto the open-air landing overlooking the parking lot. I could see the tops of the maple and magnolia trees in the U-shaped courtyard below, flanked by the 1960s brick facade of the Hult Plaza building that Arnold Law calls home. We stopped to talk more, leaning on the aluminum railing of the balcony, which is several inches too low by modern building standards. Adam joined me in surveying the surroundings. With both of us standing at nearly 6'2", the railing touched our thighs just below the tipping point of our centers of gravity. I turned away to look at the gloomy winter skyline to the west and asked, "Do you think Gerald had it in him to kill a guy for no good reason?"

Adam pondered a moment. "Gerald's a good man. But he's complicated. He's been through a lot in his life." Then he chuckled drily. "You should hear some of the stories he tells."

"Well, if he's charged, we will likely be reading those stories, either in police reports or the newspaper. I look forward to meeting him tomorrow." With that, the two of us went downstairs and in opposite directions to our cars.

CHAPTER 2
A MEETING, A
HANDSHAKE, A CLIENT

The Gerald Strebendt I met the next morning in my law office wasn't my idea of what a mixed-martial-arts fighter would look like, much less a road-rage shooter. He was slighter in stature than I would have guessed, and not as bulked-up as I would have thought, either.

As I walked out into our reception area to greet him, Gerald stood up and stuck out his hand. His grip was firm and strong. It was a good handshake. He smiled in a way that was both welcoming and nervous.

"Thanks for meeting with me on such short notice," he said. Although obviously uncomfortable with the situation, he was notably polite and respectful to me, my staff, and his fiancée Kristin Swenson, who had come with him for moral support.

I gathered more impressions of Gerald as I exchanged pleasantries with him and Kristin. First, I was surprised that the man I was sizing up was, at 34, three years younger than me. He seemed older, maybe in the way that sadness or weariness can age a person. Second, when he spoke, I was surprised to hear the tone of his voice. It wasn't gruff or deep. Instead, it was soft, and the pitch was a little higher than mine, maybe on the verge of being considered effeminate.

I remember thinking that MMA and UFC websites must be generous with their stats on fighters, because Gerald didn't look to be 5'9" tall, as his bios claimed. Though supposedly just five inches taller, I felt like a giant towering over him. He also looked to be carrying 40-50 pounds more than the 155-pound fighting weight I'd seen attributed to him online – meaning that I still probably outweighed him by 20-30 pounds. Of course, that didn't mean much. *He can still probably kill me with his bare hands*, I thought.

I then turned my attention to Kristin, Gerald's tall, thirty-ish fiancée. She was very pretty in a strong, athletic-looking way. My hunch – later proven true – was that she had met Gerald while working out in his gym. "I'm going to steal your fella here for a bit," I told her. "I hope you don't mind waiting."

Kristin laughed and dropped into a leather lobby chair, saying, "We figured that. I'm just the chauffeur."

It's standard policy in my office to exclude loved ones or friends when I meet with a client or potential client. There are all kinds of reasons for that, but the big one is protecting the attorney-client privilege. A judge can invalidate the privilege if a third party sits in on a conversation.

I shifted my perspective as Gerald and I walked the short distance to my office. To me, this is a critical moment: I only get one chance to take a juror's point of view of a would-be defendant, and never do I want to squander the opportunity. Does Gerald look reputable and reliable? Clean and careful with his appearance? In his dark-blue jeans and button-down shirt, I would say yes to both questions. His hair was short with the sides clipped close to his head, and there were no obvious tattoos or attention-getting piercings. He looked like any average guy who was beginning to soften with age. You'd hardly notice him if you passed him on the street.

Is this really a professional fighter? A road-rage killer?

I didn't pick up any bad vibes from Gerald at all, and that's saying a lot. All of us at the Arnold Law Firm are good at tuning in on the frequencies of our clients, witnesses, and adverse parties. While most people who come to us are normal people who have just screwed up somehow, we have represented or in some way worked with our fair share of folks with borderline, narcissistic or antisocial personality disorders. Consequently, our "crazy gauge" is always on and usually accurate.

Gerald didn't seem the "angry man," the "controlling manipulator," or the "likeable charmer" that we often see in violent perpetrators. He just seemed like...*a nice guy.* He came off like a typical small business owner, someone not much different from me – with one big exception, of course. He had recently shot and killed a man.

I motioned for Gerald to sit down in a client chair. "Make yourself comfortable," I said. "I'm going to run down the hall to get some paperwork."

This too, is strategic. I like to "go get paperwork" before beginning a meeting so that people have a chance to sit alone in my office and get comfortable being there. For most, it's their first appointment with an attorney and for many blue collar folks, also their first time in "some suit's office."

Sitting alone, guests can look out a large wall-to-wall window beside my desk to distant trees and hills. Or, they can survey some of the items I've strategically placed in the room to spark small talk. There's a photo of me going over 30-foot Big Brother waterfall on the White Salmon River in Washington, which often prompts the question, "Is that *you?!*" Or maybe they talk about their kids after seeing a photo of my daughter or one of her drawings. My rugby days are over, but years ago you would have found several scrum photos on display. Now only one remains to spark conversation.

I want my visitors to see me as somebody a lot like them, someone who is more than "a suit," because I am. Law degree notwithstanding, I'm just a guy who helps good people find their way past a really bad day in their lives. While the job has its moments of drama, overall it's just a lot of talking to people and staring at a computer screen. Very few of my days look anything like an episode of "Law and Order."

Outside the door of my office, while supposedly "getting papers," I ran through in my head the goals for this conversation. My first priority was to provide Gerald with information that would allow him to protect himself legally as the police investigation went forward. The second priority was to give him some general information about the law as it pertains to self-defense, which I hoped would let him rest a little easier about what lay ahead. Before walking back into the office, I stopped at the printer to pick up the jury instructions for deadly force, so Gerald could take them home and review them.

What is never a goal when first meeting with a client is getting hired. It either happens or it doesn't; we aren't there to sell ourselves. We exist to educate a client in a straightforward, honest manner about his or her rights as an American citizen. Still, experience has shown that this happens to be a pretty effective sales technique. When we answer questions with real knowledge and experience, we almost always prove ourselves to be well-equipped to handle the case.

"Okay then," I said, closing the office door behind me and sitting down in my chair behind the desk. I folded my hands in front of me, hoping that Gerald would open the conversation on his own terms, maybe with some banter, or some comment or question about things he'd seen in my office. But Gerald didn't initiate, so I took the lead with some getting-to-know-you questions. He sat in the green upholstered client chair and answered each question quietly, keeping his head, shoulders, upper body, arms, and hands still. *He's very carefully under control,* I thought.

We started by talking about how he knew my associate, Adam, who like me was a transplant from the Midwest. Then we quickly got to more relevant information. I asked, "How are you doing? Are you getting any sleep?"

"No, sir," he replied. "I haven't eaten or slept much since this happened."

I left it there. I didn't want us to stray into talking about what happened the night of the shooting. I never talk about that on a "first date."

Instead, I went back to rapport-building. I started by asking Gerald where he was from, although I already knew the answer. (It was a first for me to have a client or potential client with his own Wikipedia page.) Gerald confirmed that he was from a rural area outside Coos Bay, Oregon. This led to talking about what it was like to grow up near a coastal cattle ranch owned by his grandfather and two uncles. Plainly, he loved it.

Gerald was surprised to learn that I'm a bit of a rancher, too. This opened the door for me to tell stories of the various ways I've shocked, stabbed, cut, or otherwise broken myself while farming. I have no shortage of these stories, unfortunately. I have grabbed an electric fence while standing in a puddle of water in flip-flops. I have fallen over a fence trying to escape a rushing Angus bull that didn't appreciate my carrying away an abandoned newborn calf and seemed to enjoy the hell out of seeing me end up with splatters of fresh greenish manure on my face. I can tell the story of cleaving off a knuckle while using a handsaw to trim a rafter on a tin roof. I once got stung by dozens of our honey bees, which sent me into anaphylactic shock and required my wife to drag my near-lifeless body into the truck to drive 110 miles per hour to the nearest ER.

Any trial lawyer absolutely must be an above-average story-teller. It's a skill that most of us work to cultivate. After I ran through a couple embarrassing stories starring myself, Gerald began to respond with stories of his own, revealing more and more information about himself. And, I had to admit, the guy was a damn good storyteller in his own right.

I learned that Gerald liked building stuff and making engines sing loud. He loved being out in the woods, cutting down trees and occasionally making some side money selling firewood from the bed of his truck. I learned that he had rolled his first GMC Denali pickup about a year earlier, and that he had bought his second Denali just before the shooting. As much as he loved the new truck, he was a little heartbroken about the demise of that first one, he said, because he had purchased it right after returning from Afghanistan. He bought it with the money he made as a military contractor for Blackwater.

He's been a merc, too? This guy's credentials include not just martial arts and the military, but also Blackwater? What is a jury going to think about that?

As my head spun with potential jury questions, Gerald went on reminiscing. He told me that he loved going to the coast, where he could take his sea kayak out on the water to catch cod and snapper. He spoke of diving for abalone near Brookings, a town on the Pacific at the Oregon-California border. Apparently this prized mollusk lives in waters as shallow as eight feet, but most of the trophy eleven-inchers can only be found at 25-feet deep or more. It takes a long, frigid free dive to harvest them, Gerald told me, in waters that are always dark and full of tidal currents. Sometimes sea lions sneaked up on him mid-dive, he said, scaring the hell out of him as they brushed by.

We talked like this for a long time, maybe 30 or 45 minutes. The two of us had a lot in common. Somewhere along the way I realized that I liked the guy, and I thought a jury would too, if it came to that. There was nothing in his manner or in the stories he told to back up the internet trolls' allegations of violent tendencies. But at this point, Gerald hadn't been charged with anything and I didn't know if he would be. It all depended on what the police thought happened on that roadway that night.

I went into the meeting without any intentions of asking Gerald to talk about the shooting. I consider it a big misstep, especially at a first meeting, to ask a client or would-be client who's accused of a crime to tell me their version of events. I like to let a little time pass for building trust and rapport before asking for the truth of what happened. But I will, indeed, ask a new client what they "think" they told the police and what evidence they "believe" the police have. That's important. Hearing the actual chain of events, however, should wait at least until after my client has had time to refresh his or her recollection by reviewing the police reports.

My experience is that clients will often tell me what they think *should* have happened, what they *wish* would have happened, or *what they think I want to hear*. They do this even though the truth is usually their best defense. Then, they get stuck in their story and don't want to admit that they lied to me – which creates big problems later on, when the evidence starts to conflict with their story.

I've seen this play out plenty of times. In one instance, a long-time client of mine confessed that his initial account of a crime was made up and that, actually, something else happened. I was elated when I learned that he had lied to me! His initial story would have made him the unluckiest guy in the world, putting him in the wrong place at the wrong time with the wrong stuff in his truck. When the truth came out it was clear that he did something that was morally wrong, no doubt, but not illegal.

Ideas about morality and protecting one's personal reputation... these can put good people in prison. The lies begin when somebody does something embarrassing but not criminal. Then their unwillingness to tell the truth lands them in court, facing criminal charges. I feared that any story Gerald might tell me could make him a victim of just that sort of scenario. Though I was afraid he might want to try, there really wasn't any way to stay looking good in society's eyes when it came to explaining how a motor vehicle collision escalated into a fatal shooting.

But clients trying to save face by telling lies is not all I worry about. Studies prove that human memory is faulty, especially during traumatic events in which our most basic fight-or-flight instinct takes control. From an evolutionary standpoint, remembering every detail about what happened in a life-or-death situation doesn't matter. Research shows that what we recall most clearly is the *outcome* of a situation. That's because it's the part that is most important for natural selection: you solved the problem and you lived on to procreate. Recalling the color of the stone tool you were carving when the lion started chasing you? That was not important to our ancestors, and it's still relatively unimportant today.

As soon as I finished providing Gerald with the legal information that I thought he needed to know, I found myself itching to break my initial-consult rule. I wanted him to tell me what happened. This wasn't an impulsive urge, I assured myself; it was based on the particular nature of this case and this potential client.

Time was of the essence. The case had not yet gone to grand jury. Whoever Gerald retained would have to act quickly to try to get this incident "no-filed" (not prosecuted). Police reports and evidence in the possession of law enforcement would be hard to come by unless a charge was lodged against him, meaning that whoever represented Gerald would have to work fast to create a narrative of the shooting that challenged the government's own. Knowing Gerald's side of the story would help me – if I got the job – figure out which experts to hire and which steps to take to flesh out his case.

If Gerald's story convinced me that it was indeed a case of self-defense, I'd continue to stand foursquare against having him talk to the police. Supreme Court Justice Robert H. Jackson famously wrote that "any lawyer worth his salt will tell the suspect in no uncertain terms to make no statement to the police under any circumstances." But I might take the unusual step of recommending that Gerald voluntarily testify at grand jury. In the hundreds of cases I had defended, I had never recommended that a client do this, but that's mostly because we're usually retained *after* someone is charged. In this case, it could save the guy years of his life and tens or hundreds of thousands of dollars in legal fees. Would I do it in Gerald's case? I couldn't know, not without hearing his version of events.

As I moved toward revealing some of my thinking to Gerald, I continued to internally question my motives. Was this just me seeking to satisfy my curiosity about how a professional fighter ended up shooting a man on a darkened roadway? Was I about to open a can of worms, legally speaking, that I'd live to regret? I'm not sure I was able to reason away either question satisfactorily, but I did have a strong and positive gut feeling about the man sitting across from me. If ever a client could handle the blunt question I wanted to ask, Gerald could. He was a Marine. He had been to Afghanistan. He lived a life of rigorous martial-arts discipline and had fought profession-ally before starting his own business. Beyond the obvious experience and wisdom gained from his career path, the man seemed honest. The self-dep-recating stories he had told me showed that he was able to judge himself at arm's length, admit weaknesses and learn from his mistakes.

So, guided mainly by my sense that time was slipping away on any chance of getting the case no-filed, I did what I never do. I explained my rationale to him, and then took a deep breath and said, "Why don't you tell me what happened?"

He told me, and it was chilling.

"I'm on the way home with groceries so Kristin and I can make a nice din-ner. There's a car in front of me. It slams on its brakes. I swerve around him to the right to avoid the collision. Before I can do anything he revs up and hits my truck. I'm in shock. He just hit my brand new truck. I can hear him yelling. He is threatening me. I can't start my truck. So I grab my gun and get out. I call 911. While I'm talking to the operator he keeps coming toward me. He sees my weapon. He says he's got a gun, too. I back up, telling him to stay away. But he keeps coming. He doesn't stop. I'm fearing for my life. So I pull the trigger. And he goes down. It was self-defense, Mike. Self-defense."

As Gerald spoke I watched his eyes, his mouth, his shoulders, and his hands. I realized that he was not just telling a story of what happened. He was re-living each moment, experiencing it all again. His face displayed anger, then fear, desperation, frustration... and at last, resolve. I could see that he was sweating, and I found myself identifying with him. I could imagine myself in precisely his place.

I believe him.

Not even my skeptical attorney's mind could convince me that this was anything but a justified, self-defense shoot. If ever there was a time when someone should have been entitled to kill a person, this scenario, out on the road, in the dark, facing a man who is threatening to kill you and says he is armed... well, this was it.

After a moment I said, quietly, "Gerald, that's unbelievable... but I believe it. That sounds justified."

Then I told him a little bit about how we try cases. I explained that "we prepare every case for settlement as if we were going to trial." We win by hard work and being prepared. I told him the bare-knuckled truth: this sort of aggressive defense would be expensive and time consuming. I suggested that he meet with some other lawyers both locally and in Portland, but Gerald was shaking his head before I could finish.

"I don't want to do that," Gerald said quietly but firmly. "I want to go with you."

"Look, Gerald, don't marry the first girl that says yes to a date. You've been married and divorced, right?"

"Yeah. Not too long ago."

"Choosing a lawyer is a more difficult and important decision than choosing a spouse. You choose your spouse poorly, and the consequences are a divorce that is messy and expensive. You choose a lawyer poorly, though, and you die in prison. Get it?"

He smiled wanly. "Yes, sir. I do."

"You need to completely and totally trust whoever you choose to represent you," I continued. "If you're indicted, you could be waiting for trial in the Lane County jail for a year or two. Your relationship with your attorney definitely will be challenged."

"I want to go with you," Gerald repeated. "I know what it's like to give someone all your trust. I trained to do that as a sniper. You and your spotter give each other 110 percent. If either one messes up, you die."

"True," I said, "but the difference between that relationship and ours is that if I mess up, you go to prison, and I go home to my family and a steak dinner, complaining about what a bad day I had at work."

"Mike, you ever hear of a Muay Thai fighter named Alex Gong?"

I hadn't. Gerald went on to tell how back in the summer of 2003 somebody did a hit-and-run on Alex's parked car. Alex saw it and gave chase on foot. When he caught up with the car and confronted the driver, the next thing he saw was a gun pointed in his face. "Alex died right there, on the street," Gerald told me. "Within minutes he went from doing his own thing on the street to being dead. Boom, gone. Dead in the street."

"What happened to the shooter?" I asked.

"Some dude they thought was the guy was confronted later by the cops and he killed himself."

"That's awful."

"I know. And I think maybe I was thinking of Alex the other night, in the back of my mind. Alex got killed because it didn't occur to him that he could get shot if he ran up on that car. I wasn't going to make that mistake. I wasn't going to let some random asshole kill me out there because I wasn't prepared."

What could I say to that? Nothing, so I sat there, and waited for him to continue.

"I've talked to Adam about you, and I've asked around," Gerald said, returning the conversation to the representation issue. "I'm sitting here in your office, looking you in the eyes. You believe me, don't you?"

"Yes."

"That's important to me. I need to retain an attorney who believes me, who believes *in* me."

"Sure, I do," I said. "But your defense needs more than that."

"Look, from where I'm sitting, you've got what I want in an attorney. I can tell just sitting here that you are the kind of guy who would fight, if he had to. You and me, we are the same like that; we're not too different actually. Since you played rugby, I know you can take a punch, probably a lot of them. Dish 'em out, too."

I chuckled. "I'm way better at taking punches, actually. That's more my skill set."

"But you're a fighter. I can tell. I don't think I'm going to find many men sitting on the other side of a desk that know what it's like to take a hit and bleed. You know what that's like."

(Photo: Mike getting tackled in pursuit of loose ball; the last remaining rugby photograph in Mike's office.)

I nodded.

Gerald continued, "I'm scared, Mike. I need someone who will fight as hard as I would. When I fight, I come out of my corner like my hair's on fire. I think you do, too. You have a plan and you sound eager to jump into this. I really like that. You've told me what you can do, and would do for me. Everything I've heard, I've liked. Plus, you haven't promised me anything, which tells me that you're realistic." For the first time in the meeting, he moved his body. He lifted his forearms and shoulders ever so slightly to indicate a shrug. "My mind is made up."

I stuck my hand out, and he grabbed it. We shook hands over my desk, and then I stood up and gave him one more out.

"You know, there isn't a big rush to make the decision. You can take a few days to interview other firms. I want you to be 100 percent sure that we're the right fit for you. I don't want you to regret your choice."

"Mike, I don't regret much. I can tell you right now, I won't regret this decision."

"Well, the real test will be whether or not you regret your decision a year from now. Or five years from now."

Gerald paused. Then he fixed his gaze on me and said, "Mike, I killed a man. He deserved to be shot but apparently he didn't need to be. That's the mistake I'll regret."

CHAPTER 3

GETTING TO WORK

G erald signed the fee agreement that first day he walked into my office, January 31, 2014. That was a day that changed the course of my life, as surely as the night of January 29th had changed the course of Gerald's.

I had worked on many significant cases in my career, but none that had any real notoriety attached to it. My defendants were, at best, C-level characters in my D-level town. But this case was all over the news and my client was a local businessman with a network of customers and acquaintances. I knew that people would be asking questions of me, my attorneys and our staff, so I made sure to send out an office-wide email reminding all that the Strebendt case was just like any other case, and that we had duties of confidentiality to our client.

In the email I provided instructions about how to respond to people, but I didn't discourage anyone from discussing the case. On the contrary, I wanted to invite that discussion. I could tell already that this case needed to be thoroughly focus-grouped before going to trial. We needed as much insight as possible into our potential jurors, and I knew from experience that a lot of information could be gained even in casual conversations with friends and family – just so long as the conversations stuck to the facts that were known to the public.

I began work on the case the second Gerald walked out of my office. My initial goal, of course, was to prevent his case from ever going to a grand jury. If the district attorney did choose to take it to a grand jury, then the goal became avoiding an indictment. If he was indicted, my goal then was to turn over every stone of evidence and work toward dismissal or a plea agreement. And if all that failed, I would need to be ready for trial.

It was unusual to be starting work on a case this soon after an alleged crime. Normally, I wouldn't be retained until after the charge(s) had been filed, and I would come into the case knowing exactly what my client was alleged to have done. In this case, I could only speculate among all the possibilities: Murder, Manslaughter in the first degree ("Man I"), Man II, and Criminally Negligent Homicide. Murder was my biggest concern, of course. While Man I and Man II are very serious crimes, the length of the sentences pales when compared to what you face with Murder. There's a mandatory minimum sentence of ten years for Man I, 6 ¼ years for Man 2, and 25 to life for Murder. There was a lot at stake.

The first thing I would need to do in this case was figure out who I was going to have on my team. I would need support from an associate attorney, because I was already in deep water and struggling to swim with my current case load. I called Emilia within minutes of Gerald leaving the office.

She had to have seen that it was the office calling, because when she answered the phone, the first thing she said was, "No."

I laughed. "Aren't you at least interested in what I have to tell you?"

She didn't even hesitate. "Nope, not at all. Unless you intend to magic yourself to my house to clean up the entire box of Cheerios that Jacob just spilled on the floor, I'm not interested."

"The Springfield shooter came in today."

Now she was interested. "Really? Hey, did he tell you how to pronounce his last name? I've heard it about ten different ways in the last two days."

"*Stree*, rhymes with tree, and *bent*, like a piece of bent wire."

"*stree-BENT*." She sounded it out.

"No. *STREE-bent*. And he retained."

Now I'd gotten her full attention. "Wow, that's awesome, congrats! A murder case. How are you going to juggle it with your bazillion-count animal abuse case and your corporate case?"

"I thought you could bring in your littlest one, you know, to get some time off from managing two little guys at home. It could be a really good break for you, I think."

She didn't bite, but I'm not a quitter. Instead of pulling rank or coercing her, which I know from experience brings out her stubbornness and usually results in her doing the opposite of what I ask, I just started talking about the case. There were going to be a lot of moving parts to this defense, I told her – investigators, expert witnesses, psychologists, the list could get pretty long. Then, before she could interrupt me, I told her about my meeting with Gerald – how he looked and sounded when he told me what had happened on the Bob Straub Parkway that night. And I told her that I believed him.

When I finished, there was silence for a moment. Then Emilia ended the call by rather half-heartedly telling me that she'd "think about participating" in Gerald's defense. But, not long after we hung up, she texted me: "Did you find out if Karlin is available to work this case? He needs to get down here now." *Got her*, I thought.

Knowing that Emilia would be in the office soon enough, I started to lay out the building blocks of the case. I was in what I call the "golden hour," the first hour after a client retains me. It's a time when there are no documents to review yet, and no reports or statements crowding my mind and entrenching my beliefs about the case. Like walking into my office with the accused for the first time and viewing him as a juror would, it's another really important time when I can play the role of a fact-finder who is hearing the details of the case for the first time. If I'm going to have creative ideas about my defense strategy, they'll probably come to the fore in these first 60 minutes.

As much as I'd believed Gerald's story, I knew I wouldn't be doing him any favors by simply accepting it as he told it. I needed to *establish* the truth of his account, and yes, Emilia was right; I'd have to start by getting a forensic accident reconstructionist out to the scene. My first choice was David Karlin of the Portland based Talbott and Associates. I needed this MIT-trained engineer to drop everything, take a look at the scene, and then try to reconstruct the accident that triggered the shooting.

First and foremost, I wanted to know if the evidence supported what

Gerald said happened and when. If Karlin's results showed me I could trust Gerald's account, I could build the entire framework for his defense on that trust. Second, I wanted Karlin's report to tell me what the government likely already knew. I wouldn't be able to access any police reports until the charges got filed, which to me was too late. If we wanted to avoid charges, it was imperative that we get up to speed on the government's view of the case and fast.

Karlin agreed to drive down and meet with me. After I apologized for asking him to drop everything, he replied, "Come on, Mike, this is what we do. Besides, in case you didn't know, it rains in Oregon and that's no good for evidence. I will see you tomorrow at the latest."

That was an understatement. We have two seasons in Eugene: summer and the rainy season. Being it was January, it had rained off and on since Gerald had shot the man now identified as David Crofut. Skid marks, slide marks, bits of fabric, even the paint chips found after a collision provide clues about speed, force, and directionality in a car vs. car collision, but precipitation degrades them pretty quickly. Still, I knew that if there was evidence to find, Karlin would find it.

I met Karlin in 2009 during another death case. That one was a civil products liability suit filed against a motorcycle helmet manufacturer/distributor. My client's wife was killed after her helmet came off of her head during a car vs. motorcycle collision. Karlin established himself as the meticulous, articulate, and egghead-ish expert that I like to have explaining physics to jurors. With his glasses and accountant's manner, he looks and acts like somebody you ought to pay attention to, yet behind the scenes, his offbeat personality makes him fun to work with. I like to say that if anyone needs to attend sensitivity training, it's Karlin. He's continually cracking jokes that are so incredibly inappropriate, always delivered with such a straight face – well, you can't help but bust up laughing even in the most tragic and gruesome circumstances. I can't count the number of times he left my entire team in stitches, just from hearing some quietly outrageous comment across the walkie-talkies.

But I also respect Karlin as a military veteran who enlisted at the age of 18 – with the Israeli Defense Forces, that is. He's seen a lot, he tells it straight, and when it comes to an investigation, his opinion is not for sale.

He's told me that my theory of a case was wrong far more often than he's told me I'm right.

The next call I made was to Verne Hoyer, an investigator I'd used many times before. Verne was forced to retire from a patrol job with the Eugene Police Department when a freak wood-splitting accident blinded him in one eye. Verne's son was doing the splitting when a shard of metal broke off a cheap, Chinese-made molded steel maul and flew 20 feet to strike his dad in the eye.

Verne is a story-teller, and it's almost impossible to get him out of the office when he's on a roll. He has two claims to fame in law enforcement: he was a first responder to the University of Oregon's football stadium murder/suicide shooting in 1984 and he was involved in the apprehension of the I-5 Killer, a notorious serial murder case.

I met Verne a few years earlier when we worked together on a self-defense case in Depoe Bay, Oregon, a picturesque coastal town that claims to have the smallest natural navigable sea harbor in the world. My client, Mark Dade, was vacationing at the coast with relatives when he was accused of punching the very elderly Vietnamese owner of a local Shell gas station. Mark is a big man, and the little, wrinkled gas station owner was anything but.

The case was a great lesson in "looks may be deceiving," exemplifying how confirmation bias can totally destroy the legitimacy of an investigation. Confirmation bias is when law enforcement (or anybody) has their mind made up about an individual or a situation before hearing all the facts. It's about filtering everything you see or hear through a lens colored by your own beliefs. Psychological research shows that the only way to avoid confirmation bias is to acknowledge that you may have been influenced to a conclusion without having the facts to back it up. Then you have to actively function as your own devil's advocate, seeking out opposing evidence and viewpoints.

The local police couldn't do that in the gas station case, but Verne could. He was able to confirm what Mark and his family had told me from the beginning: that Mark had only punched the gas station owner after the little Vietnamese man had physically attacked his elderly grandfather – Mark's father, really, who had raised Mark since babyhood, when his birth parents were the victims of a double homicide. Police may have assumed that the tragic loss of his birth parents predisposed Mark to violent acts. Witnesses to the gas station incident may have assumed Mark's guilt because they saw only the part where a big white guy threw a punch at a wizened old immigrant defending his property. But, via his investigation, Verne established that this "little old man" was well-known for freaking out if a tourist used the station restroom without buying gas. Verne was able to track down witnesses to prior instances of the owner's anger, and to impeach several of the prosecution's witnesses when they changed their stories at trial. Presumably their stories changed to try to help the perceived victim, underscoring the importance of truth-seeking – without bias – in any investigation.

Now I needed Verne Hoyer's investigative skills to start locating witnesses to anything and everything that happened the night of January 29, 2014. Only two days had gone by, yet I knew that memories were fading and shifting even as I sat at my desk making phone calls. We needed to have had people located and interviewed yesterday. The longer it took us to find them, the less detail they would recall, and the less trustworthy their recollection would be. Things change. People relocate, change their job or their name, join the military, and even die before you can get a case to verdict. Just as I needed Karlin ASAP, I had to get Verne on the job immediately.

It wasn't more than three hours later that I received by phone the first bit of evidence from Verne.

"Mike, I have some news," he said. "I got a tip where Crofut was coming from before the collision – the Driftwood Pub. I talked to several witnesses there, including two bartenders who served both him and his wife, Brenda." Verne said he had also talked to the bar's owner. "He looked at the receipts and did the math, and confirmed that David Crofut may have consumed between six and eight Pyramid Hefeweizen beers immediately before the accident."

I began googling the alcohol content of a Pyramid Hef. "Were they 12, 16 or 22-ounce beers?" I asked. My previous experience in both prosecuting and defending hundreds of driving under the influence of intoxicant (DUII) cases was about to come in handy, I thought.

"16-ounce pints," Verne replied.

"Damn!" I exclaimed. "Somebody was drunk and had a motive to hit and run – to avoid a drunk-driving charge. That doesn't get us to self-defense but it might start explaining this guy's behavior. What do you want to bet he's a regular there?"

"He was starting to be a regular," Verne explained. "He and Brenda had recently moved down from the Tacoma area after he sold his tavern up there."

"What do you bet he wakes up in the morning at a .02 fairly regularly?" I asked, not really expecting an answer. I know this guy's type and his patterns from the DUIIs.

"One patron said that he had offered the Crofuts a ride home that night, worried that they'd had too much to drink," he told me. "They declined."

"Worst decision of their lives," I said.

"I'll call you back when I have more," Verne assured me. "I have a feeling there's more to the story at the bar."

With that information in my pocket, I called Springfield Detective Rick Lewis, who had been commenting to the press pretty consistently and appeared to be the lead detective on the case. The day after the shooting, Lewis was quoted as saying, "[The case] remains open and uncharged at this point because there's been a claim of self-defense."

I needed to get Karlin in to see the vehicles and I hoped that by contacting Lewis I could make that happen. I was also curious about what Lewis would be willing to tell me about the case once I told him that Gerald had hired our office to represent him.

Just by being a consumer of local TV news, I had noticed that Lewis got in front of the camera a lot more than I was accustomed to seeing from a police detective. He was a guy in his fifties with close-cropped hair, somebody who had obviously spent a lot of time in the gym getting big. He came off confident, well-spoken and fairly friendly, as most successful and well-liked officers do.

After introducing myself to Lewis, I asked, "Do you know who's in charge of the case for the District Attorney's Office?"

"Bob Lane's handling it," he told me.

"Is it being grand juried?" I asked, hoping to milk some information out of him regarding the likelihood of Gerald getting charged with something. Knowledge is power at this stage of the game and the police had a lot more of both than I did.

"You'll have to talk to Bob about that," he replied. "Do you think there's any way we could sit down and talk with Mr. Strebendt about his self-defense claim?"

"I doubt it but I can check," I told him.

After concluding the conversation with Lewis, I called the D.A.'s office. I talked to Bob Lane, the lead prosecutor on Lane County's Major Crimes Team – and found, to no surprise, that he was playing his cards closer than Lewis was. I could tell I wouldn't be seeing him on the TV news anytime soon.

Lane had never been fond of giving interviews to the press. In fact, he sometimes refused to speak about cases to anybody. In a county where there are only 28 district attorneys and hardly more than 23 practicing trial lawyers in the entire office, everybody knows everybody by record and personality type. On the job, Lane is known as a just-the-facts-ma'am kind of prosecutor, not much concerned with winning the affections of jurors. Off the job, he's the kind of guy who has earned his stripes as an introvert, choosing to work in his garden or fish with older colleagues in his spare time. Outside of his circle of friends, he's a man of few words. In fact, there's a story told of an eager young D.A. who walked into the break room once to find Lane reading a newspaper. The youngster tried to strike up a conversation, but Lane wasn't having any. Lane slowly moved the newspaper down from his face to size up the whippersnapper in front of him... and then, without uttering a sound, slowly moved the paper back up and continued reading.

With a legal pad rapidly filling with notes from these phone calls, I now had the beginnings of a trial outline. It's in part a to-do list and in part a script for trial. I'm a big believer in thinking about my opening statement, jury selection and even my closing argument, right from Day One. I encourage my associates to do the same. In my characteristic scrawl I saw a shopping list of experts to hire:

- *Firearms and ballistics*
- *Physical evidence (gun powder residue, blood/blood spatter, hair, clothes)*
- *GMC Denali (someone who knows the particulars of Gerald's truck)*
- *Psychologist (PTSD testing)*

Pondering the situation further, I added three more to-do's, all three of them very important to accomplish ASAP:

- *Establish website (to let people find us if they have information)*
- *Develop Media Plan (for getting out Gerald's side of the story)*
- *Call Peter Jarvis (our firm's ethics counsel in Portland)*

Gerald was getting slain in local and national media, even at this early stage of the case. That very morning Oregon's largest newspaper, *The Oregonian*, reported the titillating details in their headline "Minor Car Accident in Springfield Involving Former Sniper Leads to Fatal Shooting." The first paragraph identified Gerald Strebendt as a professional mixed martial artist who allegedly "gunned down" David Crofut. This article created the impression that the collision was no big deal and that this man who had the ability to defend himself with his hands used a gun to execute someone outside of the safety of a vehicle. Here was Oregon's leading media source, claiming that my client "gunned down" an unarmed man. This I would not tolerate.

KEZI-TV (Eugene's ABC affiliate) was a little more accurate, calling the collision a "crash" rather than a "minor accident." Words and descriptions matter. They have long-lasting effects on the minds of potential jurors that reporters fail to consider when they write stories. During the same TV report, Springfield Detective Lewis hinted at a motive, saying that the shooting had something to do with driving behavior before the collision, but that they were interested in learning more through their investigation. It was disappointing to see a seasoned detective portraying a purported theory of motive as fact.

These were just a few examples of the ways my jury pool had already been salted with negative, even false, publicity about what happened on that road that night. I knew from reading the psychological research that negative publicity on a client or a case causes confirmation bias and source confusion to set in very rapidly. It's crucial to get accurate, unbiased information out there as quickly as possible to level the playing field.

With this in mind, I wanted to discuss with our firm's ethics lawyer, Peter Jarvis, what I could do for Gerald in the media within the confines of the Oregon Rules of Professional Responsibility. Most lawyers with ethics questions call the free Oregon State Bar number to get advice. There you can get information on a variety of issues, including pre-trial publicity ethics, but in my experience, you get what you pay for. I prefer to call an expert and be done with it, and Jarvis is the best ethics lawyer in the Northwest. I'd rather pay him and know I'm getting a fast, accurate reading of what I can and can't do than to rely on government-paid bar advisors who may try hard but have no personal malpractice risk of their own to better incentivize them to get it right.

I wasn't a newbie here; Gerald's situation wasn't our first media case. In fact, I had one case that really galvanized my belief that the defense owes its clients every effort that is ethical to get its side of the story before the public.

Several years earlier, we defended a hit-and-run charge where our client may have acted in self-defense. Driving his Dodge pickup truck, he ran down and nearly killed a Mongol outlaw motorcycle gang member. Immediately after the incident he fled in fear for his life. He was terrified to turn himself in because he knew that the victim was a confidential police informant who perhaps worked with the same detectives that were investigating the attempted murder charge stemming from the hit-and-run. My client was also afraid to be tried or incarcerated locally, because he thought the victim had gang connections in jail.

Since my client was thought to have left the state, there was a fugitive warrant out for him. On my client's behalf I bypassed local authorities and instead contacted the U.S. Marshals, agreeing to turn in my client at the federal courthouse in downtown Eugene. When interviewed by local reporter Jack Moran about it, I said that the victim had threatened my client with violence and claimed an affiliation with the Mongols motorcycle club. The reporter then confirmed through the Mongols that the victim was indeed a former member of the biker club. The victim later showed me a large Mongols tattoo on his neck, proof of his background, and confirmed his role as an informant.

I can write about this case because it's now a matter of public record – I *made* it part of the public record by talking to the press with my client's permission. It was part of my larger Media Plan for that case. However, it instantly angered the district attorney on the case, who apparently believes that press contact is exclusively the domain of the police. There was talk of an ethics complaint against me, but it never materialized – probably an idea that was dropped after the office conducted a group reading of the ethics rule on pretrial publicity and learned how off-base they were in criticizing me. But it didn't stop the assigned D.A. from allegedly telling a colleague that my office was "walking the line, ethically speaking."

I would like to clarify that there is no "walking the line." There is no cloudy middle ground that gradually pulls you to the dark side of the bar when you approach it. It is no different than walking down a sidewalk. Technically, you are always walking the line, and you could stray into traffic and be killed instantly. But it's silly to worry about that. Just keep moving forward.

So, I say to hell with the holier-than-thou misconception among prosecutors and even some defense attorneys that a lawyer should never talk to the press. Are we to believe that the media can only be used by the government for "perp walks" or leaks of negative information from police public information officers? No, absolutely not. Aware of the psychological research on confirmation bias and source confusion, I long ago came to the conclusion that it is essentially malpractice to avoid the press when you have an innocent client. There are enough obstacles in the way of defending a client against the weight of the government. Self-imposed limitations on the use of the press should not add to the burden.

Going further, I'd say that our legal process only works fairly so long as both sides are playing the same game and having an equal opportunity to speak publicly. If only the government is playing the press game of checkers and the defense refuses to participate, the government is always going to win. Consequently, you will never, ever find me saying "no comment" when a reporter calls. It's my duty to make a move and at least use the opportunity to educate the public about the jury system and the presumption of innocence.

Later on that afternoon, I decided to add yet one more item to my growing list:

- *Polygraph?*

So-called lie-detector tests are not admissible in court in Oregon. But we weren't headed to court, not yet anyway. Would I ask Gerald to sit for a polygraph test in the hope that a finding of truthfulness would help ensure that he wouldn't face charges in the shooting? It was something I'd have to think about before even raising the possibility with Gerald.

CHAPTER 4

THE WEIGHT OF
RESPONSIBILITY

I was on autopilot that night as I drove home, deep in thought.

This wasn't just a potential murder case. This shooting was actually about seven different cases rolled into one – a motor-vehicle accident, a personal injury case, an assault case, a gun case, a drunk-driving case, and a self-defense case. The good news was that our firm was a perfect fit for it. Collectively, we'd done it all and plenty of times before. The bad news was that it would take all of us, "all hands on deck," as it were, to get Gerald the representation he needed and deserved. This defense was going to put Arnold Law to the test.

This kind of balls-to-the-walls defense was going to be costly, very costly indeed – six figures easily. Gerald had already signed paperwork that put everything he owned on the line to maintain his freedom. And when all those equities were borrowed against and still the case wasn't over… well, I wasn't quite sure what was going to happen. All I knew was that I wasn't inclined to leave the guy hanging. I felt I owed him more than that.

While I have a lot of confidence in myself and tremendous faith in my associates and legal assistants, that moment when someone puts his or her trust in me and says, effectively, "Whatever it takes, whatever it costs, let's just do it"… well, I feel it. It's a weight in my chest and sometimes even a lump in my throat.

Driving through the countryside at dusk, I was experiencing the weight of the responsibility I'd taken on. I wanted to be worthy of Gerald's trust. I wanted my firm to do such a fantastic job for him that, when it was all over, he'd shake my hand and say, "Mike, thanks. What you did for me was worth every penny."

But I knew that this was rarely the case. You don't always get what you pay for when you retain a lawyer. True, you will likely get more experience and wisdom when you hire a higher-cost attorney – somebody who's been in the business longer and handled the more-complicated cases. But I'd seen for myself that sometimes there's no relationship between what the attorney brings to the table and what sort of outcome is achieved. Sometimes a defendant is entitled to feel pretty unhappy when considering the cost-benefit analysis.

I thought back to a particular case, my first major felony case in 2009 – a high-profile engagement by local standards. It was a string of three signature crimes, each of them carjack-styled armed robberies where local women were kidnapped and taken to an ATM to withdraw money. (My wife, like lots of women in the area, was nervous about going anywhere while that offender was on the loose.) Anyway, the case was covered heavily in Eugene-Springfield and, to a lesser extent, in Portland.

My client was by no means nondescript. The victims described, and the ATM videos showed, a man who wore a New York Yankees ball cap. His face featured a prominent keloid scar or birthmark in the shape of Africa. My client had such a birthmark on his face. He was quickly arrested and pleaded guilty, along with a co-defendant. According to the plea agreement brokered by the judge, she retained the discretion to impose any of the three possible sentences consecutively or concurrently with one another, meaning that each man could get anywhere between 70 months and 210 months in prison.

What followed was a contested sentencing hearing in which we called witnesses, including an expert on future dangerousness. We spent days preparing for it and my client's mother invested heavily in our attempt to limit her son's period of incarceration. The argument was passionate, attracting media interest. It was my first time arguing a case in front of a video camera.

After presenting a half-day of carefully crafted evidence and argument, we rested our case. The judge then turned to the experienced public defender who represented the other defendant in the case. He talked for four or five minutes about his client's age, history, and other basic information. It was similar to the hundreds of DUII cases I'd been party to over the years, cases where what was on the line was two days behind bars, not 17.5 years. Does a retained attorney help you more than a court-appointed lawyer? Well, here we had a test group and a control group. All the facts and circumstances were the same – only the lawyers were different. I provided a carefully prepared, workmanlike argument for leniency. It was thorough, no stone left unturned. The public defender did demonstrably less. While I like to believe that you get what you pay for, here my weeks of preparation and hours of passionate argument did nothing for my client that his co-defendant didn't get for free. The judge ended up agreeing with the prosecutor, Bob Lane, and sentenced both defendants to the same sentence, the maximum allowed by the plea agreement.

I sincerely hoped that Gerald wouldn't share the same fate, to end up imprisoned and bankrupt, with my best efforts having done little or nothing for him. If it were inevitable for him to go to prison, a free attorney would allow him to save all of his money for commissary, I thought ruefully. At least he'd have the money to eat junk food like a king while behind bars.

Of course, I didn't allow myself to wallow for long in this sort of second-guessing. A defense attorney's success hinges partly on confidence – confidence in himself or herself as a litigator, and confidence in the strength of the case to be put forth.

I wondered, *do I want to believe his story because an innocent defendant makes it easier to come to work?*

Don't get me wrong, I don't have any problem defending people who are guilty. In such cases, I have an important job to do in our system of jurisprudence. People always ask, "How do you sleep at night?" Well, I don't lose sleep when I represent someone accused of something terrible. Everyone deserves competent representation, and the fact that I make a good living providing it certainly helps. I also know that defending the guilty helps me hone the skills I will need to defend those who truly deserve my help: the overcharged, the innocent, and the victims of political prosecutions.

But on that first day as Gerald's attorney, I knew I had gotten spoiled by having represented lots of falsely accused clients in recent years. It had been fun and exciting to work cases in which I thought there was about a 90 percent chance of a client's innocence. No moral dilemmas to face!

Then again, I could never be completely sure of a client's innocence because I, of course, wasn't there at the scene of the crime. Thinking of that, I had to laugh. Even if I *had* been there when it went down, I would still only raise it to about a 99 percent chance of innocence, and here's why: My well-trained skepticism of eyewitnesses would require me to include my own potentially lyin' eyes.

I had to admit: I was already invested in Gerald being innocent. And while I thought it was the right call to ask Gerald to tell me his version of events, I was dreading receiving the police reports. Belief in innocence is dangerous to those of us with OCD tendencies and an over-developed sense of justice. Despite my legal experience, I still maintained what could be construed as a naïve, juvenile concept of "justice" in our legal system. I knew at that time that if the reports came in, and Gerald was by all accounts innocent, that I would be losing a lot of sleep in the coming months. I also knew that if the reports came in and they contradicted Gerald's compelling recitation of his "facts," that a little part of my justice-loving heart would die. If a man could lie to me so well, and convince me so thoroughly, what did that say about me? I really wanted to believe in my fellow man, but it gets pretty hard at times. Being an optimist is tough and, too often, disappointing work.

So there was the question I had to face up to: *Could Gerald have fooled me somehow? Did he sucker me into believing him?*

I didn't think so. An attorney gets fairly practiced at spotting signs of dissembling, much less bald-faced falsehoods. Indeed, an attorney worth his or her salt is inevitably the first person to conclusively figure out that the client is lying, because you get to know the individual on a personal level and hear their story over and over again. The truth is, most folks are not very good liars. It takes a highly intelligent and manipulative sociopath or psychopath – the type of person who doesn't get caught by authorities – to maintain a lie over a long time period. Consequently, I've most likely never represented this type of individual.

A great way to expose someone's lies is to have them tell the story backwards to you. You ask them how the situation ended and then ask, "What happened before that?" then, "What happened before that?" and so on. You watch their body language. You see if they shift in their seat, avoid or maintain eye contact, and even what kind of words they choose to use.

Seldom do I go to these lengths. Most people make it pretty clear to me within the first interview that they are concealing a part of their story; as a lawyer I pick up on these signals pretty quickly. With Gerald it was different, however. I really believed what he had told me. This meant that he was either a psychopath or he was telling the truth, and I sincerely hoped that it was the latter. A psychopath with Gerald's military and martial arts training would be a very dangerous man indeed.

The days and weeks ahead would be paved with opportunities to put Gerald's story to the test. I realized as I drove out of Eugene and onto the country roads that would bring me home that I could already think of several things I would need to understand if I were to be fully convinced that David Crofut was shot in self-defense. But the one thing that I did *not* need to convince myself of was this: Defending yourself against a threat is a twilight zone unlike any other. In the heat of the moment, there is no calculation, no weighing of right and wrong, and certainly no consideration of what's allowable in the eyes of the law. All there is – and I knew this from experience – a determination to vanquish the threat, whatever it may take, and *live*.

If that assertion of mine seems especially fervent, it's because there's a story behind it.

A few years earlier, I was showing two college-aged women the amenities of our long-vacant South Hills condo, which I was hoping to rent to them. As we walked down some steps to the pool and hot tub, with the three of us deep in conversation, I suddenly stepped onto…nothing. I slipped and stumbled down the stairs, grabbing the railing to control a long fall down. It was not graceful, it was definitely painful, and I found it plenty embarrassing with the two pretty coeds looking on. It turns out that the carpet had been removed from the stairs and the wooden steps had been left exposed and covered with slippery carpet glue.

Without thinking, I angrily shouted, "Who's the fucking asshole who didn't put the warning sign at the top of the fucking stairs!?!"

Hearing no answer, I picked myself up, straightened the suit and tie I was wearing – I had come straight from the office – and turned to see two men striding toward us from the pool area. One was a scruffy, thin blond still holding a carpet tool in his hand. The other was a short, powerful-looking young man with a big mouth. "I'm the fucking asshole you were looking for!" he shouted. "Is there something you want to say to me?" With that he stepped forward aggressively, and I, my adrenaline still pumping from the fall, stepped toward him with similar aggression. A few choice words followed. The stockier carpet-layer then stood down, taking a half-step back and turning his body slightly away from me. Having thus disengaged from the potential fight, the two guys retreated into the rec center again.

"I'm sorry, it's not usually like this here," I said to the would-be tenants.

A few minutes later, as we finished the tour and began walking toward our cars, one of the young women asked me when the rec center renovation would be finished. "I don't know, but he probably does," I said, gesturing behind me to the stockier carpet-layer, who had started to walk in our direction. He heard me and responded with a smile that I should have noticed was a little too bright for the situation.

The next thing I knew, I felt something jab into the right side of my lower back and saw the flash of bright metal from the corner of my eye. *A knife,* I thought.

It was on. I was a grown man, a lawyer in a suit, engaged in a fight that threatened to become a street brawl. Was I fighting for my life? It certainly felt like it. I didn't know if this guy had another weapon and I certainly didn't take time to figure out whether I'd been injured.

I've thought many times about what I was feeling during the fight. Was I angry? Probably. Was I scared? Certainly. But the strange thing is that I couldn't remember feeling that way after it happened. What I remembered, mostly, was the absence of emotion. Instead there was just this…purposefulness. I wanted not only to stop this man but to hurt him.

After what seemed like a few minutes, the fight was over. The threat was no more. My opponent appeared injured. But I was safe…or was I? Only then did I reach behind me and touch my suit jacket where it covered my right kidney. There was something sticky there, but cool to the touch. On the ground where we had struggled, I saw a spackling knife covered in glue. That glue was on my suit and now on my hand, probably in retaliation for running my mouth at the carpet-layers back at the pool. With that realization, my lawyer brain clicked back on. I was never in any real danger. Apparently my attacker had wanted only to damage my clothing, not knife me in the back.

I quickly switched from self-defense to damage control. I told the stunned young bystanders to call 911 while I did the same. Now I could see how I had scraped and bloodied my knuckles during the fight. And though I may have sounded controlled and deliberate when I told the man that I was going to escort him to the ground, I was now shaking and so out of breath that I had difficulty answering questions from the 911 dispatcher.

I knew I didn't want to talk to the police without a lawyer present, so I tried calling my wife. When I couldn't reach her, I called my office for the help of any available associate attorney. Emilia was in the office, and arrived at the scene before the police did. Sitting in the cab of my truck together, I told Emilia what happened and what I thought I said to the 911 operator.

Officer Teresa Barrong soon arrived. We recognized each other from my time as a prosecutor for the city of Eugene. She first talked to the two coeds and then to me.

I did what I always tell my clients *not* to do. I told her my version of events. I knew I'd rather deal with the situation right then and there than let it go to court. She laughed aloud when I told her that I had said, "Sir, if you don't calm down I'm going to escort you to the ground and it's going to hurt." But she turned serious again to let me know that the girls had said the guy who confronted me by the pool was carrying a carpet knife.

Office Barrong then asked me, very seriously, "What would you have done if you had been carrying your gun? You would have been justified to shoot him." No doubt dispatch told her that the caller was a concealed weapon permit-holder who had no weapons on his person or in his vehicle. I had left my Glock 21 .45 pistol in my desk drawer before showing the condo because I didn't want to scare the tenants if they were to see it.

I said, "Teresa, if I was carrying my gun I never would have gotten in this situation to begin with. I never would have yelled and cursed at that guy and I never would have given him a reason to attack me." She nodded as if she knew exactly what I meant. It's almost a universal truth with responsible gun owners: you feel a larger responsibility to yourself, your family and society to avoid conflict when you're carrying the ultimate conflict-ending device, a tool that kills instantly. You can't just go running your mouth and get in fistfights, lest you be disarmed and killed… or left armed to kill. Your attitude changes when you're carrying. Your focus shifts.

If I'm honest, I have to say that I'm something of a trouble magnet. I took my first punch in sixth grade and, with that, got my inaugural bloody nose. There were physical skirmishes in high school and college, and in my rugby days, some "between the whistles" fights. I never threw the first punch, but I often started the fight by asking for it with my mouth. Then, when someone proved they richly deserved it, I made a point of finishing the fight or at least getting in the last communicative act. I never thought much about it. Just thought it was what men do.

Now, standing outside the condo, Officer Barrong asked me how I wanted this altercation to end. Did I wish to press charges? "I have him with a felony for unlawful use of a weapon, and a felony for criminal mischief – the damage to your clothes." As she said the last part she gestured toward the scrapes in my designer leather shoes and the drying yellow glue stains on my suit.

"How bad is he hurt?" I asked.

"They're going to take him to the hospital. He heard something pop in his knee."

"You know what?" I said. "If he comes over and apologizes to me in front of his buddies, we can call it good. A knee for some clothing – seems like a fair trade."

She was surprised by my offer, but delivered my message. Soon I was standing in front of a crew of four or five workmen, including my assailant. He put his weight on the uninjured leg to stand, and then stuck out his hand. I took it in a firm handshake.

"Man, I'm really sorry about all that," he said to me.

"Me too," I replied. "Sorry for running my mouth earlier. But I've got to say, I was a little surprised that you jumped me from behind."

That's when one of the guy's buddies piped up to say, "You got your ass kicked by a lawyer in a suit!"

"You didn't realize that he was a 220-pound rugby player!" Officer Barrong added.

Then we all laughed and parted ways. That was the end of it, or so I thought.

I'm a little embarrassed to say that this 30-second fight left me with weeks of PTSD. I had occasional flashbacks that were incapacitating, and random, inexplicable panic attacks. I also got lost in my own head, reliving every millisecond of the fight over and over again. A few days later, driving to the Portland airport with my wife and daughter, I was replaying the fight in my head when I almost drove my truck off the road at 60 miles per hour, the rumble strip jolting me out of my daytime nightmare and probably saving our lives.

Having listened to Gerald Strebendt tell his harrowing story of the shooting on Bob Straub Parkway, I now fully appreciated how different things could have been in my condo incident. Having been through it, I now understood, deep within my synapses, how subtle the difference can be between a "good story" and a deadly encounter. And because I had my own self-defense moment, and the PTSD that followed in a far lesser incident, I thought I understood at least a fraction of what Gerald Strebendt was going through... for having felt that he needed to shoot that man.

Now it was up to me to go through the process of determining whether Gerald's actions would be considered a *prima facie* case of legal self-defense, or whether we'd be looking at more of an "imperfect self-defense" claim — or, as it's sometimes put in courthouse parlance, "the summa bitch deserved killing" defense. Right now the fine points didn't seem to matter. I felt he was justified both legally and morally, and yes, I was basing that entirely on the account he gave me of the shooting.

CHAPTER 5
MANAGING THE MEDIA

O nce it became public knowledge that we had been retained to represent Gerald Strebendt, the proverbial floodgates opened and we started getting phone calls, emails, and messages about him. Our family, friends, and plenty of complete strangers felt compelled to share their impressions of him, no matter whether they knew him personally or not.

I don't have family in the area, being from Missouri originally, but Emilia was born and raised in the Eugene/Springfield area. Through her own previous martial arts experience and connections to the close knit wrestling community, she received more than a handful of calls and Facebook messages about Gerald. Nothing positive. Her own brother had called her to say that he had run into Gerald in the gym on several occasions. He'd heard, he said, that Gerald had executed Crofut on the street. "He's guilty, right? He did it, right?" She reported to me that she had listened and tried to ask good questions. It was important for us to understand the rampant misconceptions in the community about the case, so we could work to correct them.

I took these negative contacts as another sign that having a good Media Plan in place was of paramount importance in this case, just to try to correct – or offset – the misinformation swirling around in the pool of potential jurors. We needed to work on self-defense narratives, and also some that addressed Gerald's Second Amendment right to be legally armed, even just driving home from the grocery store, as he was that night.

So it was a great relief when Peter Jarvis, my ethics counsel, called to green-light my strategy regarding media. Immediately I began calling press contacts that I had developed over the years. Then I spent some time drafting a press release to accompany my conversations with reporters and also to post on our soon-to-be-established, case-related website. Jarvis assured me there was no risk to me or my law license by doing any of this. He agreed that it was in Gerald's best interest that I didn't play the coward, especially when the ethical rule constraining pretrial publicity didn't apply until right before the trial. Still, it made me nervous, sticking my neck out publicly for a client, knowing that others tended to naively think the rule was a blanket prohibition against speaking out – ever – on a client's behalf.

After we went public I immediately felt vindicated and relieved. The Media Plan bore fruit right away. The requests for interviews started coming in within hours. Television stations from the Eugene and Portland area contacted me. I also received a call from a producer of NBC's "Dateline." My newly created website began registering page views just as quickly, which was great news. I didn't know how many witnesses might be out there to find, but I knew how to help them find Gerald and me. When people googled "Gerald Strebendt" or anything about the case, I didn't want them going to some government-biased news source. I wanted them to find our portal, where the self-defense claim had been carefully and dispassionately framed. Gerald claimed he was telling the truth, so we went out to collect as many witnesses as possible and, well, I hoped that the truth would set him free.

(Photo: Mike speaks to a reporter on the condition that she does not wake the baby.)

Over at Springfield P.D., Detective Rick Lewis was still issuing all the statements related to the Strebendt case – for some reason their Public Information Officer (or "PIO"), who usually did the media contacts, was nowhere to be seen. In one interview, Lewis told local CBS affiliate KVAL-TV that "they found Crofut's body in the street, a short distance from the two vehicles involved in the crash."

A short distance away? What vision did that conjure up? A man lying dead next to his vehicle, which was far different from Gerald's tale, in which the shooting victim had moved aggressively toward him while Gerald essentially backpedaled. I knew that the location of Crofut's body would have been logged and would definitively be determined when I got the police reports. But words matter. Sloppy writing by a busy reporter can have lasting and negative effects. Already these initial impressions were going to be difficult to get out of the minds of potential jurors. Confirmation bias would set in.

As the days rolled on, law enforcement continued to release information selectively to help the government's case. For instance, in an early February interview with a local station, Lewis said, "No other weapons were found at the scene. Crofut was unarmed."

Technically, that was an accurate statement. But it wasn't a balanced statement. Lewis didn't reveal that Gerald had told 911 callers – and the passersby – that Crofut threatened to kill him. The detective didn't provide the public any details that would have been helpful to Gerald. This was a conscious choice, I believe. It was gamesmanship. Luckily, there had been no indictment yet.

I responded in kind, telling reporters that Gerald had "no choice" but to pull that trigger in self-defense. "He made the only decision that a reasonable person would make in that situation," I said, adding, "When someone threatens to kill you, you are entitled to take them at their word."

This isn't hyperbole; it's a correct statement of the law. You are justified to kill someone if you reasonably believe that they intend to kill you. In other words, if you threaten people's lives in the dark, you're doing so at your own risk.

Presumably the police already knew what we knew – that within hours of the incident, Gerald told a friend what had happened on Bob Straub Parkway. The friend was Justin Vaccaro, and at Gerald's suggestion, he was one of the first people our investigator talked to. His account supported everything we had heard from Gerald. Verne reported the following:

> On January 29, 2014, Justin Vaccaro had been working and had turned his telephone on the silent setting. After retiring for the evening, Justin awoke around 3:00 a.m. on January 30, 2014. He noticed his cell phone was flashing as though he had missed a call. The missed call was from Gerald's fiancée, Kristin Swenson, so Justin called the number back.

> It was Gerald who answered the phone, and he sounded upset and frightened. Justin asked what was going on, and Gerald [told him his account in detail]…

Gerald told Justin he had left a couple of handguns in the pickup, and Justin confirmed, when we spoke, that he and Gerald had been target practicing near Hill Creek Dam a few days before the shooting incident and this early-morning phone call... [This is a great fact, I thought. Recent target practice would help explain the presence of the AR-15 in Gerald's truck.]

When asked about how Gerald sounded on the phone that night, Justin described Gerald as "terrified and completely shaken-up." Gerald told Justin that Crofut had repeatedly told him "you're going to die tonight."

This is the story the public needs to hear, I thought to myself – not law enforcement's selective comments about the case. That only fed the trolls, who were having a field day on social media declaring Gerald's guilt, and polluting the jury pool with inaccurate speculation.

While continuing to make contacts with local and national media, I decided to put the wheels in motion to check the veracity of the account Gerald had given me. With Gerald's permission, I contacted a local polygrapher to see if we could get Gerald in to see him ASAP for an examination. As I've already said, I wouldn't have much hope of getting a "lie detector test" into court, but at the early stages of a case, they can be persuasive and even affect how the case proceeds. Law enforcement relies on them heavily and the Oregon State Police Department even employs full-time polygraphers. If Gerald could pass a polygraph, maybe we could persuade the prosecution to do the right thing and slow down or even stop the investigation.

I thought that a passed polygraph might also be useful in raising money, if it came to that. It wasn't only inevitable that Gerald would run out of money for attorney's fees and expert-witness costs, it was looking likely to happen soon, maybe even before the case went to a grand jury, if that's where it was headed. Defending a murder charge all the way through trial would cost exponentially more than all the money and assets Gerald owned. Friends and family would be more likely to support a loved one that they believe in. This I knew from experience. And people are more likely to believe in defendants who have passed a polygraph.

I also had my own reasons for wanting a polygraph test done. The results would validate my belief in my client if he passed, but it would definitely call into question my faith in Gerald if he failed. It's not that the quality of our work would change if he didn't pass. However, if he failed, the quantity of any work I ended up doing for free would change significantly. I prefer to reserve the sacrifice of my personal time for my innocent clients. When a client's innocent, I'll spend every waking moment pondering and processing the intricacies of the case. I'm less generous with my personal time, however, when there's no question that the defendant is guilty.

Now I just had to hope that Gerald could calm down enough to clear the test. Even innocent clients fail polygraphs when they're under too much stress.

CHAPTER 6
STUDYING THE SCENE

I met up with David Karlin, our forensic accident reconstructionist, soon after we were retained by Gerald. He drove us in his little Prius hybrid out to Bob Straub Parkway, on the outskirts of southeast Springfield. We arrived at midday to get the best possible look at the road, and also to look for any evidence that might be out there. I always send my experts to the scene, and I try to be there for their initial review of it. In the motorcycle crash manslaughter case for which I got a jury acquittal in 2013, we actually managed to locate and collect evidence from the scene that the government's investigators missed due to ineptitude or ignored due to confirmation bias. I still have the reassembled three-foot-long wooden post that the motorcycle struck from that case in the shop at my farm. It proved to be a vital exhibit exonerating my client.

Karlin pulled over and parked on the right shoulder just before the road split into a two-lane boulevard with a grass median in the middle. He grabbed his kit, turned to me and said, "Here, wear this." It was a reflective safety vest.

While donning the vest over my three-piece suit, I asked, "What first?"

"First we look," he replied.

While some of the details of the scene were obvious, such as the bright orange spray paint on the road, other details were not going to be so easy to spot. Karlin walked the scene like a bloodhound, bent over at the waist with eyes locked on the ground, looking carefully at the road. I followed, trying not to get hit by passing cars.

While he measured and considered, Karlin pointed out areas of interest. The area where Crofut's car and Gerald's pickup collided was after the "v" where the two southbound lanes merged into one. North of where the vehicles collided, several hundred feet away, was an intersection with stoplights, and beyond that, the city of Springfield.

In the direction where Gerald and Crofut were headed, it was open road, with just a few side streets leading into neighborhoods. If Bob Straub Parkway was a river channel, these streets were like tiny creeks feeding into it. There were a few streetlights near the corners, but staring southbound in the dark of night would have been like looking into a black hole. There were houses to either side of the road, but they were set back from the street 100 feet or more and faced away, like stout watchmen with their backs turned. Fences and shrubbery were the main features of the landscape. If it weren't for traffic, the two vehicles that crashed in the road there would have been totally on their own. Who would have noticed?

"David," I asked, "do you think the crash had something to do with the merge? Or the intersection behind us?"

"The evidence doesn't tell us anything yet, Mike," replied the engineer in his typical professor's voice. "Be patient. We go where the facts lead us."

Cars passed as Karlin and I continued exploring the ditch and the landscaped median. Each time I heard one approach I looked up for safety's sake while Karlin continued scouring the ground. He was completely comfortable working in this environment, but not me. I hoped that the paint marks and debris would allow Karlin to piece together a fairly detailed preliminary picture for me, and preferably soon, so we could get off this road.

By late the next afternoon, I had a call from Karlin. That was a surprise. It seemed too soon.

"Mike," he said. "I've got some good news, and some bad news for you."

"Bad news first," I said.

"Alright," he said. "First, while I was able to take some measurements out there, I didn't get enough to come to any conclusions. I'm going to need the police reports and photographs before I can give you any sort of concrete, usable opinion."

I understood, of course. I wanted his fastest work, yes, but also his best. "The good news?"

"The good news is that I do have a little bit of data I can give you now, something you might be able to use."

"Good. Shoot."

"I saw the markings on the road from the collision and the SPD investigation, and from them I can give you the distance between the cars and the body. Remember how the police were saying in the news that the shooting happened close to Crofut's car? That's not accurate. It was more than 80 feet."

Eighty feet? *Eighty?* I was floored. We would have a field day with that fact. What on earth had David Crofut been thinking? Why in the world was he that far away from his car if he was scared of Gerald – unless, of course, Gerald had chased him and gunned him down. That would be even worse for Gerald's case than a quick encounter near the vehicles. The best-case scenario for our side was if Gerald grabbed his rifle when he left his truck, and Crofut walked 80 feet towards a man who was brandishing a powerful weapon. Even if Gerald truly had cut off Crofut on the road, causing a crash, what had caused Crofut to leave the safety of his vehicle and approach a man armed with an assault rifle? Was the car still drivable? Was it stuck under the bumper of Gerald's truck? Was Crofut attempting to protect his wife and draw the threat of a crazed gunman away from her? Whatever he was thinking, Crofut was wrong to have picked an armed Marine sniper to follow out into the dark void of night.

After I got off the phone with Karlin, my receptionist buzzed me to tell me that I had a phone call from someone interested in the Strebendt case.

"Who is it?" I asked.

"Some guy. Says he knows Gerald. Benjamin Graiser"

I'd never heard the name, and we'd been getting lots of calls about Gerald's case, but I put on my headset and picked up the line. "This is Mike."

"Hello, sir, hello," he said nervously. "Thank you for taking my call. My name is Ben. I just gotta say, I can't believe what I'm seeing in the news."

"Hi, Ben. I know how you're feeling. This whole thing is pretty unbelievable."

"I knew Gerald, you know that? Back in the Marines. I haven't talked to him in years. But when I saw the news, I had to call, you know? I had to tell someone that I knew Gerald."

"I can pass a message on to him, if you like. Did you want to speak to him directly?"

"No, no, I don't need to do that. I just wanted to know. Is it true? What people are saying on the internet? That Gerald executed that man?"

"Ben, of course not. It was self-defense."

"Oh, thank God. Then what happened?"

"I would love to tell you the story so it would all make sense, but I can't. Everything I know is confidential, and I can't release any more specific details to you without Gerald's express permission."

"I know, I know. It's just that, well…." He paused, and took a deep breath. "I knew Gerald a long time ago, and we worked out together, you know? We drove in the car together…all the time. I never saw him do any-thing like what they're saying on the internet. That road rage stuff? I just can't believe it."

"What did you say your name was?" I was writing now.

"Ben Graiser. I'm out in North Carolina now."

"What else do you know about Gerald?"

"He's a nice guy. He'd never do the things they are printing on the internet, in the paper. Gerald doesn't get angry. Not like that, not at other drivers. He's a really easy-going guy."

"Have you ever seen Gerald, and I'll put this in my air quotes, 'road rage' on someone?"

Graiser actually laughed out loud. "Gerald? No way. He always did the driving, and you know California traffic, those California drivers. I'd be punching the dash and yelling out my window at people and Gerald, he'd just laugh at me. *I* was the road rager, from the passenger seat."

"Do you think Gerald would ever shoot someone in anger?"

"The Gerald I knew would never – never ever. Well, I suppose he would if his life was in danger, but wouldn't you? I know I would, if I had to."

I ended the call after obtaining Graiser's contact information so Verne could follow up with him. Then I grabbed my notepad and went looking for someone to tell about Karlin's news, that 80-foot measurement he'd given me. I strode down the hall until I realized that all of the offices were empty. I checked my watch. The office had closed while I was on the phone with Graiser; everybody was gone. I tried calling Gerald on his new phone, but he didn't pick up. Since I could find no one to celebrate with, I decided to go home and spend some time with my daughter before she went to bed.

As soon as I stepped into the cab of my truck, my phone rang. I had been talking on the phone all day, it seemed, but when I saw who was calling, I activated the Bluetooth so I could talk hands-free.

"Hey Dad! Can you hear me okay? I just got in the truck."

"Loud and clear. How's it going, son?"

"Well! I got some good news today. Just a small detail, nothing earth-shattering, but it helps."

"Can you talk about it?" My dad loved to talk about my cases with me.

"Nah, not yet. But when we get around to focus-grouping it, I just might."

"Darn it," he said. My father rarely cursed. "Well, I've been on Google and I saw the news articles about your guy. The case sounds pretty bad."

"There's so much I wish I could tell you, you wouldn't believe it. I can tell you, though, that I think my client is innocent. I really do."

"Well, I just can't see how any man could pull out a rifle like that and kill a man. If it were me, I doubt I would have had the wherewithal to even think of grabbing the gun, much less to use it."

"Really Dad? You wouldn't shoot someone if you thought you were going to die? You'd just let someone shoot you?"

"Well, I don't know about that. But it seems like to me that the reason he killed that guy was that he brought out the rifle. He was the one who escalated things. He made it deadly, not the other guy. He brought a rifle to a fistfight."

"It isn't that simple, Dad."

"Never is," he agreed. "Well it sounds like a lot of work. I should let you get home. You take care of yourself, okay? And remember that you got that baby girl – she needs you too, you know."

"Thanks, Dad, I know. Hey, I gotta go, I'm going to lose you here in a bit when I get off the highway to where there's no signal."

"No problem. Say hi to the girls for me. Good night."

And it did prove to be a good night, absolutely. Getting that 80-foot measurement from Karlin allowed me to give my brain a night off. I went home to Jacy and our daughter feeling free to focus only on them, instead of mentally hashing over today and worrying about tomorrow.

CHAPTER 7
TELLING TALES AND TESTING TRUTH

Over the first few weeks of the case, I had opportunities to sit with Gerald and converse about life in general – off the clock, of course. I never charge for banter. To a bystander, my conversations with Gerald could look like a waste of time. But to me, the time spent with him had a real concrete purpose. To defend Gerald, I needed to really know him – his good qualities, his less-admirable ones, his triumphs, his mistakes. I needed to get a handle on not just the truth of the story he was telling with regard to the shooting, but his general trustworthiness with any set of facts. Listening to someone tell stories can help with that, I've found. Besides, Gerald could tell a damn good story, he seemed to have a million of them. Frankly, in a short amount of time I had come to enjoy spending time listening to him talk – especially about the three elements of his life that would be of most interest to a jury, which were the Marines, Blackwater, and his stint as a professional Mixed Martial Arts fighter.

I remember one set of stories, told to me in a lighthearted three-hour session where I wasn't probing for anything in particular, just looking to get a flavor for where the guy had been and what he had done. If we stumbled across something I could use in the case, great. If not, that was fine, too.

"Tell me something interesting you did in the Marines," I said.

The topic Gerald chose was Marine Mountain Warfare Training.

"We were there preparing for a potential fight with North Korea, and one of the things we did was build snow caves and live in them during the training. But we had to understand the science behind avalanches first because we were traversing super-steep mountain slopes on skis and snowshoes."

Gerald then described testing the snow on each slope, knowing that the position of the sun continuously altered snow conditions all day long. "To test for avalanche conditions, we would dig a pie shaped wedge of snow out of a hillside about 8 or 10 feet deep and 10 to 12 feet wide. Then, in our skis, we would walk above the little ledge we'd just dug. Then we'd stop near the edge and look for layering in the freshly dug snow. If the snow has a layer of ice in between the bottom part and the fresh top, be ready. It can slough off and become the start of an avalanche."

Gerald told me, in meticulous detail, how he and his fellow trainees built a snow cave once they found a safe hillside. "You need an air hole, so you get a long stick and punch a good breathing hole through the roof above the door. You build a ledge in the wall to set a candle. The candle reflects off the inner surface of the snow cave and glazes it over, creating a warm thermal barrier against the cold."

Yes, he told me, just one candle could heat the entire cave. But it also melts the snow. "You have to keep an eye out so the dripping snow goes down the walls instead of putting the candle out. Then you build a little trench along the floor near the walls to carry away the snowmelt. If the candle goes out, check your breathing hole." He paused to chuckle. "Always check your breathing hole!"

For 30 days a cave like this would be the base of operations for a team, Gerald said. They patrolled, practiced assassination missions, and trained to weigh people and gear carefully to allow for potential high-altitude helicopter rescues in thin air that limited the lift of the rotors. By day they camouflaged themselves with two-sided white sheets – plain white for snowy landscapes and painted with wisps of gray and green to blend into areas that weren't completely snow-covered.

Cedar boughs were their friends, Gerald told me. The trainees slept on them and made snow transport from them. "We put our skis on the ground parallel to each other and tied branches across them to create a sled, then we would lie down on them and pull ourselves along with our hands – like Arctic ninjas."

"That's amazing," I said. "Can't imagine that training comes in all that handy now as a small business owner, though."

Gerald laughed. "Not really."

"I guess you would have been all set had Crofut attacked you during a snowstorm."

"No shit," he said, with another burst of laughter. "The tire tracks and footprints would prove my case!"

"Crofut's death snow-angel would have been a nice touch, too." Now we were both laughing, neither of us opposed to making light of the macabre or gruesome. A little levity is important for client and attorney morale alike, I've found. If I can't engage in a little irreverence with my client from time to time, I'll quickly become like the many prosecutors who are too serious for their own good. I'd lose the touch of realness I need to connect with a jury and to stay sane.

"Okay, then how did you get from the Marines to Blackwater?" I asked, hoping for another snippet of recollection.

Gerald said he could trace his Blackwater days back to the Marines in Okinawa, where in 1998 he met a member of 5th Force Reconnaissance, the Marine Corps' premier special ops team. The guy's name was Eric Warren, nicknamed Kicker.

"Kicker had been working with Blackwater on an OGA contract – that stands for Other Government Agency. It's a top-secret, CIA-backed agency, just google it. Anyway, he had been doing well in Iraq and had built up a good-enough reputation that he could put together his own team. He was about to sign me up with Blackwater to be under his command, but he got pulled to Hurricane Katrina. He introduced me to his friend, Jeff Wright, whose Blackwater name was Shark. Shark had the distinction of being the oldest person to ever graduate Navy SEAL school BUDS, or Basic Underwater Demolition School. He was a legend in the SEAL community and was on the cover of Reader's Digest once.

"I was set to be on Shark's team to protect some VIPs from an American company called Lincoln Metals. They saw big dollar signs in taking all of the blown-up Russian tanks and Light Armored Personnel Carriers that litter the countryside. Scrap metal was up to 10 cents a pound, and those tanks must weigh 50,000 pounds – and they're everywhere – fields of them stretching as far as the eye can see. Shark was my program manager and we went through a shooting package together at the Blackwater training facility in Moyock, North Carolina. I had to wait for USCENTCOM to issue me an armament agreement to allow me to carry explosives and machine guns in-country and it took several weeks. Shark already had his paperwork, so he went ahead to Afghanistan. By the time I got there, I was put on a counter-narcotics team."

"Did you get a nickname?"

"Boot. I was the youngest and newest guy, and in the Marines, that makes you a 'boot.'"

"Well, Boot," I said, "I imagine the Blackwater guys were a pretty interesting bunch."

"Ha, well, you should hear about my team leader, John Raynor Moore, III. He was from Bloomington, Indiana and he was a 20-year veteran of the Army's Special Forces. One night he came home and caught his wife with a psychology professor from Purdue. John was a tried-and-proven Green Beret. He was in Afghanistan with a Special Forces A-Team in October, 2001, fighting with the Northern Alliance against the Taliban. He was one of the first boots on the ground after 9/11, too. Well, he caught his wife upstairs with this Morris guy from Purdue who had his hair in a ponytail. John told his wife to get their son out of the house and he pulled out a .357 Magnum. He told Morris to sit down. Then, John shot him twice in the head, and now he's doing 20 years in an Indiana penitentiary." He nodded at me and my widened eyes as if to say, "for real!" "Google him and you can see a mugshot of what was once an American hero."

"Pretty tough company you kept there."

Gerald agreed. "The Blackwater contractors were the rock stars of both Iraq and Afghanistan. Our reps preceded us and we never, ever lost a principal. Not even the Secret Service can claim that. When Dick Cheney visited Afghanistan, the Secret Service hired Blackwater to protect him. When the FBI sent agents to investigate the Blackwater crime scene at Nisour Square in Baghdad, they still hired Blackwater to guard them. I could go down a list of Blackwater guys that got killed. Real heroes like Casey Casavant, Rod Richardson, Scott Helvenston – all legends."

He told me several other stories that were hard to believe about Blackwater and meeting celebrities. After the punchline in one interesting story, his voice trailed off. He paused and said, "That was a long time ago. A whole lifetime ago."

I told Gerald he should use his time behind bars to write some of these stories down. I thought people would enjoy reading them.

"I've thought about it, but honestly, I don't think anyone would believe me. They'd think I was making most of it up. I'm not, but how would I ever prove it?" He digressed for one more story, a brief mention of his doing some fighting as a stuntman in a made-for-Europe B-movie starring Gary Busey and Pamela Anderson. When I just looked at him and shook my head, he said, "See? Who'd believe this stuff?"

I wondered if *I* should be believing it, so I did a little fact-checking online later at the office. That Mountain Warfare training? Found it – south of Lake Tahoe, and yes, they train at up to 12,000 feet. Those Blackwater names? Found those too. Even the movie with Pamela Anderson – yup, it existed and I found Gerald's name in the IMDb.com database, an online movie-industry encyclopedia.

However, when I began looking for the friend who shot his wife's lover, John Raynor Moore III, I started coming up blank. I tried different variations of the name, still nothing. Had Gerald made this up? Finally I found an Indiana Department of Corrections inmate locator... and discovered a John R. Moore III, born 1960, sentenced and imprisoned February 12, 2010 for voluntary manslaughter.

Gerald's stories always sounded unbelievable, but so far as I could tell, they were true.

Would the polygraph show him to be telling the truth about the shooting on Bob Straub Parkway too? On the appointed day, I anxiously awaited the result.

When polygrapher Steve Hebner called me, I could tell immediately from the way Hebner greeted me that I wasn't about to receive news that Gerald had passed the exam.

"Your guy didn't fail the polygraph, but he didn't pass it, either," Hebner told me.

Shit.

Hebner voiced what I'd feared – that Gerald's extreme situational anxiety, combined with some acute post-trauma stress after the shooting, probably prevented him from getting a conclusive result, although the numbers still showed, inclusively, that he was being truthful. But we'd have to try again.

However, that wasn't all Hebner had to say. He bent my ear for almost 20 minutes about his conversation with Gerald, and told me point blank that despite the inconclusive examination, he believed Gerald was telling the truth.

This was terrific news, because if Hebner says it, you can take it to the bank. He was a veteran of more than 26 years with the Oregon State Police. He spent many of those years as a detective. He had been a polygrapher for almost 20 years, and in that time he had conducted criminal polygraph examinations for the Oregon State Police, the United States Attorney's Office, the FBI, the United States Citizenship and Immigration Services, the United States Department of Homeland Security, and other agencies.

In other words, Hebner's whole professional life was spent evaluating people's stories for veracity. And based on that experience, Hebner believed Gerald on a personal level, as only a cop's cop can do after hearing the stories of thousands of suspects over the years. He believed Gerald's version of events. What's more, he also supported Gerald's actions.

Like many police officers, Hebner was trained in the "21-foot rule." That's the distance a charging subject can cover in the time it takes an officer to recognize a threat, draw his sidearm and fire two rounds at center mass. The implication, then, is that when dealing with a weapon-wielder at anything less than 21 feet, assuming the weapon is not a firearm, the officer had better have his gun out and ready to shoot before the subject starts rushing him. If the suspect is rushing at him within 21 feet, he had better be firing, or risk that he would not be able to respond with sufficient force in time. When it comes to guns, police officers are trained to fire upon any subject who points a firearm in their direction regardless of whether a subject is within or outside the 21-foot area. The fact that a suspect might not have a weapon (either knife or firearm) is generally beside the point. The decision to fire rests in the mind of the police officer, and what he reasonably believed at the time he fired. If the subject made him believe that he had a knife or firearm, the officer would be justified in reacting accordingly.

"It was a good shoot," Hebner said, before concluding the call. If he had been in Gerald's position, he told me, he might have even fired the shot sooner. He said he was impressed that Gerald waited as long to fire as he had.

This was great input. I felt confident that the evidence would follow our perception of his innocence.

Gerald, however, was devastated to learn that the polygraph was inconclusive. "Mike," he said. "If I can't pass a polygraph, how is it that anyone will believe me?"

"But you did pass," I told him, letting my elation show. "It is just not yet scientifically valid, so it is deemed 'inconclusive.' We may not have a polygraph result to give to the D.A. yet, but in my mind, Gerald, you passed the exam. Hebner believed you. He watched you respond to the questions and he believed in your innocence. You'll pass if we do the test again when you aren't so stressed out."

"Are you sure?" he asked.

"I never guarantee anything. But I do think your chances of passing next time are excellent."

Gerald at last seemed reassured. I reiterated several times my strong feeling that we'd have a report we could use soon – after Gerald was able to process what had happened and calm down. Eating and sleeping, I advised, would be a move in the right direction.

I went through the rest of the day with some optimism, however misplaced it might be due to such underwhelming results. Hebner's comments about Gerald's exam validated my commitment to the case and reassured me that everything would come together. Eventually Gerald would be calm enough to pass – never mind that the exam wouldn't be admissible at trial – we'd find something useful to do with it. Maybe we'd even try and make some new case law if it came to that.

Near the end of the day, I had to bring myself back to focus on the "what next." The priority now was to try and stop the progression of this case before it gained momentum. I couldn't use a polygraph result to convince Bob Lane that this case shouldn't go to grand jury, because I didn't have one yet. I would have to think of something else.

CHAPTER 8

SHOULD GERALD TELL HIS STORY?

I n the office the next morning, Emilia and I began discussing in earnest the possibility of Gerald testifying at the grand jury that the District Attorney's office would likely convene. If he was innocent, as we now felt certain, why shouldn't he step forward and tell his story, in the hope of stopping the case in its tracks?

In Oregon, all felony charges must be presented to a grand jury for an indictment unless a defendant waives the process. The grand jury proceeding is secret. It's not open to the public, and its proceedings are not recorded. Nor is it open to the defense. It is, in effect, a Star Chamber, a secret tribunal. The prosecutor schedules it, and then brings forward whatever evidence of a crime he or she wishes to present, using witnesses, documents, photographs—anything allowed by statute. We never get to know if evidentiary rules are followed properly, though, because as I say, we're not allowed to be there and no record of the proceedings is ever revealed.

Grand jury reform is needed everywhere, but particularly in Oregon. Where once grand jury secrecy was aimed at protecting the people associated with the investigation who may be innocent, now the secrecy in our state and others seems mainly intended to give the government a chance to investigate and prove cases without being challenged by an adversary, a defense attorney like me. I can't examine the evidence that goes before the grand jury. I can't submit any contrary evidence to the proceedings, which is often allowed in states that have preliminary hearings instead of grand juries. If the grand jury ultimately decides that there is enough evidence for the prosecutor to get a conviction at trial, what follows is called a "true bill." The indictment is then filed and served upon the defendant with an arrest warrant. Then and only then does the accused have any right to participate in his or her own defense.

It's a flawed process, that's for sure.

Emilia and I readily accepted the fact that Gerald couldn't force himself into the grand jury – the accused had no right to testify there under then-existing Oregon law – but we knew that he could appear if he was invited by the District Attorney's office. Of course, any prosecutor would love the opportunity to get an accused in the grand jury's witness box under oath and without an attorney present. The question we were putting before ourselves was whether we too would love the opportunity for Gerald to testify at grand jury, or whether it was what it usually is – a terrible idea worthy of immediate rejection.

I came into the conversation leaning pro-testimony. Having now established that there was a distance of 80 feet from the motor vehicle collision to where David Crofut was shot, I felt more confident than ever in Gerald's story. If he were truly innocent, and there was a way to get him before the grand jury, maybe he could go free without ever getting to an indictment or an arrest. As a defense attorney, I knew it was a brave but extremely risky thing to consider. That understanding was what was keeping me on the fence. Was it worth the risk or wasn't it?

Emilia was solidly against the idea. She thought that the risk to Gerald greatly outweighed the slight chance that he could turn the tide of the case by himself.

After hashing out the pros and cons awhile, she asked me, "Mike, what's the one thing you can always trust a D.A. to do at grand jury?"

"Try to get an indictment?"

"For the most part, that's right. They wouldn't be there if there wasn't enough evidence to proceed." Emilia told me she'd seen her share of grand juries when she clerked for the D.A.'s office down in Roseburg, Oregon, and that most of the time, she saw the cases result in an indictment. "It would be a complete waste of time and resources if a D.A. took every case to grand jury, regardless of the evidence. So any D.A. that takes a case to grand jury – ours included – is doing it feeling pretty confident that he's going to get an indictment and the case is going to proceed."

I had to agree, of course. Since its creation at the time of the Magna Carta 800 years ago, the grand jury process has gradually morphed into something that does an excellent job of putting a stamp of approval on government investigations and catering to the aims of ambitious prosecutors. Cases go to trial more often than they should, based on only half the evidence that will be brought to trial. What's worse, the defense can't be sure of learning when grand jury testimony backs the defendant or impeaches a prosecution witness. Just think of how many times in a regular trial there are slightly inconsistent statements from witnesses, an important detail that differs from the story told to police, or an account that has shifted over time. It happens all the time, and the defense is there to take advantage of it. But in a grand jury proceeding, we're not there and there is no recording or transcript provided to help the defense find the discrepancies. It's all up to the D.A. to deliver the information.

In a case called *Brady vs. Maryland*, the U.S. Supreme Court ruled that it was a violation of due process not to present exculpatory, or favorable, evidence to a defendant. This is called the government's "Brady obligation." Now, since stories shift and "truth" is only for a jury to determine at trial, you would think that prosecutors are kept pretty busy alerting defendants to testimony that differs from reports. So, how many times, in the hundreds of cases that our firm has handled, has a D.A. actually notified us of inconsistent statements from a grand jury witness? Once. Only one time has a D.A. ever called me and said, "Hey, Mike, I need to tell you a useful fact for your case, something that I heard at grand jury today." That call came from Lissa Casey who, before 2012, was a prosecutor in the Lane County District Attorney's office. We hired her when she got laid off during a county budget crisis.

Though Emilia was convinced that Gerald's indictment was coming, I wasn't. "They could be taking it to grand jury because they know it's a case of self-defense and they want to hide behind the grand jury not indict-ing," I offered. It would make it easier to "circular-file" a high-profile case, I explained, because the decision not to indict would be on the grand jury's shoulders and not on the D.A.'s.

But then I recalled the official position of the Lane County D.A.'s office: they maintain it's unethical for their office to submit a case for grand jury consideration that they do not personally believe they can prove beyond a reasonable doubt. Taken at their word, it means they don't even allow a grand jury to consider something that they don't intend to take to trial.

"You're right," I then conceded to Emilia. "We should assume a lot when they take something to grand jury. As a starting point, we should assume they believe our client is guilty."

"Correct."

"So that means we are heading straight into the grip of the D.A. They use the secrecy of grand juries to get information that helps their case. They do it for the tactical advantage of learning the weaknesses in their case before a defense attorney gets involved."

"Possibly," Emilia said with a shrug. "I haven't observed that in my experience, but then again, I've never watched a grand jury consider a mur-der case."

But if Emilia thought I'd gotten off the fence, she soon saw me reclaim my perch there. "We have to remember that this is a special case, with a spe-cial client. Even if the D.A. is gunning for an indictment, Gerald himself might be able to change some minds on that grand jury."

"Possible. But it's a long shot. What's more likely is that our client will say something inconsistent with what he told somebody else. Then he's a liar. What if Gerald testified to something different than what he told 911?"

"That would be a disaster. He'd get indicted for sure."

Still deadlocked on the question of whether to have Gerald offer to tes-tify at grand jury, we brought in Jan Holcomb, one of Arnold Law's senior attorneys. She's a retired Oregon Circuit Court judge, and a former pros-ecutor who has taken plenty of cases to grand jury. One such case was the 1997 aggravated murder case of Alan Watkins, where Jan successfully prose-cuted one of Oregon's youngest aggravated murder defendants in the shoot-ing of his foster mother. Jan also presided over many a murder case in her court, including one that caused a prosecutor in another county to hand in his resignation when Jan laid partial blame for the murder of a child on the state. Oregon, she said, had failed to address child-abuse allegations – and the inaction led to a murder. Yes, her experience with murder cases involving political D.A.s was important to me and to Gerald. She knows the turf.

After listening to Gerald's account of the shooting, Jan told him that any reasonable district attorney "would have to sit up straight and listen," because he sounded very credible. "Even if this D.A. plans to indict," she advised, "your testimony could change the charge from murder to manslaughter, making a trial much more palatable to you."

"What do you mean by that?" Gerald asked.

"I mean that if you go to trial on manslaughter in the first degree you are only risking 10 years of your life rather than 25 to life for murder. It reduces the risk of trial dramatically."

Both Gerald and I understood this line of reasoning, of course, but like Emilia, I had come to believe that the risks to our client outweighed the benefits. The greatest benefit to Gerald if he testified and things went well would be if it stopped the district attorney's prosecution of him completely. That would be an enormous payoff. He could save a year of anguish awaiting trial and potentially years of jail or prison. But what if he did a great job and still got indicted? The prosecution would know our entire defense theory and could spend a year preparing a case against it. Or, more ominously, what if Gerald said just one thing wrong, just one tiny detail that differed from what he said to 911 or to friends and family? The prosecution wouldn't take that slip-up as evidence of nerves or stress, but of guilt. I had to acknowledge that the odds of Gerald screwing it up and harming his case were extremely high. But the possibility of avoiding the whole court process just by coming clean about defending himself... well, it was undeniably tantalizing.

Ultimately, I had my decision made for me when I spoke to a reliable law enforcement source who had heard some very relevant gossip through the local legal grapevine. He disclosed to me that Bob Lane, the prosecutor, had already decided to "true bill" the murder charge, meaning that he intended to indict Gerald for murder. While the grand jury was officially the body that would do the indicting, the prosecutor's power to choose what the grand jury heard basically gave the prosecutor significant leverage over the end result. This, to me, was the final indicator that the script was already written, and the outcome of the grand jury process all but predetermined.

I took a deep breath and called my client. "Gerald, I heard from a source at Springfield," I began, "and it's not good news. Bob Lane plans to 'true bill' this."

"Your source, is he credible?"

I named the source, and Gerald was speechless. I could almost hear the hope trickling out of him during his stunned silence.

"I am pretty damn sure the deck is stacked against you at this point," I continued, "I can't be in there with you in the grand jury room. I can't listen to what you say, or object to anything, even if the question wouldn't be allowed in any other court proceeding. In other words, there's just too much risk in testifying at grand jury. I can't advise you to do this."

Gerald heard me, but he wasn't accepting my advice. His voice strengthening with conviction, he asked, "Why? Why can't I do this?"

Candidly, I said, "I'm afraid for you, Gerald. I'm afraid of what might happen to you in there. I won't be able to do my job for you, standing on the other side of the door."

Then Gerald laughed derisively. "I'm too stupid to be afraid."

"We're talking about the rest of your life."

I understood that Judge Holcomb's words had been persuasive with Gerald. But I wasn't at all happy with the position he was taking. I continued trying to convince him that testifying was a bad idea. It would basically be a deposition taken by the D.A., I said. I didn't want him to go in there before our accident reconstruction was complete. I didn't want him to go on the record until we had the facts to back up his version of what had happened. I reminded him that stress and trauma can be hard on memories. Clients don't always remember everything, or what they remember can be erroneous. Mistakes can be made. Not lies, mind you, mistakes. It's just how it is.

Nonetheless, I knew the decision was Gerald's, and I left him to ponder it. A few days later I heard back from him. While considering what to do, Gerald had gone salmon fishing with a former prosecutor at the Lane County D.A.'s Office. The guy was an acquaintance of Gerald's who still helped out on cases now and then (it's a small town). Speaking with this former prosecutor convinced Gerald once again that he would be a good witness for himself. The prosecutor had advised him to testify, Gerald told me, and he wanted to do it. He wanted me to call the D.A.'s office and make the overture.

Now, I'll admit that if I were Gerald, I'd have wanted to testify too. My wife would have probably throttled me before it could happen, but I would have wanted to. I began crafting a set of ground rules before agreeing to make our client available:

- We would limit Gerald's testimony to the time between exiting the vehicle and pulling the trigger. This would reduce our exposure to "facts" and evidence that the D.A. might have that we did not. I was still reluctant to fully accept the allegation of the intentional ramming by Crofut. It just seemed too good for the case to be true.

- We wanted Gerald to have unlimited opportunities to take breaks and meet with counsel during the testimony. We needed to be on hand to advise him.

- We wanted Gerald to be able to review the transcript of the 911 call before testifying. It was a public record that wouldn't be available to us until the investigation was complete. We reasoned that police officers get to review their notes and reports before going before a grand jury, so why couldn't our client have access to his own words that night?

- Finally, we insisted that Gerald's testimony be recorded to provide context for any statements he might make, avoiding the question of whether he said or didn't say something.

Assistant District Attorney Bob Lane called me back, and unfortunately, the conversation was not what Emilia or I would call constructive. He wanted no limitations placed on Gerald's testimony. None of my conditions were acceptable to him. Why? "It's just not done that way," he said. If ever I had doubted it, I now had to entertain this strong possibility: Lane was after an indictment, probably even an indictment on a murder charge.

It was time for me to take my own advice and stop hoping for the best. I needed to prepare for the worst and advise my client to do the same.

Lane, a short man in his late fifties with a cop mustache, is a seasoned prosecutor. His track record is strong, but it includes some notable losses that would seem to be the result of his hardheaded insistence on letting a jury make the tough decisions. For example, in 2012, Lane tried and lost a locally high-profile case involving a young woman who allegedly gave birth and either killed the baby or failed to get medical help to save it. A first jury was hung after learning of a coerced police confession by the Springfield Police Department in the case. Lane tried the case again, only to have the young woman quickly acquitted.

If Lane wouldn't let Gerald see the transcript of the 911 call, if he wouldn't let Gerald confer with me during breaks, and if he wouldn't even agree to record Gerald's testimony, there was only one conclusion to reach: Lane was only interested in gathering evidence for his case, not at getting to the truth. His confirmation bias firmly in place, Lane apparently believed he knew the truth already and any contrary facts he may have encountered were matters he could set aside as irrelevant or unimportant. I found it most galling that Lane was barring the door to me and my advice, even during breaks. Opportunities to speak with counsel are common accommodations for a federal grand jury target or subject, which is sadly beyond the scope of experience of most D.A.'s I've encountered. (Most are career prosecutors who haven't seen much outside their little county fiefdoms). I think a lot of D.A.'s in Oregon could learn something from reading the United States Attorney Manual, which discusses the "appearance of unfairness" in denying a suspect's request to testify before the grand jury.

I took one more shot with Lane, encouraging him to subpoena the bartenders who had served David Crofut and his wife that night. They would detail, I said, how intoxicated both were at the time of the motor vehicle collision. I'm sad to report that Lane declined to do this, along with everything else he said no to.

Unable to reach an agreement on accommodations, Lane and I ended the call knowing that this grand jury would proceed without Gerald's testimony.

CHAPTER 9

A NEW KIND OF DEPLOYMENT

Over the days that followed Deputy D.A. Bob Lane's refusal to accept the conditions under which Gerald would be granted his wish to testify before the grand jury, I was in a dark mood and I wasn't reluctant to share it with the rest of my office. It's never fun to feel your client has a right to tell his story, yet also know that it's not safe for him to do so.

Still, I have a rather irritating tendency to begin looking on the bright side before too long. As I told Emilia, there was one to be found here, if we looked for it.

"What else did we learn from Bob Lane in that phone call?" I asked her.

Emilia's usually pretty quick and this time was no exception. "That Gerald should prepare for an extended concrete vacation?"

"Ha, no. While Lane may be a smart man and a great litigator, he has a complete lack of strategic vision. He might as well have flat-out told us that he either doesn't know or doesn't care about strategy."

He made this obvious, I thought, by passing up an opportunity to get a suspect under oath and mostly on his terms. A smart, strategy-minded prosecutor would have rolled out the red carpet, catered lunch at the grand jury visit while giving the suspect a foot massage, all to get the defendant under oath. It's an opportunity that no prosecutor should pass up. What was the downside for him? Yes, Gerald would get to see all the evidence, but if he chose to testify at trial, he'd get access to all that before taking the stand anyway. And Lane and his team would have gotten a preview of what Gerald had to say, which would be a big leg up on their trial preparation. Our cards would have all been on the table and we would have been committed to a defense theory.

What do I mean by "committed to a defense theory?" Well, sometimes the truth is not the best defense. Often an innocent client's story is unbelievable because they are misremembering or the facts are just that bizarre. Sometimes you don't argue the big conspiracy theory that is likely true, because it's better to argue incompetence or something else. Even when you don't make that decision until the middle of trial you never, ever tell the other side. It's like showing your playbook to the opposing football coach. To quote Lane himself: It's just not done.

The Lane County Grand Jury was convened at the beginning of March to consider the shooting death of David Crofut. We knew the date because Gerald's fiancée, Kristin, received a subpoena to appear and testify.

I was in my office when I got a call that week from Verne Hoyer, who was pretty indignant about something.

"Get this!" Verne said. "I just got off the phone with Oneta Boyles, you know, the gal who drove through the scene and called 911. She testified at grand jury yesterday. You know what she told me? She told me that before she testified, the SPD detectives let her listen to her 911 call."

"You're shitting me."

"Straight up, that's what she said."

"Thanks. Write a report and call me later."

I hung up, and walked around my desk to the window. God, I was angry. I watched the cars traveling up onto the Ferry Street Bridge and out of sight, and the ones coming toward me, funneling east and west from the off ramps. It was calming to watch, like life blood, always flowing. I needed that calm. If I didn't find it pretty quickly, I was going to throw my computer through the window.

The government had prepped all of its witnesses, given them the accommodations, let them refresh their recollections, yet Gerald was not deemed to be entitled to any of this. He didn't even have access to any of the evidence yet! I felt glad then, gladder than ever, that Gerald had not gone to testify at grand jury. It would have been akin to sending a lamb to the slaughter, because I now knew with close to certainty what I had begun to suspect – that Gerald would be charged with murder, not manslaughter in the first or second degree, and certainly not criminally negligent homicide. The deck was stacked and Lady Justice wasn't dealing these cards.

The next evening, as I was driving home from a 52-count felony case in Columbia County, northwest of Portland, I received a text from Kristin. Gerald had been arrested. She said he had been taken into custody during a traffic stop.

Most likely, this ride with Kristin was the last time for a long time that Gerald would be in a vehicle without the accompaniment of handcuffs and leg chains.

CHAPTER 10

DISCOVERY AND THE
"PARADE OF HORRIBLES"

Gerald Strebendt was arraigned on March 7th. When I read the murder indictment handed down by the grand jury, I was enraged all
over again. From what I could see, Deputy D.A. Bob Lane didn't
call any of the witnesses that I had asked him to. The fix was in; no need for
me to fight my cynicism on that anymore. Letting Gerald testify at grand
jury was a terrible idea from the get-go. Under no circumstances would
Gerald be talking to anyone in the government about anything from here
on, unless we decided to have him tell it to the jury at trial. And trial, unfortunately, was where this was headed.

It was time to dig in deeper on the evidence. It was time to shift the
focus from the D.A. to Gerald's eventual jury, and figure out what that
group of people will need to exonerate my client.

Most defense cases come to me, as I've said, after arrest and around the
time of arraignment. Typically, that's when you get hired, after somebody's
been arrested or charged, so all the reports and evidence are available right
from the start.

But Gerald Strebendt's case had been different. There was a solid month
between the shooting on January 29th and his arraignment on March

7th, after which he was remanded to custody in the Lane County Jail to await a trial that could be years away. During those weeks before the grand jury indictment, we were doing whatever we could to head off the possibility that Gerald would be charged and tried, and we were doing it on our own. Nothing was available from the government to help us develop our case. But now that our best efforts had failed — now that Gerald was indicted, arrested and arraigned — we began receiving what evidence the D.A. and the Springfield Police Department had on Gerald (or thought they had). Taken together, these reports, statements and documents are what's called discovery.

When the discovery became available, I put everything aside to immerse myself in it, hoping the documents would help me understand some of the key questions in the case — the main one being why David Crofut would have followed Gerald 80 feet beyond their two vehicles, threatening that he, too, had a weapon. Was he armed? Was he drunk, as we strongly suspected? What could the police investigation tell me that would help me defend Gerald? What surprises might the paperwork hold?

Perhaps fittingly, the first file I reviewed included photos of my own client taken at the police department, the night of the shooting. The images showed Gerald at all angles, from both sides and then facing the camera. His eyes stood out. They were empty, blank, unfocused — truly the thousand-yard stare of a trauma victim. Retired Marine Sergeant Major Joe Houle, the Vietnam veteran who coined the term, described the look on soldiers' faces as deadened, as though "the life had been sucked out of them." I made a note in my trial outline to show these photos to the jury. Gerald looked terrible, and not like a cold-blooded killer.

Next I listened to the tape of the 911 call that Gerald had made that night, and I understood even better why Gerald looked so traumatized. It was seven minutes of stress and terror. Gerald sounded like a man in abject fear. His words dominated, interrupted only by questions from first one dispatcher, then another. He sounded polite, intelligent and very, very apprehensive. To me, the things said on the tape completely substantiated Gerald's story and how he told it to Justin Vaccaro on the phone. He was driving home when the motorist in front of him slammed on his brakes, forcing Gerald to go around him on the right. Then the motorist rammed his truck. Then the guy got out of his truck and threatened Gerald. Gerald feared he had a gun, partly because the guy said he did. In the tape, Gerald tells the dispatcher that he's got his rifle in his hands, but the other motorist won't quit advancing on him. You can hear Gerald repeatedly telling his eventual victim to "stay back, sir." Then there is noise, static, and Gerald cried out for an ambulance.

Also in this first batch of discovery, I found the usual crime scene photos and police reports detailing the handling of evidence. I grouped them and, for the moment, set them aside. Then I came upon the SPD's reports on interviews done with witnesses who had driven by the scene. I skimmed these for new information, but didn't find any on the first pass. Everybody spoke of a car, a truck, a man with a rifle saying "get back," and another man not getting back and not wanting a 911 call to be made, apparently determined to handle the situation himself. These reports would get a detailed look later on, with the help of investigators and experts.

Then I found what no defense attorney wants to find: page after page of interviews with witnesses who have bad things to say about your client. In my career I've come to call evidence like this "The Parade of Horribles." I can say that in all of my years as a defense attorney, I had never received such a Parade as I did in Gerald's case:

- **Riley Omlid** talked about Gerald getting mad at other drivers. Riley, the friend from whom Gerald was going to borrow DVDs on the night of the shooting, was quoted as telling police that he had seen Gerald behaving in ways that suggested actual or potential road-raging. He also said Gerald had boasted about shooting incidents that occurred while in the Marines or working for Blackwater.

- There was a report from the **North Bend Police Department** that Gerald once beat up a homeless man in his mother's garage. Investigators there believed it was a vigilante-style assault because of the victim's sex-offender status.

- **Bill Hammond** said that he had experienced an in-person disagreement with Gerald about tires. Gerald confronted him aggressively, and called him out. He said, "Want to box...fat fuck?" Hammond called Gerald "a loose cannon" and was not surprised to hear that Gerald had killed someone.

- **William Pitts** said that while driving on South "A" Street in Springfield, Gerald tailgated, gestured, and yelled at him. Pitts reported that Gerald threw a cup of coffee at his vehicle.

- **William Richey**, a security guard, said he was confronted by Gerald when investigating some damage to a nearby property. Gerald was hostile, getting in Richey's face to scream, "You fat fuck, you rent-a-pig, come on attack me, you have a gun, I will fuck you up." Richey thought Gerald was completely out of control.

- **Dale "Duce" Madras** said that he was punched repeatedly and pinned to the ground by Gerald after Madras had an argument with William Pressley at an auto body shop called West Side Classics. Madras also claimed that Gerald smashed the driver's side window of his car while Madras was attempting to call 911 and flee the scene.

- **Walter Stenger**, an un-employed and probably homeless man, said that he was jumped by Gerald and punched several times when he approached West Side Classics looking for work.

- **Kevin Shields and Tina Ramsdal**, neighbors of Gerald's, said they turned into the cul-de-sac where all three lived, only to have Gerald cut them off with his pickup truck, accusing them of "following" or "stalking" him.

- **Tina Ramsdal** told of two more incidents. In one, she said that Gerald, apparently intoxicated, boasted of killing people for a living and of shooting numerous people while in the military. She told police she feared that he would kill her. In the second incident, Gerald, again allegedly drunk, had left the door to his pickup truck open, leaving "at least eight guns" in plain sight. Ramsdal said she spent 10 minutes pounding on his door to come close the truck, fearing that a child would get ahold of one or more of his guns.

- **Kenneth Caudell** said he responded to Gerald's Craigslist ad for tires. When they met, the two men argued about the tires. Gerald became hostile, called Caudell an "idiot," and attempted to start a physical fight. Caudell had contact with Gerald again a few months later, and Gerald again approached him aggressively, stood extremely close to him, and attempted to lure him into a fight. At the time, Caudell was 65 years old. Gerald was 33.

- **James Antsy** called law enforcement after hearing about the case in the news and claimed he helped raise Gerald with his own children. Antsy reported that Gerald bragged to him about killing people as a hired mercenary. He also told police that Gerald "always had an instinct for wanting to kill" and that Gerald had killed animals as a child. He called Gerald "macho" and said that he had a "bad temper."

- Screenshots of **Gerald's Facebook page** showed that he had posted several pictures of himself shooting or holding rifles or other weapons. He also posted a picture of himself drinking a Corona while he held up what appeared to be an angry note from another driver.

- **Michael and Jean Cunningham** said they were taking a back road in nearby Pleasant Hill, Oregon, behind the local pizza joint, when they had contact with Gerald on July 4, 2013. Gerald was standing in the road, talking to another male in a vehicle. Cunningham honked at Gerald to let Gerald know he was coming through, and Gerald responded by aggressively approaching the Cunningham's truck and punching out Cunningham's driver-side mirror.

- **Lane County Sheriff's Deputy Charles Douglass** observed Gerald speeding on the freeway in his pickup truck, weaving in and out of traffic without using turn signals, and tailgating to coerce the drivers to move out of his way. The deputy initiated a traffic stop. According to his report, Gerald yelled at the deputy, calling him an "asshole" and a "douchebag." Gerald even threatened to write the deputy a ticket. Deputy Douglass wrote in his report that he was worried Gerald would come out of his truck to confront him. He wrote the ticket quickly and ended the contact, and then requested that an officer safety alert be placed in a database for the benefit of law enforcement agents who might have future contact with Gerald.

- There were also pages of reports showing that Gerald had **called 911 on his neighbors** multiple times to say that he had observed domestic violence, drunken driving, and a fire. Sometimes, if police didn't arrive quickly, Gerald stepped in physically.

- Gerald followed an out-of-control driver and later allegedly told **Deputy Derrald Mann** that he was prepared to run the man's car off the road if it had become necessary.

- **Kim Charbonneau** told of a September 2013 incident in which she and her husband had been in a dispute with Gerald regarding traffic rules for emergency vehicles.

- In an alarming and eerily similar incident, **Nicholas Johnson**, a disabled veteran, said he had just been released from the hospital in 2004 and was driving home to the Oregon Coast when he came into contact with Gerald. According to Johnson, Gerald drove up behind him and started tailgating him. Johnson said that he tried to let Gerald by, but Gerald stayed right behind him. Johnson said he was concerned enough that he drove past his house, not wanting Gerald to know where he lived, and not wanting to risk getting assaulted by stopping. Eventually he pulled over, he said, and watched as Gerald stopped in the middle of the road and pulled a rifle out of his truck. It was Gerald who called the police, though, reporting Johnson as the aggressor and saying Johnson was the one who brandished a firearm.

- Gerald's own ex-wife, **Rachel Chilton**, recounted various alleged incidents of "road rage," including brake checking, cutting people off, and numerous other incidents that allegedly occurred "as much as three to five times a week." Chilton specifically referred to a 2011 incident in which Gerald allegedly road-raged while pulling Rachel's loaded horse trailer.

- In a **Facebook posting** from just a handful of days before the killing, Gerald had written, "If you like to drive slow guess what? You should be in the slow lane. If you want to drive greater than the speed limit guess what? You should be in my lane. If you get this confused somehow guess what? I will strike hard and fast like a cobra should an opportunity present itself."

This is a disaster. I'm starting to see where the road-rage allegation has been coming from.

I had to ask myself: Were all of these people just attention-seekers, people who wanted to be part of what passed as a "high-profile" case locally? Hindsight is always 20-20 and people tend to shape their past memories to fit the framework of the information they find in the present. There's research that proves it. But was it even possible for all of those people to be mistaken... lying... just plain wrong?

Unfortunately, all of these incidents were relevant to Gerald's self-defense claim — that is, if we couldn't keep them out of court. Since the standard of self-defense is what a reasonable person in Gerald's position would do, his history and temperament, for better or worse, mattered. The acts described in the Parade of Horribles posed quite a high hurdle, not just for our defense case, but for any juror who might want to find Gerald not guilty. If we couldn't get at least some of the Horribles excluded from the trial on legal grounds, I was concerned that the jury would have great difficulty focusing on the exculpatory evidence that we were gathering from the incident itself.

Hell, I was having my own difficulty separating the Gerald I thought I knew from this new and very disturbing evidence against him! As high as I had been when I heard the polygrapher say he believed Gerald's story of innocence, well, I was now every bit that low or lower.

Like others who saw the list, I found it incredible — absolutely astonishing — that Gerald had never been convicted of a crime. We knew that Gerald had been in continual contact with law enforcement for pretty much his entire adult life, and while some of these contacts were positive — ones where Gerald had been helpful to his fellow man and assisted law enforcement by providing self-defense training – this list of "bad acts" completely overshadowed anything good we'd heard about the guy. Clearly, this helpful teacher, mentor, and good citizen had another side. He obviously had a tendency to let his mouth get him in trouble, and sometimes his fists came along for the ride.

The rest of my defense team was just as devastated by the Parade of Horribles as I was. But, as is often the case, as we met to discuss the new evidence, Emilia pointed me back in the right direction. "Having a big mouth is a far cry from killing. Just because a man is an asshole doesn't make him a murderer."

I agreed. But how would we handle this? How would the prosecution try and use all of this evidence? Lacking a solid plan, I ended the meeting with instructions: "Let's work up some of the 'good Gerald' stories we've been hearing. And let's find out if David Crofut has any skeletons in his closet."

A CONCRETE BOX

Visiting Gerald in jail was difficult for me. The guy was going to be twiddling his thumbs in jail for a long time, unless we could get him bailed out. Because of the seriousness of the charge and his notoriety as a professional fighter, he'd be doing all of his time in solitary-confinement. As a defense attorney, you never get used to seeing your client in custody, especially when you think your client is innocent.

Yes, innocent. Despite being shaken by the government's case against Gerald, I still thought the shooting was justified, even with the Parade of Horribles. I kept reminding myself that what happened at the scene that night had to be judged separately from whatever "bad acts" had been alleged against Gerald in his past. But damn. It was really hard to get past that list, with so many of the bad acts lending credence to the government's road-rage theory of the case.

When I visited Gerald, I learned that the Parade had knocked Gerald back on his heels, too. He had mitigating details to offer in most of the stories, and some of them he flat-out disputed. But in each encounter listed in the discovery, there was a kernel of truth in what the reports said, and Gerald readily admitted it. Yet he fiercely maintained that he was innocent of murder, reminding me again and again of the ways that he tried to de-escalate the situation before firing his weapon that night on Bob Straub

Parkway. Crofut wouldn't quit coming at him. It looked like he had a weapon. Crofut even grabbed at the rifle in the seconds before Gerald fired. What was he to do?

The actual evidence we'd gathered so far seemed to support what polygrapher Hebner had said, that it was "a good shoot." Crofut had to have been drunk, given his earlier consumption. Passersby described Crofut as the angry one. But from the indictment, it was clear that the D.A. had presented to the grand jury none of the evidence we suggested he should. Gerald already knew how pissed I was about that. He and I had often talked about the grand jury and the problems I had with how it was conducted. Today I had another bit of news, and it wasn't good. I tried to come in looking and sounding upbeat. I hoped he'd do the same.

When Gerald arrived in the attorney visiting room and sat down, I noticed immediately that he looked thinner than the last time I'd seen him.

"What's up, man? How you doing? You losing weight?"

"Yeah, well, the food isn't exactly gourmet and I'm not that hungry. They've got me in solitary, you know. Have you seen what the cells are like in there?"

"I've never toured it. But Emilia has, and she didn't choose to extend her stay. Not impressed."

He smiled wryly. "It's basically a concrete box with a metal door. No bars, just concrete blocks. I've been counting those blocks and there are 532 or so, depending whether you combine the half-pieces at the floor and the ceiling."

"Do you have a window?

"There's a small one up high, but I can't climb up to look out or anything. I mean, I could, but if they catch me doing it they'll put me in a cell that has no windows and I'd never get any natural light in at all."

"The cell's pretty small, I suppose."

Gerald shrugged, as if to say, "Compared to what?" He guessed maybe 8 feet by 10 feet. "I suppose a tall guy could touch both sides at the same time. It's big enough to do push-ups on the floor, but not too much else."

"Toilet? Decent bed?"

"There's a steel toilet. The bed is actually a poured concrete slab that sticks out of the wall, covered with a pretty thin foam mattress, only a few inches thick, and the pillow is made of the same stuff. The blanket is the definition of threadbare. I can see right through it."

"They let you out of there at all?"

"If I behave, I get what they call 'day room' once a day. They'll walk me down to another room that's a bit bigger, with a shower and a phone. I usually call Kristin, and then try to walk around as much as I can. I'll shower, get cleaned up…."

"Anyone ever in there to talk to?"

"Sometimes one or two guys, who also don't get to be out with the rest of the population." He shot me a look to emphasize how surreal it was to be rated among the worst of the worst, then continued. "The guards know I'm not going to fight, and these guys aren't violent either, so sometimes they put us in together. Mostly sex offenders. Fucked up, yes, but not violent."

The trouble with day room, Gerald continued, was its lack of privacy. "If you need to pee or shit, there's no stall, no doors. And there are these long windows on one wall that open to the hall. I'm not supposed to look out of the windows or I'll lose day room, but I see people out there – women staff, sometimes civilians. So I just wait to use the toilet until I get back to my room." The shower wasn't as private as it could be either, he added. "In the shower is where they give me my allergy meds. The nurse is female, and she basically has to watch me eat it, make sure I swallow it. You don't hold onto your dignity long in here," he said.

"We'll get you out," I said lightly but fervently. "We'll get this behind you."

Gerald looked up and said, "Anything new?"

"Not really," I answered. "Nothing in particular." After a moment I added, "Well, we do need to talk about money."

With that, I let Gerald know that my firm's fees had already eaten up the funds he'd put in trust for his defense. We'd burned through everything he had in a matter of weeks. "But that means nothing," I quickly reassured him. "I'm asking the court to find you indigent and appoint me as your lawyer so the state will pay the bills." The $46 an hour I'd make in that role was about a tenth of my going rate, but we didn't dwell on that. I told Gerald he could rest assured that as long as he wanted me, he had me for the duration.

With that conversation having dwindled into awkward silence, Gerald surprised me by leaning back in his chair to ask, "Read any good books lately?"

I snorted. "Do I look like I have time to read anything but 'The Gerald Strebendt Story' these days?"

"I've been reading the discovery too," he replied, "but my mind needed a break. I started borrowing books from this little cart they bring by every week, and that's pretty much all I do in my cell – read books."

"So what do you like to read?" I asked Gerald.

"Everything. History, fiction, anything. I hated English in high school, so it's ironic that I love to read now. I barely read anything as a kid. I think that hampered me."

"What are you working on now?"

"I've got a few books going, but I just finished 'Into the Wild,' by Jon Krakauer. It's about that hippie kid who got around the country hitchhiking and died up in Alaska trying to live off the land."

"I read it and I saw the movie too," I said. "I thought the guy was an idiot – interesting, but an idiot."

"No! He was really smart, he went to Emory, and some of the books and authors he mentioned were ones that have had a real impact on me. I really think he could have made it. It wasn't impossible."

"People talk about how his off-the-grid stuff was so romantic," I scoffed. "Whatever. Surviving is hard work. I only dabble in farming but I watched my grandpa and my uncle farm in Iowa, and it's hard work, even with modern machinery. Play-surviving is fun. Tilling my pasture is fun. Real surviving is scary and hard. I think his death was a waste."

"Maybe, but I still think what he did was pretty amazing. He wasn't afraid to die doing what he believed in. I can respect that." He slumped back in the plastic chair and slid his arms off the table to fall to his sides. "*What. A. Life.*"

"People ought to prepare, though." I countered. "Why not take a sat phone? He didn't have to use it. He could starve all he wanted to. But when he needed it, it would have saved his life."

"Mike, it was 1992 and normal hikers didn't have satellite phones. But, just think, though," Gerald said, getting philosophical on me. "How many people these days will suffer and even die for what they believe in?"

Our conversation moved on, but in my head I was stuck on what Gerald had said a few moments before: "What a life." Gerald should talk,

I was thinking. By now I had a pretty good biography on my client, both from the work of my investigators and from Gerald's own words. It was the story of a man determined to grow up and out of his meager circumstances to become somebody – ideally, somebody strong enough to fight what was wrong and defend what was right.

CHAPTER 12

THE BEGINNING OF GERALD STREBENDT

N ow that Gerald was in jail, we had plenty of time to talk about his life, and what brought him to that moment in the dark. As he had told me in our very first meeting, Gerald called "the Bay Area" his home – Coos Bay, Oregon, not the San Francisco Bay Area. It's a semi-rural setting on the coast of southern Oregon. He was born March 1, 1979 to Debby and William Strebendt. Debby married William just after her 18th birthday, but it wasn't a marriage made in heaven. They had divorced by the time Gerald was two. Gerald reported that his father participated in child-rearing sporadically after the split, and that William put considerable effort into not paying his child support. That left Debby struggling to support her little family, which included not just Gerald but an older brother, Doug. Without William's help, Gerald told us, there often wasn't enough food to eat.

The first place Gerald remembers living was in a trailer park called "The Firs" in Hauser, Oregon. There his most significant memory was walking in a windstorm with his mom and brother, and losing some of the family's Christmas presents. Around the time he was three years old, Gerald, his brother, and mother moved up in the world. They got out of their single-wide trailer and into a double-wide that his mother's boyfriend, "Buzz", helped get them into. Gerald has fond memories of the "Sand-N-Wood" trailer park, where the new double-wide was parked. He recalls days spent roaming around unsupervised, carrying a handmade bow and arrow, and his slingshot.

When the price of gas increased and limited Buzz's ability to visit, Debby Strebendt and her young family moved to North Bend to live with Buzz, his parents, and his grandparents in low-income housing. Gerald waited in line with his mother at the local community center for food, taking home bricks of cheese, powdered milk, and bread. Gerald's mother did not drive, so if Buzz wasn't driving, they walked.

Gerald and Doug idolized their new father figure. Buzz was a long-haul trucker who let the boys play with knives and BB guns. He also took the boys along on his questionable adventures. The boys were with him back in the trailer park days, for example, when Buzz used his spiked boots to climb the telephone poles to connect cable TV for not just Debby and the kids, but everybody else in the trailer park who wanted it too. "It's not stealing," he told the boys. He also took the boys along when he raided construction sites at night to haul away 2x4s and other easily transported supplies. This too was okay, he told Gerald and Doug, because "it's just scraps."

Visits from William, Gerald's father, were infrequent and much anticipated by his sons. But William was a man with a lot of sharp edges. According to Gerald, he drank a lot and once drove a vehicle through the wall and into the bedroom of their trailer. Did these things really happen? I couldn't be sure. Still, the impact of his parents' separation on Gerald was undeniably bruising. Gerald recalls being berated for any perceived weakness, especially whenever he admitted to cold, hunger or fear. Gerald came to believe that he was weak, definitely too weak to take care of his mother. It didn't help that Gerald was a small kid. His eventual height would be just below 5 foot 9 inches, and he was slow getting there.

Somewhere in the early 1980s, not long after it completed its theatrical release and went to VHS, Gerald saw "First Blood," the Sylvester Stallone/Rambo action flick. From that day forward, he wanted to be a soldier. It would be many years before he even knew that there were different branches of the military, but as he grew, the goal stayed constant – a soldier he would be. Most of Gerald's clothes in his young years were handmade by his grandmother, so he cajoled her into using camouflage fabric, like a soldier would wear. He also convinced her to sew large pockets into the shirts and pants to hold his slingshot, sticks, rocks, a small pen knife, and even lizards and snakes when he could find them.

In walking to and from grade school in North Bend, Gerald discovered a gun shop called the Ammo Bunker. It was owned by a man named Steve McMullan. Gerald began to stop by the store every day, and the habit continued into Gerald's early teens. If he was going to be a soldier, he explained to McMullan, he would need to know all about guns. Gerald was 10 or 11 when he bought his first rifle, a Ruger 10-22. Gerald's grandmother signed for it, but the boy himself paid for it with $150 he had earned from delivering newspapers.

On January 11, 1993, Gerald was pulled out of school by the vice-principal who told him that McMullan had been brutally attacked by a robber and was hospitalized. Everybody knew that Gerald spent a lot of time at the Ammo Bunker; it was a small town. Gerald left school and ran to the shop. When he arrived, it was still swarming with police and blood was splattered on the snow of the sidewalk. It was there that Gerald learned that Jason Ray Dizick had tried to murder McMullan by slashing his throat.

Gerald told me about his memories of standing outside of the gun shop, ankle deep in the bloody snow. If it hadn't been for the snowfall that day, he wouldn't have gotten a rare ride to school. He would have been walking, and he believes that he would have stopped by the Ammo Bunker as he had so many times before. It could have been his blood there in the snow. It was then and there, standing in the snow spattered with the blood of a man he cared for and admired, that Gerald made a decision: Never would he be anybody's victim. He would make himself strong. He would learn to protect himself. He would never let someone hurt him or someone he loved – not if he could do anything to prevent it.

And yes, guns would come to play a role in this resolve of Gerald's. While he got his first rifle in elementary school, it wasn't until almost the 7th grade that he really learned how to use it. During an outdoor education program at school, he worked with a precision air rifle and learned all the necessary gun-safety rules, including the most important: "Never point a rifle at anything you do not intend to shoot."

Then, in his freshman year of high school, Gerald came across a book that further shaped his life. By then he was in Idaho, trying out a stint of living with his dad for awhile. The book was a bit of local Idaho history called "Give a Boy a Gun: A True Story of Law and Disorder in the American West" by Jack Olson. The story told of Claude Lafayette Dallas, Jr., a young man raised in Upper Michigan whose father's philosophy was "give a boy a gun and you're makin' a man." Dallas worked as a cowpuncher and handyman on several ranches in the rugged border areas of Nevada, Idaho, and Oregon. There he got involved in poaching and he was eventually contacted by two game wardens. He killed the two men, and went on the run. The book reports that Dallas made the decision to shoot the wardens only after they wantonly killed his mule during his arrest. In reading the book, Gerald empathized strongly with Dallas. While he didn't agree with Dallas' decision to kill the wardens, he understood the frustration and anger the lonely Dallas must have felt when the wardens uncaringly shot his mule. For the first time in his short life, Gerald realized that the lines between right and wrong were gray and justice was often in what remedies a person could find for himself.

In talking to Gerald, I learned that he was named after his great uncle, who died in 2012 leaving behind a large, working ranch on the oceanfront north of Port Orford, Oregon. It was 1,180 acres with 600 cattle on it, and it had been in the family since 1941. Amazingly, the ranch had managed to retain its right to the beach at high tide, which is very unusual in our state. When Oregon declared all beaches from Washington to California public, Gerald's family sued and prevailed. It's still a place, Gerald said, where Japanese glass fishing floats wash up onto the sand, from the tiniest ones to the huge 52-inchers. When I thought more about it, I realized that not only did Gerald tell me this story to provide me another window into how much he loved the beautiful outdoors we're blessed with in Oregon, he also was showing me once again how his life and his values revolved around standing up for one's self, and admiring those who do.

Each time I visited Gerald in jail, I tried to fill in a few gaps in his life story. That's largely how I pieced together everything I knew so far. These weren't interviews with him, they were conversations, and aside from the pain of seeing him stuck in solitary and losing weight, I enjoyed the time we spent together. Talking seemed to do Gerald good, and it did good things for my morale, too.

"You said you wanted to become a soldier since you were a little kid," I began one day. "Why did you choose the Marines?"

"The Marines have the toughest reputation in the world," Gerald replied. "Their snipers are by far the best. I wanted to be the best sniper, so that's where I chose to go."

"That simple?"

Gerald's face told me it wasn't simple at all. "With all the time I have in here to think, I've come to the conclusion that I probably joined up because I wanted to show my dad that I was a man, that I was tough. But it's also true that I wanted to be a sniper."

When it came time to decide which branch of the military suited him, Gerald visited the local Pony Village Mall, where all the recruiters were lined up like a gauntlet, easy to visit with and compare. "I had just been kicked out of school for throwing eggs at the seniors," Gerald said, setting the context. "They graduated a week before the end of the school year, and they drove circles around the campus throwing their eggs. I skipped class, went to Safeway, bought a dozen eggs and ambushed them." He laughed at the memory. "I went all Godfather-toll-booth on them. But the police came and I got caught... and kicked out! So I walked down to the mall to join the military.

"The recruiters liked the fact that I had fought back [with the eggs]," Gerald continued. "It didn't bother them in the least that I had just been kicked out of school. They told me their stories about getting kicked out of college, out of bars, and even certain countries." First up, the Army: "They were nice guys, but nothing about the Rangers or Green Berets excited me." Next, the Air Force: "They were skinny-fat guys – you know, lean guys with guts – who smoked and hadn't ever punched anyone in the face. I ruled them out immediately." After that, the Navy: "There some weasel of a sea-man said, 'You can be a sailor and go into foreign ports and experience many different foreign women.'" Gerald shook his head and chuckled. "Uh, that wasn't all that persuasive for me. I had never even experienced an American woman; what would I do with a foreign woman? I ran out of there as fast as I could.

"Then I walked into the Marines office. I saw two Marines in there, standing nose to nose, looking like they were about to fight. One was Staff Sgt. Walls and the other Staff Sgt. Boening. Walls had the whole half of his scalp melted off and Boening was anybody's idea of a huge muscle-bound Marine. I watched them from the door. Walls turned his attention from Boening, saw me and spat out, 'What!?' It was like I was bothering them. I said I was interested in the Marines, and that I wanted to know what the Marines could offer me. They looked at each other, and burst out laughing. Walls said to Boening, 'This guy wants to know what the Marines has to offer him!' They laughed some more. Then he turned his laser eyes on me, and demanded, 'What the fuck do you have to offer my beloved Marine Corps?' I was hooked."

Because Gerald was too young to join up immediately, he went into a delayed entry program that allowed him to finish high school. While he waited to turn 18, he drove Humvees out on the sand dunes and shot M-16s and ran and swam – not just *with* the Marines, but as one of them.

Then, the Marines and Gerald fulfilled his dream of going to sniper school. In his spare time, he began training in Brazilian Jiu-Jitsu. After leaving the Marines, he fought professionally in the MMA. And then he came back to Oregon and opened an MMA gym, which probably would have been his lifelong career had not Gerald become briefly and tragically acquainted with a man named David Crofut. But those stories would have to wait for other days. I had to get back to work. Just as I needed to get to know my client in order to prepare his defense, I needed to get to know the shooting victim that the prosecution would be presenting in court. Good guy? Bad guy? Or something in between?

CHAPTER 13
WHO WAS DAVID CROFUT?

Right after the shooting, when I first learned the name of the man Gerald Strebendt shot on Bob Straub Parkway, I did what most of us do nowadays – I googled his name and looked up his page on Facebook. On the social media site I saw what appeared to be a very average, gray-haired Caucasian man. His profile photos and others posted of him online give the impression of a middle-class man drinking beers with friends, wearing sunglasses on a bright day outdoors, and cozying up to his younger-looking wife, Brenda, who appeared plumpish but carefully made up and coiffed. David Crofut, in the photos, was always smiling. He was born on September 15, 1960, making him 53 on the night he died.

Then I found the man's obituary and several tributes online, in which Crofut was described as a "great businessman" who had "a wonderful family, wife and friends." Having heard Gerald's account of the shooting, it was hard to square what I was reading with what I believed to be Gerald's accurate, truthful recounting… of how a victim became a predator, and a man with an assault rifle his prey.

In the days after Gerald's arrest and arraignment, I saw frequently David Crofut in death. Skipping around among the digital discovery files on my computer, I could not avoid the photos taken by police at the scene. The area had been photographed before David Crofut's body was removed, and the images of the deceased man lying on the street were grotesque. He was flat on his back on the wet pavement. His right eye was whole and fixed, staring at nothing. The left side of his head was in pieces sprayed all over the road. Blood pooled a few feet away on the pavement, but it looked like someone had dropped a bucket of it, the way it sprayed off to the sides. Some of his brains clung to his torso, looking for all the world like grayish scrambled eggs. One of his hands rested over his chest, while the other lay next to him on the ground. Even having seen him alive and healthy on Facebook, it was a struggle to imagine what he looked like alive. The body just looked vulnerable, and very dead.

The autopsy confirmed that at 53 years old he was 5'8" tall and weighed 175 pounds. That made him about the same height as Gerald, though Gerald likely outweighed him. Reading further into the report shed no light on what occurred before Gerald pulled the trigger, but it was clear that Crofut died quickly – if not immediately – after being shot. Pieces of his skull's shattered bony fragments had been found all over the road, ditch and median. There was so much debris, in fact, that I doubt that all of it was documented, much less collected as evidence. Some of it probably left the scene on tires, since both an ambulance and a fire truck, with its helpful ladder and spotlight, had driven through the debris field. Investigators, too, walked amid the blood, bits of hair, and skull fragments, unintentionally disturbing and redistributing them. The tow truck drivers, called to remove the vehicles from the scene, actually knelt in the human debris as they hooked up their chains.

The report revealed that David and Brenda Crofut resided on Mt. Vernon Rd. I entered their address on Google Maps and asked for directions to the scene of the shooting, just to estimate the distance between the two locations. The Crofut home was located just past where Gerald shot David. From the location of the home, I surmised that Crofut and his wife were on their way home. Crofut's house was just a half-mile away from the where first responders located his body lying on the road.

Further into the reports, I learned that Gerald wasn't the only one to call 911 that night. Brenda Crofut also called, and I was shocked to hear the belligerent, drunken-sounding salvos she launched at an undeserving dispatcher. The tape captures her wheezing, wailing and screaming as she discovered the splattered, exploded remains of her husband. She called for help. She also sought forgiveness for some now meaningless sin committed against her husband.

DISPATCHER: 911. What's the address of the emergency?

MS. CROFUT: It's like, um, 59th – 5979 Mt. Vernon Road. Fuck, I don't know. But this white guy just pulled a gun on us. I don't know.

DISPATCHER: Are you involved?

MS. CROFUT: Oh, yeah. It's like my car is – we – this guy pulled out in front of us and we hit him and we heard gunshots and I see somebody and (inaudible).

DISPATCHER: Brenda. Brenda, what's going on right now?

MS. CROFUT: I think he's dead. Oh, fuck. He shot him in his head. He's dead. Fuck. Help us, bitch. Please, please, please (inaudible).

DISPATCHER: Brenda, what is going on? We have the call. Tell me what's going on.

MS. CROFUT: (Inaudible) somebody shot this – this man shot my husband.

DISPATCHER: Okay.

MS. CROFUT: Please (inaudible).

DISPATCHER: Stay in the car. Okay? We have officers and fire coming.

MS. CROFUT: 5939 Mt. Vernon Road. Fuck, just get here. My husband.

DISPATCHER: Okay. Stay on the phone with me. Okay? Are you in your car? Stay in your car. Brenda?

MS. CROFUT: Please.

DISPATCHER: I'm getting you over to the dispatcher. They're on their way.

MS. CROFUT: (Inaudible.)

DISPATCHER: Okay? Stay on the phone with me.

MS. CROFUT: (Inaudible.)

DISPATCHER: Okay. Brenda, they're coming. Okay?

MS. CROFUT: (Inaudible) right there. I'm scared. (Inaudible.)

DISPATCHER: What vehicle are you in?

MS. CROFUT: Oh, my god. What happened (inaudible) fucking (inaudible) you fucking (inaudible). Help us. Please, please, please, please. He's a fucking asshole. Oh (inaudible). Please. I don't know (inaudible). Please, please.

DISPATCHER: I –

MS. CROFUT: I am so sorry. Oh. My – (inaudible). I am so sorry. Oh. Oh. (Inaudible.)

DISPATCHER: Yeah. Brenda.

MS. CROFUT: Oh, he's crazy. (Inaudible) in the street. I am a nurse. His brains are on the roadway. (Inaudible.) Help us.

DISPATCHER: Brenda.

MS. CROFUT: Oh, I can't do it.

DISPATCHER: Brenda, can you hear me?

MS. CROFUT: No. I can't – I am. And I can't. My heart is (inaudible).

DISPATCHER: Brenda, can you hear me? I have help coming to you.

MS. CROFUT: I know – I know and (inaudible). Oh (inaudible).

*He's dead. Oh, help. His brains are flowing out in the driving. It's so
fucking sick.*

DISPATCHER: Brenda, can you hear me?

*MS. CROFUT: (Inaudible) brains out. (Inaudible.) I can't do any-
thing. (Inaudible.) Oh. He has no (inaudible). Fuck you, bitch. I hope
he goes to jail for the rest of your life because you blew my husband's
brains out. And I'm a nurse and you're a fucking asshole. And I don't
even know what else to tell you. I will never, ever forgive you for what
you did to me. It don't matter. I will never forgive you. He fucking
killed my husband. And I can't (inaudible). Fuck him.*

I had seen this man alive in photos, and I had seen him destroyed by
a bullet, his head practically turned inside out on a street. I had heard his
wife's raging grief and disgust, too. Now I needed to learn everything about
who this man really was, in the hope of understanding what led to his altercation with Gerald.

I knew that if we could prove that Gerald had reacted to something
David Crofut had done or said, then we'd have a better chance of getting
Gerald acquitted at trial. So I began working to flesh out what David and
Brenda did that night, beyond drinking at the Driftwood. Also, I'd look
into whatever I could learn about his character. What kind of person was
he? A peaceful man? A stubborn man? An aggressive man? Once we knew
what we were dealing with, we'd go about figuring out how to get the evidence admitted at the trial.

Getting character evidence admitted at trial is a difficult and technical
process. I knew from experience that a judge's primary concern is whether a
jury could be misled by inflammatory evidence of personality problems or
past transgressions, perhaps to the point of over-emphasizing it and reaching a verdict that isn't supported by the facts of the case. It's a reasonable
concern. But I knew that dead men tell no tales, and David's wife sounded
too drunk to provide an accurate account of what happened. So all I had
to work with was Gerald's story… and whatever I could learn about David
to indicate his personality, his background, his physical and mental health,
and his state of mind that night. Knowing that I was going to be plenty

busy processing the evidence from the scene itself, I handed off the David Crofut investigation to Emilia.

After looking through what we had on hand and the possible avenues of investigation leading from them, Emilia quickly recommended more manpower. I agreed. We needed people running down witnesses and following up on leads in various locations scattered from Oregon to Washington and half a continent away in the Midwest. It was more than Verne could handle alone. We hired experienced local investigators Patricia Jaqua and Jeff Dodge. Emilia gave the investigative team their assignments, maintained contact with them to track their progress, and directed their work. On the occasions when the investigators couldn't locate a witness or find the answer, Emilia did the work herself.

There were plenty of slammed doors and unreturned phone calls. As is typical in a serious criminal case involving death, few of the Crofuts' family members, friends, or neighbors were willing to speak with anyone associated with Gerald's defense team. We couldn't use ruses to gain information, or hide who we were and who we represented. This left us working mainly from the discovery documents we had already received, online research, public records requests, court records, and whatever else my investigative team could put together.

From the Washington divorce records, we learned that David Paul Crofut ended his education after the eighth grade. Somewhere around the tender age of 16, David married his first wife, Kathy, in 1978. About 10 months later, David's only son, Michael, was born. With a family to support, David enrolled in union carpet-laying school, and he began work in that trade upon completion. In 1992, he started his own carpet-installation business.

Kathy and David apparently worked hard to gain financial security. By the time their 20-year marriage unraveled in 1998, their son was finishing his college degree and the Crofuts had a business and multiple rental properties to divvy up. Their marriage may have failed, but they had succeeded in creating a productive and relatively prosperous life for themselves and their son.

The divorce papers, however, provided unsettling details about David and Kathy's life together. Kathy alleged, under oath, that on November 7,

1998, David grabbed her by the shoulders and threw her across a room, bruising her. She also stated that on November 12, 1998, David became enraged in the early morning and pulled a phone out of the wall and threw it. She also claimed that he prevented her from calling the police for assistance. On other occasions, David allegedly threw her clothes out of the house, grabbed her purse and dumped it out to look through its contents, and put his foot on her to keep her down. Once, when she called police and they responded, but they did not arrest him. Kathy called David "controlling." Responding, David claimed that police would have arrested Kathy had he not intervened on her behalf during at least one of their three visits to the Crofut home.

While all of these allegations and counter-allegations could be passed off as just the result of a toxic relationship, we did find evidence that David had an explosive temper that followed him into his second marriage.

David met Brenda Martinez, the woman who was to become his second wife, around 1999. She was the mother of two children by her previous husband. On January 23, 2006, shortly before their decision to marry, Brenda's then-17-year-old daughter, Joanna, called 911 to report that Brenda and David were involved in a physical fight. She said the fight had started with her, and that she (Joanna) and David had argued loudly before he struck her multiple times with a closed fist. Brenda later told police that it was she and Joanna that had been fighting, not David and Joanna, and that Joanna had attacked her after she had slapped Joanna across the face. Brenda claimed that David intervened only to separate them and to protect Brenda from Joanna.

We located court pleadings in a Washington trust case that confirmed that Brenda was no stranger to violence in her relationships. Well before David Crofut came along, Brenda told the Pierce County Superior Court that the father of Brenda's children abused her, and tried to kill her by stabbing her.

I can only speculate what attracted Brenda to David. Perhaps Brenda had come to expect violence in her relationships. Or, maybe she felt that a woman with two children should avoid setting the bar too high when it comes to suitors. Though her relationship with David was turbulent, Brenda may have appreciated the financial security and social stability afforded her by this attractive, hard-working and reasonably successful businessman. But the road ahead for them was to be difficult. The court documents we located told us that Brenda and David struggled to parent Brenda's children, both of whom reportedly ran away frequently, skipped school, stole, fought, and did drugs. Both were in and out of the juvenile justice system. Brenda's son was eventually charged with a crime in adult court, and sentenced to prison time. She and David spent countless hours and thousands of dollars on attorneys to get these kids through their difficult years of early adulthood. Reading this, I could only imagine the strain it would have put on a marriage.

Through a public records request, we found a veritable gold mine of a police report in the state of Washington. Nine months before David Crofut died, on April 14, 2013, Brenda called 911 to report that she and David were having an argument and that he was throwing things around the house. Before hanging up abruptly, she told the dispatcher that David had a gun – not on his person, but outside in his truck. When dispatch called back, daughter Joanna answered. She said that Brenda and David were drunk and that she was afraid David would kill Brenda and then himself. He had recently held a gun to her mother's head, she said, and made a murder-suicide threat at that time. When officers arrived, they found Brenda alive and, aside from being very intoxicated and incoherent, well. The condition of the Tacoma house, however, confirmed daughter Joanna's account. Police reported seeing overturned bookcases, a toppled 52" television, broken picture frames, and smashed flower pots. What had brought this on? Brenda told police that David was upset that she was having an affair and hadn't ended it. She said he had previously scared her by driving very fast with her as his passenger, threatening all the while that he would kill them both.

Fast-forward, now, to the night of the shooting and what we were able to piece together of the couple's day. On January 29, 2014, Brenda Crofut left her home health care nursing job early, planning to go home and pick up her husband. Together they would do some shopping to prepare for a Super Bowl party four days later. At Eugene's Cash & Carry, a wholesale market, they picked up food and snacks. Then, on the way home at about

4 p.m., they stopped at the Driftwood Bar and Grill on Springfield's Main Street, where they would spend the rest of their afternoon and early evening.

Over the hours that she served them, bartender Kathy Uhlman learned a lot about her two customers. David said he had just received his Oregon Driver's License and that later in the week he planned to apply for his contractor's license and start working. She heard that they had just succeeded in selling their Tacoma home, and that they were planning a Super Bowl party at their new place. David talked about a shooting that had occurred in his Tacoma business, which led him to reconsider the wisdom of owning a bar. It was the shooting, he said, that caused him to sell his business and move to Eugene/Springfield.

Driftwood patron Ken Smith also became acquainted with the Crofuts that night. He sat at the bar with them, he told investigators, commenting that David seemed to have done quite well on the video-poker machine, having won about $200. He, too, had been told that the Crofuts had sold their home in Tacoma that day.

After bartender Uhlman ended her shift, Meg Disario took over serving the Crofuts. When the SPD officer asked her if she had seen David Crofut engage in any confrontations with anyone at the bar, Disario disclosed that the only one she had observed was with his wife, Brenda.

That made me wonder: Had David and Brenda Crofut been arguing in the car that night? That I would never know. But the discovery had certainly indicated past marital strife, including fights, threats, and a history of drinking. In the Washington police report, Brenda had accused him of aggressive driving, too. While photos of this innocuous-looking man certainly didn't make Crofut seem like someone who could be abusive or prone to road rage, the details in the reports certainly did raise questions in my mind.

He sounds like a guy capable of ramming somebody's truck and engaging in an angry confrontation. But, following Gerald 80 feet from the collision, when he knew Gerald was armed? What on earth could he have been thinking?

Then again, maybe he wasn't thinking at all. The two bartenders who served David Crofut confirmed what Verne had told me back in the beginning – that that they had served him about eight 16-ounce beers over the period of three to four hours. For a man of medium height and build, that much beer in a three- to four-hour period is a lot. It would be a lot even for somebody like me, five inches taller and 40 to 50 pounds heavier. I could not and would not drink anywhere close to a gallon of beer and drive.

How drunk was he? The county medical examiner who performed Crofut's autopsy, Dr. Daniel Davis, finally had my answer for me. He reported a blood alcohol content (BAC) of 0.15 percent at the time of death. That's almost twice the legal limit in Oregon of 0.08 percent.

This, to me, was a big point in Gerald's favor as I prepared his case. No matter what jurors might decide had happened that night on the Parkway, they were bound to have a problem with the victim driving drunk – falling-down drunk for most people, in fact. They'd dislike him for that. They'd be prone to ask more questions about his actions that night, simply because Crofut was drunk and Gerald was sober. Advantage: Gerald.

But I was also angry that this critical information hadn't been presented to the grand jury. They never knew that Crofut was drunk. Why? Because the medical examiner's report was dated four weeks *after* the D.A. had taken the case to the grand jury!

Now, in an ideal, judicially unbiased world, the D.A. wouldn't have gone to the grand jury before the results of an autopsy were in hand. He would have wanted to know whatever he could about Crofut's condition that night before moving the case forward. Having already waited more than a month to go to grand jury, what would it have hurt to wait another week or two to have the autopsy and the toxicology results in hand?

In my opinion, the D.A.'s office simply assembled their "best facts" for the grand jury, the ones that would get them their indictment. I consider this morally, if not ethically, unscrupulous. But it's standard operating procedure, because the public doesn't know and most defense attorneys are unwilling to kick up a fuss about it.

Of course, I can't be absolutely sure the grand jury didn't know about Crofut's blood alcohol level. I wasn't there and there isn't a recording of the proceedings. But it didn't show up in the D.A.'s notes provided to us in discovery, and that date on the report – it certainly suggests that the grand jury heard the case without knowing the victim drank four quarts of beer before the incident. Frankly, I doubt it would have mattered if they had, though. As the saying goes, "The grand jury would indict a ham sandwich if the D.A. asked them to." When a D.A. wants an indictment, he or she gets it.

But there turned out to be more that the grand jury should have known. Another thing I learned as I read the crime lab report was that Crofut also had a drug called venlafaxine in his blood. It was a familiar name, one I'd recently encountered in a DUII case. Venlafaxine is a serotonin and nor-epinephrine re-uptake inhibitor (SNRI) used to treat depression, anxiety and panic disorders. It is more commonly known by its commercial name, Effexor. Side effects include dizziness, nervousness, and anxiety. Serious side effects of the drug could include agitation and hallucinations. Patients were advised not to mix Effexor and alcohol.

Just a tad important, perhaps, in a self-defense shooting case where the victim was drunk?

I'd need an expert to help me really understand the drug-alcohol inter-action, so I called Dr. Robert Julien. Dr. Julien has been a hair's breadth from retiring for as long as I have known him. In addition to his medical degree, he has a Ph.D. in pharmacology, the science of how drugs work. His book on the effect of drugs on the brain and behavior, "A Primer of Drug Action," was first published in 1975 and has been in continuous circulation for more than 40 years.

While I was making arrangements with Dr. Julien on the phone and sending him the necessary police reports and toxicology results, I received word of a missed call. A man named Greg Stewart had phoned about Gerald's case. I didn't know Stewart, but I returned the call. He proved to be the owner of the Dexter Club, a roadhouse that sits down the road from the local reservoir.

"I heard that your investigator was out pounding the pavement, look-ing for people who knew Gerald."

After I confirmed that Verne Hoyer was indeed out there asking ques-tions, Stewart told me he was following up by phone because he hadn't been around to talk to Verne. His wife had offered what she could, "but she doesn't know Gerald all that well."

"And you do?"

"Yes. Yes, sir, I do. I mean, as well as I do any of my regulars. I've seen him in here a lot since I bought the Club a few years ago."

I figured I might as well cut to the chase. "You ever see him drunk?"

"Sure, I have, a time or two, I imagine."

"What kind of a drunk is he?"

"Normal I guess." Stewart paused. Then he said, "You know, now that I really think about it, the only time I really saw Gerald in here drunk was on his birthday. His friends threw him a party. He'd never had a 'grown-up' birthday party before, someone told me. So he really let loose."

Made it to his thirties without ever having a birthday party as an adult?

I continued. "Did you ever see him get aggressive?"

"While drunk?"

"Ever."

"Not at my business. Gerald never gave me any problems. And in my work, you know that there are people who give me problems. Those people, I don't like to see them come in the door. But Gerald, he's always welcome here. He's a good person and a good customer."

I thanked the man for phoning the office, got his contact info, and then hung up and went back to work on the discovery documents. It was only a few hours later that my receptionist buzzed to tell me Dr. Julien was on the line.

Already? That was quick. And I said so when I picked up the call.

"I got the reports you sent me," he began. "I didn't spend a lot of time looking at the reports about the scene; I just looked at the urine and blood."

"What do you think?"

"A 0.15 BAC is very intoxicated, likely with behavioral disinhibition, like fighting, assault, aggression and so forth. I'd expect to see some cognitive inhibition, but not blackout at this level."

With that, Dr. Julien turned to the levels of venlafaxine (Effexor) in Crofut's blood, launching into a technical explanation of how many milligrams of the drug Crofut would have had to take to produce his blood level of 0.402 milligrams per liter. The upshot: even if Crofut had been prescribed the maximum daily dose of 225 milligrams, "there is no way that his levels should have been up that high."

"Does that mean that he was overdosing on the drug?"

"Overdose is really a loaded word," Dr. Julien replied. "I don't really have any way to know at this point how much he was taking. I do know, however, that some people are just physically slow metabolizers. That could be the reason why the level was so high in his blood. I doubt anyone ever tested him to check his levels."

"How would that have affected him? Would it have an effect?"

"You mean physically? Or in his behavior?

"Both."

"Well, at this level, you could see serotonin syndrome, in addition to the other side effects, such as dizziness, nervousness, and anxiety."

"What's serotonin syndrome?"

"It's a broad term for any group of symptoms that indicate issues like a drug overdose. The syndrome can be characterized by tremors, muscle jerks, rigidity, rapid heart rate, agitation, confusion, disorientation, and hallucinations."

Then Dr. Julien provided a caveat: Post-mortem blood tests for venlafaxine can vary depending on whether the blood taken is cardiac or femoral. And the report wasn't clear as to where the blood was drawn. It was possible, he said, that Crofut's venlafaxine level wasn't as high as it appeared. He knew I'd want to be aware of that before I used it in court.

Still, Dr. Julien had plenty to offer me for Gerald's defense. First and foremost, he thought the drug combined with alcohol could have been a factor in what happened that night. "Regardless of whether the level measured was inflated because of the sample, when combined with his BAC, it could account for his aggressive behavior." Second, he let me know that this drug is known for a particular effect.

"Of all the antidepressants, venlafaxine is the drug most commonly associated with a manic flip in persons diagnosed with bipolar disorder. Was this guy bipolar? I have personally testified in two cases of homicides where a bipolar defendant experienced such a manic flip."

"What's 'manic flip?'"

Dr. Julien explained that a person experiencing a "manic flip" or a "manic switch" could experience insomnia, perceptual abnormalities, and psychosis. In other words, a manic flip could explain to a skeptical jury why it was that David Crofut jumped from his car and advanced on an armed man, grabbing at the gun pointed at him. I knew from reviewing case law that Crofut's mental condition (or illness) could be admissible if it went to the heart of our factual theory of the case and tended to complete the picture regarding our defendant's account of the incident. I didn't think that we'd be allowed to offer much if any of the evidence we'd gathered that pointed to Crofut being a violent asshole. But if his aggressive behaviors were the result of a mental illness, or the inappropriate levels of his depression medication, maybe we would be able to get the evidence before the jurors, and maybe it would prove to them that Gerald acted reasonably when he fired.

The key word there, of course, is "reasonably." To win the day, we needed to be able to prove that what Gerald chose to do was appropriate and understandable – reasonable given the situation. We had to get the jury to understand why Gerald pulled the trigger, and I thought that Dr. Julien's testimony regarding the BAC and the outrageously high venlafaxine level might just have found us a way.

After I got off the phone with Dr. Julien and returned to the discovery files, I noticed something additional in the medical examiner's report. The office's investigator, Elizabeth Whisenhunt, had observed and reported an unknown quantity of cash in David Crofut's left front pants pocket, and more cash on the ground at the scene, next to his right hand. A cell phone was on the ground, too, on Crofut's left side. Had Crofut had the cash or his cell phone in hand when he was killed? Had Gerald seen Crofut grab for something in his pocket? Had Crofut tried to give him cash? Maybe some of his winnings from video poker? Is that what Gerald had seen him reach for?

What I also read in that report obliterated any remaining respect or sympathy I had for David's widow. Whisenhunt reported in the interview she conducted with Brenda Crofut that despite all accounts that she was drunk, so drunk that the bartender at the Driftwood cut her off, she denied being inebriated. Despite David's 0.15 percent BAC, she also denied that he was intoxicated. Having listened to her slurred and belligerent call to 911, I considered this ridiculous and downright despicable.

But some of the rest of what she said was quite helpful to Gerald's case, especially what she said in an interview with a Springfield detective. Brenda denied seeing anything unusual before the crash, despite being a passenger in the car, the one and only eyewitness to what occurred before the collision. She didn't mention any brake-checking or tailgating, both of which are typical behaviors leading motorists to become violent. On the contrary, she told the detective that David had been *driving normally*, until he was cut off by a vehicle from the right side. She said the vehicle turned in front of them, and they struck the left rear portion of the vehicle.

Aside from the Parade of Horribles, how had this become a "road rage" case? Where on earth was the actual evidence of road rage?

CHAPTER 14

RE-EXAMINING THE EVIDENCE FROM THE SCENE

Working a defense case requires the continual gathering of evidence. It also requires that we periodically stop to consider where things stand. That's how you figure out what is missing, and what questions remain unanswered.

I met with Emilia to review everything we'd received either in discovery or through reports from our own investigators and experts. Piece by piece, detail by detail, we sought to establish our own understanding of what occurred in this shooting case and how we would use the evidence to defend Gerald against a charge of murder.

The Timing

Whatever happened, it sure happened quickly.

Before the incident, Gerald left his Northwest Training Center MMA gym (519 Main St., Springfield) at about 7:30 p.m. He drove his Denali pickup to the Safeway store near 54th and Main, which is less than a mile away from where Crofut died. Gerald bought a few groceries, including greens, shrimp and scallops, planning to have a nice dinner and a movie at home with his fiancée, Kristin. His receipt for the purchase is time stamped 7:53 p.m. The recording of his 911 call begins at 7:57 p.m. The shot that killed Crofut was fired at about 7:59 p.m. Assuming that all the clocks are synced – and that's a big assumption – Gerald loaded his truck with groceries, drove out of the parking lot, turned right onto Bob Straub Parkway, drove less than a mile, got in a car crash, and then called 911 – all within four minutes. Crofut was lying dead on the pavement just six minutes after Gerald purchased the ingredients for a romantic home-cooked meal.

The Witnesses

Local resident **Oneta Boyles** called 911 after she drove through the scene:

MS. BOYLES: There's a guy out here on the highway with an assault rifle. We went around it and I came here and I called 911.

DISPATCHER: There's an assault rifle?

MS. BOYLES: The guy's backing up and the other guy's – in front of me. And he just got out of the rig with an assault rifle and the car rammed into him. And the guy's backing up and he's going, "Get away from me. Get away from me." And he goes, "I'm not going to hurt you. I just want to talk to you." "Get away from me." He's got this assault rifle, so I got around him and came here.

DISPATCHER: Huh.

MS. BOYLES: And the car – the pickup slammed on his brakes, so the pickup's like this. It's just right out here, back a little ways. And the car slammed into him. And the car guy says, "This crazy guy slammed on his brakes, and I'm getting out of the car to talk to him, and he pulls out of his car with an assault rifle and he's over in the other lane."

Anita Staples, who lived nearby, called 911 after hearing a gunshot:

DISPATCHER: 911. What's the address of the emergency?

MS. STAPLES: Um, it's the – the parkway right outside where I live. We're on 926 South 59th Street. What is it? What is the name, Mom?

DISPATCHER: What are you calling to report?

MS. STAPLES: A car crashed. Two cars are in a crash out there and they're arguing, and we thought we heard a gunshot and they were talking about a rifle.

DISPATCHER: What is your name?

MS. STAPLES: Anita Staples.

DISPATCHER: Did you hear gunshots?

MS. STAPLES: I just heard it sounded like a gunshot.

DISPATCHER: How long did you hear that?

MS. STAPLES: There's — there's cars moving along slowly now. Just like right before I called you.

DISPATCHER: Okay.

MS. STAPLES: But I heard them out there arguing. One guy says the other guy pulled out in front of him and then he slammed on his brakes. And they're talking about, "Show me that rifle." And the other guy's going, "Don't come near me."

Now Emilia and I needed to compare these 911 calls with those made by Gerald and Brenda Crofut:

- The transcript of Gerald's call to 911 confirmed that Gerald had told the dispatcher that Crofut had "hit him on purpose."

- Crofut's wife, Brenda, claimed that David had been driving normally. She said she hadn't noticed anything unusual until Gerald cut them off from the right and turned in front of them, causing the collision.

The discrepancy between the two calls, of course, needed to be explored. The jury would want to hear our explanation for the differences.

Meanwhile, there was the matter of Gerald's pickup and Crofut's sedan, and how they got where they were. Police on the scene said they arrived to find the two vehicles stopped in the roadway. Gerald's Denali pickup was in front, angled into traffic toward the median of the now-single lane of slowly moving traffic. Crofut's medium-sized Nissan Rogue was smashed into the rear of Gerald's pickup. The forces of the crash were significant enough that a tow truck was required to separate the vehicles.

I had to admit, given the position of the vehicles in the roadway, it certainly seemed like Brenda's story was plausible. The Denali, huge and black, stretched across the entire lane of travel. The driver's-side door was left standing open. If I had happened upon the crash as a bystander, I would have assumed, as other witnesses did, that Gerald's Denali had been stopped there for the purpose of cutting off Crofut.

Was there something that triggered a confrontation between these two vehicles? Working backward from the collision, Emilia and I turned to additional witness statements:

- Witness **Nick Dysert** said that he saw the vehicles driven by Gerald and the Crofuts at an intersection a few minutes before the crash. He said that he observed the Crofuts take a right onto Bob Straub, and then saw Gerald make an illegal right from the left turn lane, going after them at a high rate of speed. Dysert turned onto Bob Straub after them, heading home, and accelerated quickly to 60 mph (in a 45 mph zone). The other cars quickly outpaced him and he lost sight of them before turning off into his neighborhood.

- **Bill Powell**, another witness, said that he had been driving a car in front of Gerald and the Crofuts. He saw Gerald pass Crofut's car on the right and then suddenly slam on the brakes.

We also looked at how the police had tried to sort out what happened that night. After Gerald was taken into custody, the police stayed on-scene to collect what evidence they could. They photographed the vehicles. They looked for skid marks on the road. They jacked up the pickup and tried to spin the tires, perhaps to see if the truck had been in park at the time of the crash – which might suggest that Gerald intentionally stopped to confront the other driver.

Working under spotlights in the dark, investigators took stock of the damage to each vehicle and collected many of the smashed parts and bits of debris found in the roadway. They even observed that some mud from the undercarriage of Gerald's truck had fallen and marked where it landed. Using a laser mapping system, they plotted all of the evidence they found, the width of the lane of travel, the location of the shoulder, the placement of the vehicles in the lane, and the proximity of all of this to Crofut's body. Only then were the vehicles towed to the Springfield Police Department.

Based on the lack of tire marks on the pavement, law enforcement's accident reconstruction expert concluded that Gerald's truck had been completely stopped when the Crofuts crashed into the rear of the truck. But there was one set of data unavailable when he made the determination: the "black box" data from the two vehicles.

A few days after the shooting, when a search warrant had been obtained, Springfield P.D. arranged to have data downloaded from the Airbag Control Modules (ACMs) in the vehicles. This so-called "black box" data can be obtained from U.S.-made vehicles manufactured after 1998. The small airbag-controlling computer is generally found under the driver's seat. The device monitors data from the vehicle's sensors. When the vehicle gets involved in a collision that meets the computer's criteria for airbag deployment, the airbags inflate. The information recorded by the sensors can be downloaded to understand what happened. Each vehicle has a different sensitivity setting given how big it is and how it's used. Trucks tend to require more G-forces to trigger an airbag event than smaller cars, simply because we wouldn't want someone off-roading in a truck to have airbags exploding when they were simply driving on rough terrain.

In the crash involving Gerald's Denali and Crofut's Nissan Rogue, only the ACM from the Nissan yielded any data. Gerald's ACM did not, and that was most likely because whatever happened to the Denali on the roadway didn't meet the criteria of the ACM computer. This may have been because the Denali was much, much heavier than the Nissan, or the forces on the Denali weren't significant because the impact occurred at a relatively low speed. Or, because it was more of a rear-impact collision, perhaps there was no need to deploy an airbag to protect the driver, making it a "nonevent" from the computer's point of view. Regardless, the lack of data on the Denali ACM definitely indicated what *didn't* happen – namely, the high-speed, dramatic, sudden-stop crash that Brenda Crofut described.

This may seem like good news for our side, but not necessarily. For an innocent man, the absence of data hurts. Any stone turned over can produce something helpful to a defense, but that's of no help when there aren't any stones.

Meanwhile, the review of the Nissan data showed that, from the perspective of that vehicle's ACM, a triggering "event" *had* occurred. The device stored five seconds of data before the crash, yielding the following information:

1. At five seconds before impact, the Nissan was traveling at 0 mph, meaning the Crofut vehicle was at a complete stop in the roadway. His accelerator was not yet pressed down.

2. At four seconds before the impact, Crofut began to push down on the accelerator.

3. At 3.5 seconds before the impact, Crofut pushed the accelerator to 100 percent. This means he "floored it," "put the pedal to the metal." He was not pressing on the brake pedal at this time.

4. At two seconds before impact, Crofut's accelerator was still on the floor.

5. At one second before impact, Crofut's accelerator was still on the floor.

6. At 0.5 seconds before impact, the accelerator was on the floor, and the steering input showed –250.0 degrees. This means he cranked the steering wheel hard to the right, assuming that data point was accurate.

7. At impact, Crofut's accelerator was still on the floor. He was not pressing the brake pedal. The steering input showed –67.1 degrees. It either meant that Crofut jerked the steering wheel back from the hard right (several revolutions of the steering wheel) in literally a split second, or it meant that there was something wrong with -250.0 data.

The data was telling us that that *our client had been truthful* about how the crash occurred. Thanks to the ACM data, it was now indisputable that Crofut had brought his car to a complete stop, and then slammed his foot down on the gas pedal. Why did he brake? Why did he floor it? Conclusive answers to these questions eluded us, but one thing was certain: David Crofut's wife, Brenda, had lied to law enforcement investigators about how the accident occurred. She said everything was normal until Gerald cut them off, causing the crash. She didn't mention anything at all about David stopping, then ramming the back of Gerald's vehicle. Was this Brenda lying shamelessly? Or was she so drunk that she just missed all of that completely?

Our forensic reconstructionist, David Karlin, was the guy most likely to be able to answer some of our remaining questions for us. The main one: Why was Gerald's truck angled in front of the Nissan? Had Gerald indeed cut off the Crofuts, as it appeared to witnesses and was alleged by Brenda Crofut? Had he blocked the lane before Crofut rammed him?

The Springfield Police certainly thought Gerald's actions precipitated the encounter. Their investigation led them to believe that the Denali had come to a controlled stop at a 24-degree angle to the center of the lane of traffic, and that the Denali's final rest position was not affected by the impact with the Nissan. Having found no skid or tire marks from braking, the police concluded that there had been no braking or skidding. In their view, Gerald had indeed cut Crofut off.

Not so, said Karlin. He showed us a digital animation he'd made of the vehicle crash, incorporating the Nissan's ACM data. Karlin's opinion was that Gerald had been stopped to the right of the Crofut's vehicle, on the right side of the road, when the Nissan impacted the Denali – at an angle – with enough force to push the bed of the truck to the right. That's what made it appear that Gerald had pulled back into the lane before stopping. Karlin was confident that *Gerald's truck had been pointed straight down the road before the collision*, not engaged in cutting off Crofut's Nissan. He also explained that the "hard right" 250-degree steering wheel data was an "error message" and was explained as such in the ACM data "if you look hard enough.'

How to account for the differing opinions? At the risk of sounding snarky, I'd say it's the difference between actual physics and confirmation bias. While government investigators saw only what they expected to see, we actually did the analysis.

But we had no explanation for why Crofut would ram the back of Gerald's Denali. What man in his right mind would do such a thing? The car was intended to be Brenda Crofut's work vehicle and it was new to them; they'd had it less than a month. They didn't even have an official Oregon license plate installed. The temporary tag visible in law enforcement photos showed an effective date of December 31, 2013, not even a month before the shooting.

How will the prosecution handle the intentional ramming? Argue that Crofut was frightened, trying to escape? They might not know that the "hard right" turn was an error message. We might not play that card until trial.

CHAPTER 15

CORPUS PERPLEXUS

WARNING: GRAPHIC CRIME SCENE PHOTO BELOW

A key question that needed to be answered, one crucial to the success of the self-defense case I was preparing for Gerald Strebendt: Where was Crofut when the shot was fired? This Whatever the answer, it would be something I needed to be ready to explain to the jury within my theory of the case.

In trying to sort out the dynamics of the crash, I spent a lot of time looking at the diagramming of the body position, comparing it to the police photographs. The photos show Crofut lying on his back, his gruesomely damaged face looking upward. His feet, I noticed, were pointed toward the vehicles. If he had been shot and fell backward with the force of the blast, it would put the shooter between him and the vehicles. That wasn't good. How could he claim self-defense if when he pulled the trigger, Gerald was closer to the safety of the vehicles than he was to Crofut? Verne Hoyer, our investigator, suggested that maybe the SPD reconstructionist had put the body on the diagram facing the wrong way. Like me and Emilia, Verne thought that Crofut's feet should have been pointing away from the vehicles. People fall away from a powerful rifle blast, at least that's how it is in the movies. To go with that head-scratcher was this one: Why was there a large puddle of blood flowing away from Crofut in each direction along with a pile of grayish brain matter a foot or two away from Crofut's body? It was puzzling me.

I took that question to Don Schuessler, our physical evidence forensic expert. Schuessler agreed, the blood and brains seemed oddly separate from Crofut's body, and just too far away. I sent him out to the scene with Verne to look at the grade of the road, to see if there was some sort of rise or dip in the pavement to explain the distance of the human debris from the body. The word I got back was no – if the grade of the road had allowed blood to flow away from the body, it wouldn't have pooled on both sides of the head. It would have gone toward the side of the road in one direction.

More likely, the blood pooled where Crofut fell. But, how to explain the distance, the disconnection, between blood and body? I couldn't.

Emilia happened to walk into my office to drop off some correspondence as I was in the midst of trying to make sense of it all. "How are you?" she asked.

"Bad," I grumbled. "The body position doesn't make sense."

"Check your assumptions," she suggested, in her blunt but cheerful way. Then she turned on her heel and left.

My assumptions? What am I assuming that I shouldn't be?

Well, I wanted the evidence to be that Gerald was on the far edge of the scene, and that Crofut was between him and the vehicles. That's what made sense for Gerald's self-defense case. Had I been wrong to assume that the police diagram was correct? That the body was where they said it was? A mistake seemed unlikely in a case of this notoriety, so I put that possibility aside. But what else had we assumed?

Then it hit me. We had assumed that the photographs of Crofut showed him as he had fallen. *What if someone had rolled Crofut over before the photos were taken?* I pulled the photo of Crofut closer to my eyes to really study it. Lo and behold, there were drawstrings on the hood of Crofut's sweatshirt, and they were strewn to one side, together, both of them pointing in the same direction.

They likely wouldn't look like that unless somebody rolled the body over!

Since the road only sloped one direction, away from the yellow fog line, gravity would only draw the blood pool one direction. Therefore, there are most likely two blood pools – the first one next to visible brains adjacent to the fog line and the second next to Crofut's final resting spot as pictured. Yes, it made total sense now. Generally, the way you try to administer aid to somebody is with them on their back. After he had shot Crofut, Gerald told the 911 dispatcher that he thought Crofut was armed, but he couldn't see for sure because when Crofut was shot, *"He fell on his chest with his hands underneath him."* Yes! And after that, someone rolled the victim over, almost certainly for the purpose of rendering aid.

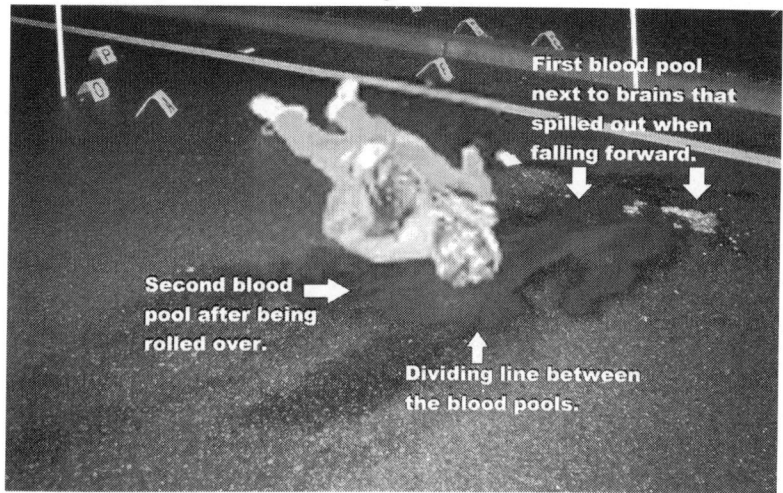

(Photo: Police photo including work-product notations by Gerald's attorneys.)

Quickly I flipped through some relevant reports to look for anything I may have missed regarding moving the body, but there was nothing. There had been no mention whatsoever of anyone touching the body or moving it. If it had been moved, it would have to be an EMT or a member of the police department who did it, and almost unfailingly, that sort of thing is noted in reports. But perhaps there had been an omission, so I asked Verne to check.

But there was another possibility. Maybe Brenda Crofut was the person who moved her husband, maybe even before police and EMTs arrived. She told the 911 dispatcher that she was a nurse. In the digital photos provided to me in the discovery process I found a photo of Brenda's boots, which were collected as evidence that night. They showed dark blotches on the toes that could be blood. Perhaps she was bloodied trying to roll her husband over to check his condition? EMTs could have done it, too, but Verne was later able to eliminate that possibility. None of the EMTs who responded to the call remembered any need to roll Crofut over.

It had to have been Brenda. How else would he end up on his back with the strings of his hoodie both pointing to the same side?

Still, there was a problem. What this seemed to suggest was that Crofut had been shot and fallen forward, landing on his face with his feet pointed toward the vehicles. If this was true, did it also mean that he was shot in the back of the head, with Gerald behind him? If so, it would be the worst possible scenario for the case. If the evidence proved that Crofut had been facing the dark night instead of Gerald when the shot was fired, Gerald was guilty and he was going to prison, maybe for life.

I called Schuessler again and asked him to come to my office. We looked through the photos together, and then I disclosed my worst fear to him. Schuessler looked at me incredulously for a second, then he began to laugh. Yes, he actually laughed at me. "Mike, he got shot from the front," he said. "The medical examiner believes that one .223 round from the AR-15 entered his forehead on the left side. Look, if you can stand it, at the photos of his face. If he'd been hit from behind, there wouldn't be any of his face left at all."

This was a huge relief to me. But I knew I still hadn't addressed and answered the question that was continuing to make the rounds on the street and over the internet: Had David Crofut's shooting been an execution?

To try to dispense with the allegation in that rumor, I spent a long time staring at the positions of the vehicles and the body – literally staring – just thinking, imagining and strategizing around the various possibilities. Gerald claimed that he had exited his truck, and that Crofut had followed him away from his own vehicle, even though he knew Gerald was armed. How I could explain that to a jury within my theory of the case – well, it was so far escaping me. Frustrated, I yelled for Emilia, whose office was only a few doors away. She came with a notepad in her hand and a baby on her arm.

"I'll help you, but you have to keep it down," she said, nodding toward her sleeping son. "If you wake him, we're done."

I quickly assented, and began to explain both my problem and my process.

"I had Verne make a diagram," Emilia offered. "You know he is an accident reconstructionist like Dave, right? Well, check the file. It shows the precise locations of all of the evidence logged by SPD."

I got it out and together we looked at it. After a few moments, Emilia said, "Do you remember back in high school, when teachers used to use transparencies and a projector? Could you make a page for all of the evidence, so that we can add things that are important and remove the pieces that are distracting?"

"Why?" I asked, not exactly up for an art project.

"Because I think you are getting overwhelmed by the forest," she said. "Right now the discovery either gives us one piece at a time or all the pieces at once. You can't tell the difference between a piece of bone and a quarter on the side of the road." You need to be able to focus on just the pieces that are important." I took her advice. Lacking the actual transparency pages, which were basically clear pages of plastic, I dug through our supply closet and found clear notebook sleeves. After cutting the pockets into single sheets, I traced the roadway from our laser map. Then I added a page just for the body and the vehicles. I did one for the gun, another for the skull and hair, and yet another for the other logged evidence.

When I was finished, the most useful of all of the transparency pages was the one showing the location of all the bone, brains and skull. With the page showing the pieces of Crofut laid over the top of the road, I could see clearly that almost all the skull and skin was located between the cars and the body. It seemed obvious to me that the shooter, Gerald, had been facing the vehicles when he pulled the trigger. That put Crofut, the victim, exactly where I needed him to be – between Gerald and the vehicles.

Both men had apparently gone on foot southbound down the road as they left the safety of their vehicles – away from Brenda Crofut and the accident scene. We took the spread of the evidence to corroborate Gerald's story that he was backing away from Crofut and the vehicles, since it seemed obvious that the bone and brains had been blown in the opposite direction. While I would need to confirm this with an expert, I couldn't imagine a scenario that would put Gerald, the shooter, in the midst of the debris field. Even with some blowback, my basic understanding of the physics just didn't seem to support almost *all* of the bone and other debris blowing in the direction of the shooter. So, yes, I felt confident that Crofut was between Gerald and the cars, just as Gerald had claimed.

But I still had to satisfy my curiosity as to how a man could get shot at close range with such a powerful rifle and not fall backwards. I talked with Schuessler, Hoyer and Karlin separately about this. Each of them confirmed for me that it was entirely possible that Crofut had fallen forward, despite what happens in the cinema. "Movies are not real life," Schuessler chided me. "There's hardly any mass to a .223 bullet compared to a man." I took the gentle razzing in stride, knowing that I had to ask the "dumb" questions if I wanted to get an answer that worked not just for me but for Gerald's jurors.

Emilia spoke up with an additional thought, and it was one that would fit neatly into my evolving trial strategy. "Wouldn't it be more likely for Crofut to fall forward when the shot struck him if he was already moving forward?"

I logged the question as a good one to ask, but jumped quickly to thinking about how the evidence might prove that Crofut was indeed walking forward when he was shot. Would one of his shoes have more blood spatter on it than the other if he had one foot forward? I zoomed in on the photos we had received in discovery. I thought that his right shoe did show more spatter on it than the left. I logged my observations, and then asked my assistant to start the process of setting up an in-person evidence review of the clothing and shoes. I'd have Schuessler take a closer look.

In the process of working through these many questions, something new and potentially important occurred to me. No one had searched Brenda Crofut. No one had looked into her purse. I jotted questions onto the pad that constituted my trial outline:

Had Crofut been carrying or holding a weapon when he was shot?

Did Brenda put a gun in her purse when she saw what had happened?

Did Crofut own firearms that would fit into Brenda's purse or pocket? And if so, can I get them swabbed for blood?

I made a note to write to the D.A.'s office and SPD, asking them to go get Crofut's guns, if he had any, and test them for blood.

That pretty much completed my review of the government-gathered evidence in discovery, so I moved on to the witness statements returned by Verne Hoyer. I suppose I could imagine a scenario where Crofut could have been marched out 80 feet at the point of a gun before he was shot, but I was pleased to see that such a scenario didn't fit with any of the additional witness statements we had gathered:

Witness Oneta Boyles, who eventually called 911, said that she approached the scene in her vehicle, traveling southbound, in the same direction as Gerald and Crofut. She slowed her vehicle then drove around the stopped cars as she moved along the west roadway edge.

Wait a second. Boyles said she drove around the stopped cars? Didn't the law enforcement witnesses claim that the southbound lane was completely blocked?

To me, their description sounded exaggerated in order to try and make the location of Gerald's parked pickup sound way worse than it actually was. I made notes in my outline to cross-examine the cops on that point.

Furthermore, as Mrs. Boyles passed the Nissan Rogue, she noticed the driver door was open with the interior dome lights activated. Mrs. Boyles observed no one in the vehicle.

What? Brenda Crofut told police she sat in the car until she heard the gunshot, then got out to find her husband dead. Was she a part of this somehow?

Mrs. Boyles stated that she continued driving slowly past the pickup where she then observed a man (Crofut) standing near the left front fender of the pickup. Mrs. Boyles rolled down her window and asked him if he needed her to call 911. According to Mrs. Boyles, David Crofut indicated "no."

Huh. That is an interesting detail. Crofut gets into an accident with a supposed road-raging driver and doesn't want the police to respond? Why wouldn't he have wanted someone to call 911? He was in the middle of the road. A man had a gun. Why wouldn't he want the cops there, if only to protect his wife?

It occurred to me that maybe Crofut knew he was too drunk to be driving. Or maybe he realized that he had committed a major screw-up by letting his aggression take over to the point that he rammed Gerald's pickup with Brenda's new-to-her Nissan. Who knows? Maybe he wasn't supposed to be driving that car of hers at all.

While Mrs. Boyles was at the scene, David Crofut started walking toward her stopped position, a short distance of 4 to 6 feet. He then paused in front of the pickup, and Mrs. Boyles recalls David Crofut stating, "I just want to know why he slammed on his brakes... I just want to talk to him." Crofut gestured toward the center of the roadway or median as he made the comment. When asked if she observed anyone else in the area when speaking with David Crofut, Mrs. Boyles said she did not – until she heard a person say, "Don't come any closer, man... don't come any closer." It was then that Mrs. Boyles saw Gerald standing at or in the median of the parkway. She observed a rifle in his right hand and that he was talking to someone on what appeared to be a cell phone. Mrs. Boyles described Gerald as facing towards David Crofut, backing up slowly as he scuffed his feet in the dirt of the median, all the while continuing to talk on the phone and warn David Crofut not to come any closer. Mrs. Boyles remembered seeing the door on the driver's side of the pickup open, with the interior dome light illuminating the interior. David Crofut, she said, seemed to be acting the "macho type" – sort of puffed up. When she was interviewed she demonstrated what she meant, putting her hands and arms to her side, raising her shoulder and arching the arm out to her sides similar to a weight lifter.

"Macho." What a great word to be able to say over and over again to the jury. I can ask Mrs. Boyles to demonstrate with her hands and arms what she meant, just like she did for Verne.

Witness Jill Tennefoss-Favre told Verne that she too had come upon the stopped vehicles as she was driving southbound on Bob Straub. Both men were alive and standing upright when she drove through the scene. Jill passed the smaller vehicle and then the pickup, noticing that all the headlights were on and Crofut was standing in front of the pickup, appearing angry. She said he was yelling at Gerald, who was standing in the median talking on a cell phone. Crofut was waving his arms above his head, she said, and she described Crofut's actions as "intimidating" towards Gerald. The last thing she saw before clearing the scene was Crofut advancing towards Gerald, still flailing his arms above his head and yelling.

Both of these were great interviews for Gerald's self-defense case. Given the statements of Tennefoss-Favre and Boyles, I thought we could, at last, set aside the "execution" theories of the internet. I was savoring the milestone when the office receptionist buzzed my phone. "I've got a lady on the phone, says her name is Ethyl Gladstone. Says she knows Gerald and wants to tell you something. That's all she'll tell me. She sounds elderly and a little hard of hearing, so speak up.'"

I picked up the phone. "This is Mike."

I heard nothing at first, then a frail-sounding woman's voice. "Hello? Hello? Is anyone there?" It sounded like she had been trying to figure out if anybody was still on the line, not knowing she'd been put on hold.

I repeated myself, louder this time. "This is Mike Arnold!"

"Oh, hello there, sorry about that. I'm a little hard of hearing."

"No problem. How can I help you?" I shouted.

"What? What did you say?"

"I said, how can I help you?!" I was practically yelling.

"I can barely hear you, dear. Oh well, I'll just hope you can hear me and tell you what I called to tell you."

I didn't say anything, since it wouldn't matter.

"I knew Gerald. You know, that guy who killed that man out in Springfield. I met him last year. I was out on the street putting nickels in the meters, because I like to do that. The city is too aggressive on the whole parking ticket thing, and I like to help people a little if I can. So one day I put a nickel in the meter where this big black pickup was parked, and a man came out of the coffee shop and asked me what I was doing. I told him that I was trying to keep him from getting a ticket. He hugged me and pulled me over to a table and we talked for a long time about whatever. He tried to buy me coffee but I told him no, I get it for free at the rest home. And then I went back to my work with the nickels, and he drove away. It must have been really loud, that truck, because even I could hear it, as deaf as I am. I never saw him again after that, but on Mother's Day, he left me the biggest bouquet of lilies at the home. They lasted for weeks in my room, and they made it smell so good! Anyway, that's what I called to say. I don't know what's going on with Gerald, but he did that for me and I thought someone should know. Thank you, you were a dear, letting me ramble on so."

I told her she'd made my day, and she had.

Marine sniper, UFC fighter, neighborhood angry guy… and friend to old ladies? My client is, indeed, a multi-dimensional character.

CHAPTER 16
IDENTIFYING KEY ISSUES

By this point, I felt I had gotten my arms around the basic shape of the case. With the discovery in hand, I could clearly see the outline of the government's murder case against Gerald. I also felt I understood the chain of events that led to the shooting, but of course, only from Gerald's perspective. While I continued to believe him when he said that he shot David Crofut in self-defense, accepting that essential part of the case didn't mean that I automatically believed every bit of what Gerald told me — especially not since seeing the Parade of Horribles.

Discrepancies and omissions wouldn't make him a liar. Humans are not video recorders. Generally speaking, witnesses provide poor evidence. In fact, research has established that the human brain only remembers parts of an event and then fills in the blanks from reasonable inferences. The result is what we call "memories," though only a fraction of any account is actually seen and coded by the brain in that way.

Having now done some testing of Gerald's truthfulness, just by listening to his stories, taking my own measure of the man, and checking some key facts afterward, it was time to begin digging deeper into the questions surrounding what happened that night on Bob Straub Parkway. It was time, in other words, for me to actively challenge my own confirmation bias. It wouldn't do Gerald any good for me to create an echo chamber made up of his statements and my own beliefs. I needed to prepare the case that was best for my client, and that means looking carefully at the difference between what I think I know and would like to prove… and what can be actually proven. Often, they're not the same things.

Three big questions presented themselves right away:

Why didn't Gerald drive away?

Why did he grab the rifle?

Couldn't he have avoided the shooting by using his martial arts skills on Crofut?

I began my deeper dive by looking at what Gerald did in the seconds after the crash. He told me he had tried to start his pickup and leave, because Crofut had gotten out of his car and started to yell at him. When the truck "wouldn't start" as Gerald put it, and Crofut was still yelling, Gerald went for his rifle. In other words, he felt threatened and sought to arm himself in self-defense.

I did think there was another possible motive in grabbing the rifle – especially since discovery had shown us that Gerald could have chosen a handgun that was also in the cab of the truck. Wasn't it likely that Gerald's main thought was to scare the shit out of David Crofut? To let the sniper rifle and scope do the talking and watch as Crofut pissed his pants and ran away? For sure, I thought. Gerald knew plenty about the persuasive powers of a show of force. He'd had plenty of opportunities in the Marines, in MMA and while working for Blackwater, to learn how to control a situation by becoming the scariest dude in the room.

Of course, on the night of January 29, 2014, David Crofut didn't scare – at least not enough to slink off into the night as Gerald might have hoped. No, Crofut did what no normal, reasonable human being in the same situation would have done: he kept coming.

By the time Gerald realized that visibly arming himself hadn't worked, he was already out of his truck and moving away from it with Crofut following him. At this point, Gerald may have panicked. He didn't have a Plan B. He was holding what was obviously a rifle in his hands, and still the guy who had just rammed his truck was yelling and continuing to advance. What was going to make David Crofut stop?

That's all speculation. Speculation without evidence is worthless. What matters in this case is what matters in any case – what we can actually prove.

I steered back toward the evidence. While I may have been right that Gerald chose his weapon with scaring Crofut in mind, I knew that the better narrative for the jury was a simpler one with less aggression implied – that Gerald left his dead truck and, in fear, grabbed the gun he felt most comfortable with, the rifle similar to the one he had used in Afghanistan.

Sometimes we don't choose the "right" tool, we choose the one we know and like. I see myself doing this on the farm all the time.

That dead truck and those martial arts skills – these would have to be investigative considerations for another day. Each would require professional analysis and expert input. Having at least provisionally satisfied myself that I could explain why Gerald chose the assault rifle – which would be a key question in any juror's mind – I knocked off for the afternoon and took time to go visit Gerald in jail.

The visit was a check-in, basically. When I've got a client in jail, I try to stop by for a conversation, just to try to combat the inevitable loneliness and stress of incarceration. Verne and Emilia, as well as other attorneys from my office, were making periodic visits, too.

This time, before leaving the office, I grabbed a file containing photos of Gerald that I had asked him to provide me, just for purposes of getting to know him and to find out how he sees himself. Maybe I'd learn something by going over them with him.

I find that the photographs a person chooses to retain can tell you a lot about who they think they are and what is important to them. Especially in the new era of digital (throwaway) photography, setting aside a handful of special digital or printed photographs is significant. To prepare Gerald's defense, I had asked him and his fiancée, Kristin, for as many photos and videos as they could provide. We'd use them in our attempts to raise money for his defense, since Gerald was well known not just locally, but also on the coast where he grew up, and in the social circles that stemmed from his time in the Marines, his MMA training, and his UFC bouts. The photos would also become exhibits at trial.

By and large, the photos we received at Arnold Law weren't homey photos – the family events were notably missing from Gerald's collection.

Instead, most of the photos came from Gerald's MMA/UFC life, his military stints, and times spent hunting, fishing and shooting guns. The MMA/UFC photos were most striking. They tended to show Gerald in the ring, with his muscles, veins and tattoos proudly displayed. He is usually straddling and sometimes choking his opponents. Sometimes his fists are up in a ready position. Other pictures from his MMA life show him while training – lots of kicking, punching, elbowing, and kneeing. There were also photos of Gerald standing next to recognizable celebrities, people he met through MMA/UFC. In the military-related photos I was given, Gerald is in uniform, usually shooting or holding a large gun. In the Gerald-the-outdoorsman photos, he's holding trophy fish. All of the pictures depicted a man at the peak of his strength and ability, surrounded by others of significance in his various worlds. Overall, Gerald looked dominant. And he looked very capable of taking out an armed or unarmed man.

As we shuffled through the photos together, Gerald described what we were seeing and filled in with anecdotes here and there. He wasn't particularly modest or self-effacing about the images; he seemed proud of what they said about him. So it maybe came as a little bit of a surprise when I told Gerald that these were the kinds of photos that would be used by the government to show jurors what a dangerous, physically capable predator he was. The prosecution would use them, I said, to plant a seed of belief in the jury, one that could grow into a murder conviction.

Gerald was sobered by what I was saying, but not surprised.

I told him that it was going to be my job to use these same photos – perhaps along with some others – to tell an alternate story of the man I was representing. "That's why I like it when you tell me stories," I explained. "It gives me a fuller picture than… well, what somebody might assume from looking at these."

From there I switched gears. "Do you know," I asked, "what wins most trials?"

Gerald shrugged. "A good attorney?"

"No. Research says that the lawyers only win the case 10 percent of the time, at least according to the survey I saw. This doesn't take into account the other factors the jurors might have said were important in the case, like the specific things that the attorneys spoon-fed them in court. No, what really wins trials, hands down, is the popularity contest. A jury has to want to help you out. They have to want to be on your side. Pretty people, likeable people, people that jurors trust…that's who gets helped out by the jury. It's human nature."

I continued, "So if you ever wonder why I'm happy to sit here and listen to you tell your stories, that's why. It's not because you're fun to talk to — though you are. I just know that we can better convince a jury if we can find ways to humanize you within our self-defense narrative."

But it would take more than just the stories that Gerald remembered and chose to tell me. I knew I had to get ahold of the stories that Gerald would rather not tell, because these too would play a role in getting jurors to see him sympathetically. In a tone of warning, I said, "I'm going to have to look into your background and find the stories that will show people what really makes you tick, the incidents and circumstances that have made you who you are."

Gerald nodded. "Absolutely. No problem."

"Some of it will probably take us places you don't really want to go," I warned him. "Childhood. People who influenced you, including your mom and even your dad, who I know is kind of a mixed character in your life. Mistakes you made. Brushes with the law. All that stuff."

Again Gerald nodded. "Do what you need to do. It's fine with me. Whatever it takes, Mike, do it. I'll own my past."

CHAPTER 17

MUZZLED JUSTICE

There are many procedural considerations in the process of getting a defendant from arraignment to trial. Whether or not to testify at grand jury was one pre-indictment issue to address. Another issue arose soon after the arraignment on the indictment – deciding whether or not to try to disqualify a potential judge in the case.

Considering whether to file the necessary affidavit to disqualify a judge is one of those things that, as a defense attorney, you normally consider for about two seconds and rush to check off your trial strategy list. It's not something you do just because you feel like it. It's not like striking a juror in jury selection. Judges don't like getting "affidavited." They consider it an affront (at least in Lane County) because every judge believes himself or herself to be beyond reproach – and many of them are. But in Gerald's case, I wasn't so quick to dismiss the possibility of trying to disqualify Judge Debra Vogt. She had been assigned to our case. I was very concerned.

Judge Vogt had been a judge for almost 10 years, and at the time Gerald's case came along, she was the district's chief criminal judge. Before that she had been a prosecutor for the Lane County District Attorney's Office. I had tried cases with her before, and I knew her to be tough on attorneys and defendants alike. While I'd had good experiences with her in the courtroom, I also had some concerns about her recent rulings on cases.

It looked to me like she was increasingly coming down on the side of the State. In fact, I thought it had gotten to the point that she was acting less like an impartial judge and more like another prosecutor. Still, filing an affidavit against her would be a big, potentially dangerous step. Such actions can cause retribution, not just from the judge himself or herself, but even from other judges in the county. It's not something you do unless you really think that judge poses a threat to your client – and you think the threat is so significant that it's worth risking that your decision will have adverse effects on other clients in the future.

I brought my concerns to my wife, Jacy, and the other attorneys in our office. Together we discussed the pros and cons. I thought the idea deserved serious consideration. Again, I pointed out that Judge Vogt was tough. Perhaps she was the one judge brave enough to stand up to the D.A. and his weak case without worrying about saving face. The discussion resulted in only one clear consensus, and that was it should be up to Gerald to decide. Did he want to roll the dice on this judge? Was it a risk to put his future in her hands, or was it more of a risk to his future to ask her to step aside? At this point she was a known entity, and as Sun Tzu, author of *The Art of War*, would say in this situation: If you know the enemy and know yourself, you need not fear the results of a hundred battles.

In the end, Gerald decided not to file the affidavit, and we supported his decision. I wish we hadn't. I view the assignment of Judge Vogt to his case as the most significant hurdle we faced in trying to win Gerald's freedom.

Shortly after Gerald's arraignment we filed our first pleading, a motion requesting a bail hearing from which bail would be set. Bail may be denied in a murder case in Oregon, so long as the State can prove with sufficient evidence that the individual is guilty (or at least that the circumstantial evidence of guilt is strong). In my review of the facts, a self-defense case seemed evident, and the evidence of murder was not strong. I thought we had a good shot at bail if the judge followed the law. If we didn't get it, at least we would learn some things about the government's case, and perhaps even get an opportunity to cross-examine the state's witnesses at the hearing.

Judge Vogt immediately called the attorneys into her chambers to discuss the issue of the bail hearing. She and the district attorney said they didn't want me to turn the hearing into a "deposition" of the State's witnesses. She said that she would determine the question of bail on the basis of affidavits alone. I told them I couldn't cross-examine pieces of paper but she denied our request for a hearing for live witnesses nonetheless.

In response to our motion for bail, the State filed an affidavit signed by Springfield Detective George Crolly, the same Springfield detective accused of coercing a confession in Bob Lane's dead fake baby case. The 18-page affidavit summarized the State's case, and included several instances of the Parade of Horribles, the alleged bad acts of Gerald in the years preceding the shooting. The State's lone affidavit, filed by one detective in a case that involved multiple members of law enforcement and several eyewitnesses, contained an intentional omission of one of the most important and legally significant facts of this case: Crofut was at a complete stop on the highway before putting the pedal to the metal and ramming Gerald's truck at maximum acceleration.

Crolly also made a misleading and self-serving omission of a key fact in another officer's report. Compare what Detective Crolly swore to under oath, versus what the report by Officer Jed Wilson really said:

Crolly: "The data shows that the accelerator was applied at about -3.5 seconds before the event and a steady increase in speed began and continued up to the event."

Wilson: "The data shows that a *maximum value* of accelerator was applied at about -3.5 seconds before the event and a steady increase in speed began and continued up to the event."

It was apparent that Detective Crolly cut and pasted this actual portion of Officer Wilson's report and chose to intentionally delete the phrase "a maximum value of." This was not just a mistaken paraphrasing of Officer Wilson's statement. It was an intentional omission of a relevant, key fact: from a full stop, Crofut floored his accelerator to ram Gerald's truck. Det. Crolly politely declined to comment for the purposes of this book.

Additionally, Crolly's affidavit spent a large portion of space alleging improper character evidence. While the rules of evidence do not apply to a release hearing, it was still important to note that none of these purported incidents have anything to do with Gerald firing a firearm in self-defense, and clearly would not be admissible at trial under the established bad acts case law (assuming the State could even meet the proof threshold that these previous events had even happened). The last five pages of Detective Crolly's affidavit were a clear attempt to distract the Court from the evidence demonstrating Gerald's reasonable and defensive demeanor, as evidenced through witness statements and his 911 call.

In response to the State's Affidavit, we filed several documents in an attempt to convince the judge that (1) Gerald had acted in self-defense, and (2) that the State had not produced sufficient evidence to hold Gerald pending trial without bail. In order to convince a jury to convict Gerald at trial, the State would have to disprove beyond a reasonable doubt that Gerald had not acted in self-defense. Based on the State's evidence alone, there was enough evidence supporting a viable self-defense claim. The Court could not rightfully conclude that there was a strong presumption or proof evident of murder. In fact, there was actually a stronger case for self-defense than for murder.

Along with my arguments, I made multiple filings. I filed an affidavit signed by Jacy about her review of the discovery, evidence from the 911 call, and an article published jointly by the Lane County regional law enforcement agents about Deadly Use of Force. I filed an affidavit signed by our investigator Verne Hoyer confirming the information he learned about the decedent's level of alcohol consumption prior to the crash and shooting. I filed an affidavit signed by Emerald Valley Armory owner Raye Gunter about the appropriate use of deadly force in these circumstances.

Finally, I filed a multiple-page affidavit signed by Gerald. Generally, a defendant accused of a crime will preserve his right to remain silent during the pendency of (the run-up to) the proceedings. Gerald told the court many details and summarized the situation as follows: "I was in fear for my life when I fired my rifle on January 29, 2014. I believed that David Crofut was going to kill me."

In reply to the Affidavit, I also argued that the Court could not evaluate the strength of the State's evidence and whether it was clear and convincing that this individual was guilty of murder without also evaluating their actions from a self-defense angle. In other words, although the State had the burden in this case, that burden had to be examined in light of the fact that a person cannot be guilty of murder if their actions were justified. A person's actions are not criminal if they are privileged under the law. If a person's actions are not criminal, then he is not guilty of the crime. If he is not guilty of the crime, then the presumption of his guilt cannot be strong and the proof of his guilt cannot be evident.

In my pleadings, I closed with:

Mr. Strebendt was justified in firing his rifle. When an angry and hostile stranger acts aggressively towards you, tells you he has a weapon and threatens to kill you, you are entitled to take him at his word.

After all of this evidence was filed, Judge Vogt reacted – and not in a way that we could have anticipated. On April 1, 2014, she entered a Trial Management Order, something that had not been requested by any party to the case. It was something she did entirely on her own. This Order found that extrajudicial statements about the case would have a substantial likelihood of materially prejudicing the imminent fact-finding process. She ordered that counsel, as well as their employees and investigators, not make any comment concerning the evidence, case theories, exhibits, testimony, or court filings regarding Gerald Strebendt's murder case. She also ordered specifically that the prohibition include commenting to persons in the news media and social media.

This trial management order was a gag order, entered against me because of the aggressive way that we had responded to the State's Affidavit. While most attorneys wouldn't have done much of anything at the bail-hearing level, we had actually done some work for Gerald. It was relatively unusual in our county for a defense team to file multiple affidavits and actually discuss the evidence, and I strongly suspect that Judge Vogt believed our purpose in filing these affidavits was not to defend Gerald, but, rather, to leak information about the case to the press. She undoubtedly suspected me to be selfishly seeking media attention, or hoping to wrongfully pollute the jury pool. Or both.

But, what should I have done instead? To this day I don't understand how one could expect an attorney to address the requirements of the statute without discussing in detail the prejudices of the evidence filed by the State. I felt I had to skewer any State evidence that might be used to show that Gerald was likely to be guilty, and therefore not eligible for bail. It was my job as Gerald's defense attorney. How else was he going to get bail and be released from jail? He was presumed innocent unless proven guilty in the eyes of the law.

This Trial Management Order fell on us like a ton of bricks, crushing our plans for seeking public assistance in developing the case. This shooting happened on a dark road surrounded by neighborhoods. Multiple cars passed by after the shooting. The photos taken by police showed citizens walking on the bike path along the road. We knew that there had to be witnesses out there that SPD had not talked to – people who might not seek us out to tell us what we had seen because they assumed Gerald was guilty. Thanks to this gag order, we had no way to reach out to them without great risk to ourselves by way of criminal contempt charges. By blocking our access to the press and social media, Judge Vogt really did a disservice to Gerald and his defense.

The bad news continued, unfortunately.

On April 2, a day later, the Judge denied our motion for release.

Instead of holding a public hearing to deny the motion, Judge Vogt again refused our request to allow the defense to call witnesses to challenge the State's witnesses in open court. In addition, she ordered that all documentation filed after March 19 pertaining to our request for bail and Gerald's release from jail be sealed and made unavailable to the public. In other words, Judge Vogt chose to protect the secrecy of the facts of the case over Gerald's right to truly fight for his life and freedom in the likely many months before his trial.

To say that I was disappointed in Judge Vogt's handling of this matter was… well, it would be more of an understatement than when I said I was shocked at the gag order. Article 1, Sect. 10 of the Oregon Constitution states that "[n]o court shall be secret." Gerald and I were concerned that she was hiding from public accountability to protect herself and the district attorney, but we could only speculate.

On April 18, I filed an objection to Judge Vogt's Trial Management Order and requested oral argument. I argued that the order requiring certain secret, sealed court documents was unlawful and unconstitutional. Gerald had Sixth Amendment and Oregon rights to a public trial, I argued, including all critical proceedings along the way.

The rights I refer to are fundamental, centered on a historical belief that public criminal proceedings should operate as a check against malevolent government-run justice systems – the kind the founders had seen in

England's Star Chamber tribunals in the 16th and 17th centuries. In recent years, this right to public proceedings has come to the fore regarding alleged Al Qaeda captives at Guantanamo Bay in Cuba, but it's not something that often involves American citizens, particularly ones who served in the military to protect our freedoms.

Our nation's founders believed that the right to public proceedings benefits both the public and the accused. On Gerald's behalf, we argued that both he and the public needed the press to have access to the proceedings in his case. A bail hearing, in particular, is a critical part of any case, requiring the government to show the public why a defendant must remain in jail instead of becoming eligible for bail before trial. Such critical decisions, we said, should not be made behind closed doors, relying on documents that are kept secret. The U.S. Constitution does not support it.

And finally, both the Oregon Constitution and the First Amendment of the United States Constitution provide for the right to free speech. The Oregon Constitution's right is actually more strongly worded and interpreted than the U.S. Constitution's. We argued that Judge Vogt's Trial Management Orders violated the free speech rights of Gerald, his counsel, and his agents. They also posed a prior restraint on friends and family, we said, by causing them to fear harming Gerald or creating a false contempt-of-court allegation against themselves by contacting the press. We added:

Even a narrowly-tailored order, which this order is not, improperly curtails Mr. Strebendt's rights to adequately defend himself (See Due Process Clause, 14th Amend. U.S. Constitution). The order in its present form prohibited a public framing of the trial issues in order to request witnesses to come forward that may assist in his defense. When a person is innocent, most if not all witnesses will have some sort of exculpatory information, and Mr. Strebendt has a right to publicly seek such witnesses. For free media assistance, the only way to get something published would be to frame it as a matter of public importance, which requires a disclosure of certain facts and case theories. An additional way is through social media requests and campaigns.

Perhaps the most galling thing about Judge Vogt's gag order was how it went beyond just Gerald or his attorneys talking to the press. It inhibited investigators and attorneys from posing certain questions or stating certain facts to witnesses for fear that they, in turn, would contact the media

— leading to possible contempt charges being charged against everyone involved in this media game of telephone. The effect of this part of the order actually chilled our efforts to investigate Gerald's case, we argued. It created the fear that any interview could be mentioned on Facebook or to the media and that the court could bring charges against an investigator or attorney, just for doing his or her job. To me, this was an obvious curtailment of Gerald's ability to have a constitutionally adequate investigation conducted on his behalf without creating a conflict of interest (fear of government contempt reprisals) for investigators and agents. Additionally, we argued that the order infringed on Gerald's ability to adequately secure his choice of counsel. He had a constitutional right to hire the attorney of his choice. That "fair opportunity" should necessarily include his right to fundraise through protected speech. If he couldn't publicly comment on the case, he couldn't raise money, we argued. And if he couldn't raise money, he couldn't afford to secure his choice of counsel.

All of these arguments were implicitly rejected by Judge Vogt. She did not rule on my request, and she did not hold argument as I had requested. I circled the wagons with my team. With the advice of ethics and appellate counsel, we filed a petition for *mandamus* relief from the Oregon Supreme Court, challenging the gag order and the secrecy of the file. Our petition was denied and secrecy prevailed... but not for long.

BAD NEWS, GREAT NEWS

After the bail hearing and the imposition of the gag order, I struggled to find ways to continue searching for witnesses to what happened on Bob Straub Parkway that night in January of 2014. That's pretty hard to do when you can't do media interviews, hold news conferences or even post on Facebook.

Necessity being the mother of invention, I did manage to seek some additional witnesses without violating the gag order. I posted Verne, my investigator, and his grandchildren at the crash site with a big sign for many hours over a period of days. No passing motorist could miss it – or them. The media reported it and we got dozens of calls from people who were onsite before, during and after the shooting. In the process, we talked to at least one witness who had contacted the Springfield Police Department with her information and *never received a returned phone call.* That's proof positive, if you ask me, that it's a miscarriage of justice to keep defense counsel from talking about the case and calling for witnesses to come forward.

Having to rely on the State to find and produce your witnesses is not just wrong, it's unconstitutional.

(Photos: Verné Hoyer's grandchildren Trinity, Seth, and Sofiya.)

The gag order also hobbled my ability to help Gerald raise money for his defense. As much as I'd like to say I'm more interested in justice than money, we do have lights to keep on at the office; the law firm doesn't run on principles of justice alone. I knew there had to be people out there who had connections to Gerald through the Marines, MMA and UFC – people who might want to help the guy out. But, the judge had me completely hamstrung. I couldn't do anything to reach out to them. To convince a donor that Gerald was worth investing in, I would have to convince the donor of Gerald's innocence which would be in violation of the gag order.

Gerald's fiancée, Kristin, was a lifesaver. When things got dire, she and her mother put their own money into Gerald's trust account. Kristin also took over Gerald's Facebook page, posting updates and information that I couldn't share – things she learned from Gerald during his daily calls made from the "day room." I was impressed by this woman's steadfastness and fortitude. When most people would have high-tailed it for the hills, Kristin dug in with Gerald, offering essentially everything she had, and when the money was gone, she offered herself, her time, her support.

I could see why Gerald was in love with her and so devoted to her. For hours he talked to me about her intelligence, beauty, and the way that their personalities fit together. He was desperate to get out of jail and get back to her. He felt like he was letting her down by not being there for her, for not supporting her through the everyday challenges of life. There wasn't much he could do for her, but he did everything he could. It included having me get back the clothing and personal items that were seized from Gerald on the night of the shooting. He wanted her to sell them and put the money toward paying her bills.

To distract him from the despair of being separated from Kristin, I kept reminding him of the reasons I felt he stood a good chance at trial on the murder charge. There was the ACM data proving that Crofut rammed Gerald's truck, the toxicology tests confirming that the so-called victim was at almost twice the legal limit of intoxication at the time of the crash, and the fact that Crofut walked more than 80 feet from his vehicle, following a man with a gun, before he was killed. There were so many weaknesses in the State's case, and we were poised to exploit all of them.

However, these discussions also forced us to confront the elephant in the room: If the State's case was so bad, why did the government push so hard to bring a case against Gerald?

I thought that the reason had more to do with Gerald himself than it did with the evidence in the case. Gerald Strebendt, the man, was far from perfect. The so-called Parade of Horribles proved that. Hell, my own very strong belief in Gerald's innocence took a battering when the list arrived with discovery. Gerald's Parade of Horribles list was longer and more damning than any I'd seen before. Over the months, I'd had many colleagues and investigators agree – this was incredibly daunting stuff to be up against in court. That's why we were going to move heaven and earth to keep as much of the list out of court as possible.

But if we fail...

It had gotten to the point that I was actively shielding my experts from the Parade if it didn't relate to their analysis or opinion. Some who had seen it in passing in the discovery found the evidence so significant and so persuasive that it gave them actual pause. By that I mean it totally rocked their ability to stay objective and help us build Gerald's defense. When you've got people reacting like that, people who have been handling criminal cases longer than I've been alive, well, it rapidly becomes clear that you have to eliminate the distraction if the work's going to get done impartially.

But not everything problematic for our case resided in the Parade of Horribles – there were other troubles, too. Some weeks after the discovery arrived in the office, we received an Oregon State Police Laboratory report on Gerald's firearm, and the news wasn't good. In fact, it was a new piece of evidence that posed a fairly significant challenge to our theory of the case. It made it look like Crofut was by no means up in Gerald's face when he got shot. Would this make it more difficult for us to argue that Gerald shot Crofut in self-defense? It well might.

The state crime lab had fired the Sig Sauer rifle using the ammunition seized from the scene and found that gunpowder particles were no longer observed at a distance of 84 inches, or seven feet. Examining Crofut's sweat-shirt and pants, no gunpowder residue was found, meaning that Crofut was likely to have been standing more than seven feet away when the bullet exploded his head.

When someone pulls a trigger, the firing pin strikes the bullet cartridge primer, which ignites. The flames then ignite the gunpowder in the cartridge case. This reaction creates a gas that expands and creates pressure in the barrel. The gas flows down the barrel in the path of least resistance pushing the bullet in front of it. The bullet pops out of the barrel like the CO2-propelled cork in a bottle of champagne. The residues of this chemical reaction are also expelled from the barrel of the gun in a cone-shaped pattern, slowing down due to air friction while falling down due to gravity. The more concentrated the residues are on a target, such as a victim's clothing, the closer the target was to the shooter.

The conclusion to be drawn from the crime lab's examination? That Gerald and Crofut were seven or more feet apart when Gerald pulled the trigger. The State would pounce on this, no doubt about it. The D.A. would argue that this test result ruled out a shot fired at close range during a struggle for the gun, or a shot fired when Crofut was advancing and almost upon Gerald. The government would argue that Gerald could not possibly have feared for his life – not reasonably, anyway – if Crofut was that far away.

Well, if seven or more feet is a distance too far away to be considered self-defense, what's the standard for murder? Seven feet and one inch? Ten feet? How would a jury make the determination?

What constitutes "legal self-defense" depends heavily upon the state you are in, the circumstances of the self-defense, and… the prosecutor who tries the case. Some prosecutors in self-defense cases mislead jurors by having them take into account the defendant's emotional state at the time of the assault/self-defense. For example, I have heard prosecutors argue to jurors that if someone is angry or acting out of anger that means he or she wasn't truly afraid of dying. That simply is not true. Anger and fear aren't binary or mutually exclusive and many anthropologists, psychologists, and evolutionary biologists will tell you that both emotions probably evolved from the same kinds of stimuli. This anger-versus-fear quandary was likely what played a major role in motivating the government to prosecute Gerald, given his sordid and frequent encounters with other drivers. On the night of the shooting, was Gerald angry over issues that arose while driving? Did that make his response road rage? Was he scared for his life? Or was he seeking retribution because somebody banged up his new Denali? To prevail at trial, we would have to nail down the specifics of what exactly happened that night, and find ways to fit each piece neatly into our self-defense narrative.

After the initial round of pretrial release motions were denied, and with the Parade of Horribles and the seven-foot gunpowder lab result in hand, to say that the team was feeling weary and downtrodden was an understatement. While the case was generally on track and moving forward just fine, Gerald was still in jail, and his trial was still a long, long time away. Some days it really got to me.

On one such day, I was sitting in the leather reading chair I keep in the corner of my office, feet up, trying to motivate myself back to the computer to work. It crossed my mind that maybe I should get out of the office altogether, maybe go see Gerald in jail and see if it didn't get me re-energized for another mile or two of this particular marathon. But I just couldn't muster the energy to do anything at all. So there I sat, leaning my head back, looking at the ceiling – that is, until I heard footsteps and saw the top of my office door swing open. I didn't look down to see who it was.

"What!?" I barked, hoping that it wasn't my law partner/wife that I was being rude to.

"Well aren't you a peach," said Emilia, standing in the doorway. I looked down from my ceiling focus to see her leaning against the door jamb, with a yellow legal pad and pen in her hand, as always. I also saw that she had a few pieces of white paper.

"I'm a rotten peach; get used to it," I said, and closed my eyes.

"Regretting taking on this case?"

"Sometimes," I admitted, with a big sigh. "I just want to be able to do something for him, you know? He's in jail, and there isn't anything I can do about that. He's in solitary, and he'll be there until his trial date. It's not right."

"It's bad, you know, all the stuff he's done."

"He didn't do all that," I spat back. I was being rude again, I couldn't help it. I hadn't gotten any decent sleep in… how long?

"At the very least, he did some of it, I think," Emilia said carefully. "But I think I have something that might help the case, if you can stop acting like a four-year-old for a few minutes to take a look."

She handed me the white sheaf of paperwork, then walked over to the chair where Gerald had sat the last time he'd been to my office, months ago when he was still a free man. In my hands, I saw what appeared to be a report from the Oregon State Police Crime Lab.

Could it really be good news this time?

Looking closer, I could see that the report contained DNA test results. The lab had tested the swabs that the government had taken from Gerald's rifle and compared them to DNA gathered during Crofut's autopsy. As I skimmed through the document, I sat up a little, then all the way up. "Does this report say what I think it says?" I asked, the pitch of my voice heading toward teenage-boy range.

"You're the expert, boss. I'm just the help around here," Emilia said, wryly.

"It says that one of the swabs, the Q-tips that they brushed on Gerald's gun, contained Crofut's DNA… but not his blood." I read a little more. "It says that Crofut's touch DNA was found on the gun."

"And…?" She asked.

Now I was out of the chair and standing up. "This report says that David Crofut touched the gun."

Emilia nodded slowly, as if to say, "Now you're catching on." After a moment, she added, "What will you do with this?"

"I don't know. I mean, we can use it at trial, sure…"

I stopped to consider what the scenario would have looked like; namely, how Crofut could have possibly gotten close enough to grab Gerald's gun. Gerald had told the 911 dispatcher that Crofut had grabbed for his gun. Gerald had told me that Crofut had actually succeeded in grabbing his gun. But honestly, I had never really believed this part of the story. I'd seen that ballistics report, the one that found no gunpowder residue on Crofut, the one that said this meant Crofut was standing seven or more feet away from Gerald at the time he was killed. My team and I were working toward test-firing the weapon ourselves to confirm the residue data and challenge the government's report, but now, not only did the DNA corroborate our self-defense theory, it made Gerald's actions more reasonable.

Gerald had been facing David Crofut with a military-style rifle. Gerald was telling Crofut to stay away from him, to get back. Faced with a big gun, David Crofut did not retreat to safety like a normal human being desirous of staying alive. Instead, he kept coming toward Gerald. He got so close to Gerald, in fact, that he actually touched Gerald's gun with his hand!

I turned it over in my head again: Two men. Out there in the dark. One of them with a rifle in his hand. Gerald was on the phone with 911 yelling at his adversary to get back… and Crofut didn't stop! What man in his right mind would see another man with a gun – whether it was pointed at him or at the ground – and keep coming? Contrast Crofut with Oneta Boyle and the other 911 callers: After hearing and seeing that there was a man with a gun on the road, all they wanted was to get away from the crazy guy. They reacted like normal people react. David Crofut did not. He kept coming, and now we knew he'd grabbed the gun.

I would have shot the guy in this situation. Hell, a police officer would, too! Go grab a cop's gun in the dead of night and threaten to kill him, and I bet you end up with more than one new hole.

I thought back to my conversation with Steve Hebner, the cop-turned-polygrapher. Police are taught the 21-foot rule, he said, which basically says that a subject with a weapon on the attack should be shot if he or she gets seven yards from your gun, is charging and showing no signs of stopping.

You can't even wait a second, because the attacker can close the distance in not much longer than that. Yet Gerald stood his ground and let Crofut get close enough – at least at some point in the confrontation – *to touch his rifle*.

I read the report a third time, just making sure I understood it. With glee I noted the absolute certainty of the report. It completely ruled out any possibility that the DNA collected from the rifle's hand guard came from blood. Why was this good news? Because it saved us a lot of additional argument at trial. With this confirmation from the lab, we could easily show that this DNA wasn't just blowback from the shot that killed Crofut. There wasn't any blood. It was what's called touch DNA, and thanks to these test results, all we had to argue was how it got on the rifle.

Not only was the news good for our case, the timing was incredible. We'd just gotten disappointing results from some of our own swab testing. Gerald had told us that he saw Crofut get into his truck after Gerald had gotten out and moved away from it. One of the reasons Gerald had thought that Crofut was armed was that Crofut could have taken one of Gerald's own guns out of the truck – he was especially concerned that Crofut might have found the handgun that Gerald kept in the center console. But when we swabbed the surfaces that Crofut could have touched inside Gerald's Denali, we came up empty-handed. Crofut's DNA was nowhere to be found. It was a setback, because it meant we couldn't establish that Crofut had gotten anywhere near the guns in Gerald's truck. It suggested that, despite what Crofut may have said about having a gun, not only did he not have one, we couldn't prove that he'd tried to get one. Gerald still looked like a potential murderer.

But now we had Crofut getting close enough to Gerald to actually grab his gun. That made it a whole helluva lot harder for the State to paint Gerald as the aggressor.

I had to go tell Gerald. I checked the time to make sure visiting hours for attorneys were still in effect and ran out of the office. I got halfway down the stairs before running back to find Emilia and drag her out of the office with me.

As we drove to the jail, Emilia and I tried to anticipate the State's arguments. I thought that the prosecutor might argue that the DNA had gotten on the rifle during an exchange of blows. I didn't really mind that argument, because it still meant that Crofut was in close range to Gerald, even knowing that Gerald had had his firearm out. Coming at a man with a gun was crazy, making Gerald's response – shooting Crofut – reasonable.

The prosecutor also might argue that the DNA wasn't the result of Crofut touching Gerald's rifle at all, but instead, the result of someone else first touching Crofut and then the gun. If an accidental transfer like that occurred, it was most likely the result of an SPD investigator touching the body and then the gun. I loved that argument, too, because it suggested a bungled investigation, mishandled evidence.

Emilia, always the joy-killer, suggested another possibility. "Maybe Gerald did it himself by touching Crofut after he had killed him, either to check for a pulse or because he wanted to get Crofut's DNA on the gun for his self-defense claim."

I made a face at her. I didn't want to think that Gerald could be devious and forward-thinking enough to have planned his defense against a murder charge even before the mist of blood had settled. Furthermore, while anything is possible, I told Emilia I thought her cynical explanation was unlikely. Brenda Crofut never said anything about Gerald getting that close to her husband's body while she was at the scene, and there had been nothing in Gerald's 911 call about him getting close to the body.

As I saw it, the State's options were limited. Either admit that Crofut advanced on Gerald and grabbed the gun, or admit that their crime scene investigation was completely botched. From the perspective of Gerald's defense, what's not to like?

On arrival at the jail we fairly ran up the stairs to the metal detector. After requesting to see Gerald, there was nothing to do but wait. I could barely stay seated in my chair. But when he came in, dressed in his greens and shower shoes, looking in need of a haircut and a decent meal, I played it cool.

"How's it going, man?" I asked. Emilia said nothing, just continued sitting there with a small smile on her face. Apparently she had no intention of stealing my thunder. She was going to let me break the good news.

Gerald shrugged, the way he always did when I greeted him in this way. "Jail is a great way to lose weight," he quipped. "I'll be back to my fighting weight in no time."

"It's all that Nutraloaf, that mystery meat garbage they're feeding you," I retorted.

"Whatcha got?" Gerald asked, sensing we had news. He gestured toward the sheets of paper in his hand, much like the ones he usually brought to meetings with us. "I have some notes for you, too."

I said nothing, just handed him the crime lab paperwork. I watched as he looked at it, read it and re-read it. I felt like a little kid at Christmas... until Gerald looked up with a frown, seeming confused. "I'm not sure what this says. Crofut's DNA was on the gun? Sure it was. His DNA was everywhere."

I took the paperwork back, and laid it on the table between us. I pointed to the section that ruled out blood. "Look here. Look at this. Not blood. Crofut had to *touch* the rifle to get his DNA on there."

Then Emilia piped up. "Or someone touched Crofut, then touched the gun."

Gerald sat back. "This is good, right?"

I nodded and let a smile creep across my face. "Very good."

"So what's our trial date again? When's a jury going to hear about this? When do we get to tell a jury that we can prove that Crofut grabbed my gun, just like I said he did?"

That, unfortunately, was the worst part of the entire thing. This evidence that we were so excited about, the crime lab report that we were sure would help get Gerald acquitted... we knew that many months would go by before it would ever see the light of day in a courtroom. We admitted as much to Gerald, and after answering his questions and collecting his notes, we left the jail significantly less exuberant than we'd gone in.

Driving back to the office, Emilia asked the million-dollar question: "If Crofut got shot after grabbing Gerald's gun, why is the State prosecuting this case? Isn't this a classic example of self-defense? I mean, who wouldn't shoot, if someone had tried to take your gun away and kept coming at you, even when they'd been warned not to?

I gave her the only answer I'd been able to come up with. "They didn't know about the DNA when the case got filed. They didn't even have the blood-alcohol level on Crofut back. I've said it before, and I'll say it again. They should have waited for the test results."

"Can't they move to dismiss the case now?"

"They absolutely should," I said, nodding. "But I don't think they will, because they think he's guilty. It's got to be the bad acts. They are looking at him as a bad guy. They don't know for sure what happened out there, but they know he's got this history of being aggressive, violent, and of course, all that bad driving. That's the only explanation."

But I still felt we had the upper hand. "I wouldn't want to be Bob Lane standing in front of a jury talking about a victim who had been drunk, had purposefully rammed Gerald's truck, and not only followed Gerald into the dark, but grabbed Gerald's gun." But as we saw in the 2012 fake baby case, Bob Lane doesn't mind letting a jury answer the tough questions.

CHAPTER 19

ANOTHER BAIL REQUEST AND
SOME UNEXPECTED PUBLICITY

At Arnold Law, experience had taught us that we were going to struggle with Judge Vogt over just about anything we might want to do — whether it was to get a new bail hearing or to examine witnesses on the bail question, or both. This was likely true even with the new and extremely persuasive evidence we had received, the touch DNA that proved David Crofut had touched Gerald Strebendt's rifle before Gerald killed him.

As much as I assumed that any motion I could make would fail in Judge Vogt's court, I felt we had to make a record. If somehow the outcome of the effort was bail for Gerald, it would be well worth spending the time and taking the chance. Should Judge Vogt deny the motion, as we had good reason to believe she would, we knew we would at least have a viable issue for the Oregon Supreme Court to consider if we immediately mandamused (appealed) the bail denial.

By now spring was turning to summer. We were almost six months past the shooting. Gerald was still sitting in solitary confinement in the county jail, reading his books, counting the concrete blocks that made up his walls, and hoping that nothing would happen to cost him his dayroom privileges. That's where he could get to a phone and call his fiancée, Kristin, which was always the highlight of the week for him. It was painful to imagine him having been in these circumstances for so long. I would have done anything to get him out of his limbo.

We went ahead and filed a second request for a bail hearing, highlighting the new touch DNA evidence found on the rifle. We were very clear about the reasons we were requesting the new hearing, and we specified – as we had before – that we would like to have live witnesses present to testify.

Again, as expected, bail was denied, and again, it happened in secret without a hearing.

Having gotten wind of new activity in the Strebendt case – or just wondering what was going on – the local newspaper, *The Register-Guard*, had its attorneys move to intervene "for the limited purpose of opposing continued closure of judicial and public records." Gag orders of the sort Judge Vogt had imposed were highly unusual and, in the paper's view, they ran counter to the tenets of press freedom. But nothing changed. The newspaper's motion to intervene was denied by another judge, the Honorable Maurice K. Merten, without explanation or even the findings of fact that the newspaper had requested. As a testament to the small world of Lane County, Judge Merten is Judge Vogt's mentor, and she served as his judicial clerk as a new lawyer back in 1994.

Some time after that, I learned from reporter Jack Moran at *The Register-Guard* that he had gotten access to an un-redacted version of a document related to an earlier pleading and asked me to comment. It was the Oregon Attorney General's memorandum in opposition to our *mandamus* petition, retrieved from the records office of the Oregon Supreme Court. Upon hearing that the press had seen documents that clearly fell under Judge Vogt's Trial Management Order, I notified the state's high court by fax. Department of Justice (DOJ) staff attorney Stephen P. Armitage subsequently explained to the parties via email that there had been a mistake. The court had only released the redacted version of the AG's memorandum, but the redaction was ineffectively done, making it possible for someone to remove the black bars and see the original document. The email read:

Thank you for your letter of August 7. I have reviewed the email that court personnel sent to the Eugene Register Guard and confirmed that the version of the state's memorandum sent out was the redacted version filed with the court on July 10. I have since been told that the redactions made by the state in that memorandum may not have been effective in deleting the underlying text. I can assure you, however, that the only version we sent to the media was the redacted one.

Like Armitage, I was certain that the newspaper's ability to read the document was somebody's mistake, probably the result of a clerical worker not understanding how to properly redact a document.

A day later on August 8, 2014, *The Register-Guard* published a front-page story describing the facts they were able to glean from the portion of the AG's memo that was supposed to have been redacted. The article essentially posted the entire factual meat of the prosecution's case. The cat was out of the bag, so to speak, yet we were unable to reply to the story in any way. I wondered, what was the point of having a gag order when most of the facts the court intended to keep out of public view have been publicized in the most visible way? It seemed illogical to me. But the gag order stayed in effect. Nothing changed.

I, of course, had nothing to do with the release of the redacted portions of the government's memorandum. I did figure out how it happened, but only after I had been told that one or more reporters were able to read the document. After learning of the mistake or glitch, I checked the electronic copy of the memorandum that I had received, and confirmed that I too could access the redacted information. Apparently someone in the DOJ had used Adobe Acrobat or some other PDF software to place black boxes over the text that was to remain confidential to the case. All it took was to highlight the blacked-out text, copy it, and paste it to a Word document – and *voila!* The un-redacted text appeared. It was simple to do. I suspected that The R-G reporter(s) simply decided to play around with the formatting and see what they could do. Very clever. Maybe they do this regularly with redacted material.

Of course, you might wonder if I gave the reporter the idea to try the copy-and-paste maneuver. I didn't. I didn't even know it was possible. What's more, even if I *did* know how to defeat the redaction, and even if I *did* want to tell a reporter about it, what good would it have done my client? None. While the redacted material that was released through the news media did contain some positive information about Gerald's self-defense case, the majority of the material was decidedly negative about Gerald and harmful to his case. This included the Parade of Horribles. Why would I want to engineer the release of information that was harmful to my client, especially since I was working hard to get this very same information excluded at trial?

Despite my obvious non-involvement in the redaction debacle, a source at the court stated that Judge Vogt did believe that I was behind it. She thought I had somehow orchestrated the release of the document with the goal of circumventing her gag order or in order to secure a change in venue. Yes, I had vehemently opposed her gag order; I believed then and will always believe that First Amendment rights are retained by American citizens, even when they are charged with crimes. I also believe that defendants have the right to direct their attorneys to speak publicly about their cases, if it serves that client and the case. However, I, sadly, do not have the power over government clerks at the Oregon Supreme Court. As Occam's Razor would say, when you have a choice between government conspiracy and government incompetence, the simplest explanation is likely the correct one. Nonetheless, Gerald might be facing a conspiracy of government incompetence.

CHAPTER 20
THE MAKING OF THE FINISHING MACHINE

What news coverage there was of the shooting case and Gerald's role in it inevitably included the acronyms MMA and UFC right behind or even in front of Gerald's name. These identifiers weren't unfamiliar to me, and a goodly chunk of the public probably had some understanding of their meaning. But what did it really signify to be trained in Mixed Martial Arts? What did it tell us to know that Gerald fought in the Ultimate Fighting Championships?

Above all, what should we make of the fact that "The Finishing Machine" was Gerald's fighting nickname? We had to be ready to explain to a jury exactly what all of this meant – and, of course, what it didn't mean.

From the beginning of this case, I'd plunged into the research of Gerald's background with gusto, probably digging deeper than I needed to, just because it was interesting. I thought it was pretty cool that Gerald had trained to reach an elite level in what the public knows as "cage-fighting." To me, excellence is always something worth striving for and, when achieved, it's worthy of high respect. But did his having contended in UFC-sponsored match-ups make him somebody who would always be looking for a fight, as police seemed to assume? Did training in MMA make him a trained killer, as some members of the public seemed to think? That's what I needed to find out.

From the get-go, Gerald never seemed to fit the stereotype of the MMA/UFC fighter – not to me, and not to Emilia, either. But we had to step away from our own confirmation bias and find out what was really true. From our earliest days in the case we had heard rumblings that Gerald may have been involved in some unsavory activities while part of his fighting crowd back in the day – and even Gerald's own stories seemed to confirm this. (Remember the Picasso-in-the-trunk story, in which one of Gerald's friends stood by while the painting was extorted from the "Girls Gone Wild" guy?) But there was something worse. There were accusations that he may have evaded responsibility for someone's death in a California murder case. But what had led Gerald to his first brush with a murder case?

The first time Gerald ever saw a UFC fight was about 1996, around the time that the new concept of Mixed Martial Arts was first gaining some national and international traction. He was 17 and hanging out with the two sons of James Antsy. Antsy's was a name I knew from the Parade of Horribles. He was already a potential witness in Gerald's murder case, having called the Springfield Police Department with wild claims that he raised Gerald with his own sons and that Gerald was a born killer. Gerald had already told me that the "I raised Gerald" stuff was untrue. The rest, of course, would need to be proven in court.

Gerald and the Antsy brothers had rented a VHS tape of one of the initial UFC fights, one of which featured a skinny little Brazilian guy, Royce Gracie, who seemed to be beating everybody. There he was in the 25-to-30-foot UFC ring, caged in with an opponent, fighting a no-holds-barred match and notching win after win. Gerald, who had been a wrestler since fifth grade, immediately felt an affinity with this sort of man-on-man fighting in a confined space. Gracie and another top-ranked fighter that Gerald began following, Frank Shamrock, looked like Greek gods to Gerald – so athletic, so powerful, so fast, so effective. That day, watching a video, Gerald found himself some new heroes. He came away excited to learn Brazilian Jiu-Jitsu, Gracie's specialty. He dreamed of becoming every bit as strong and invulnerable as the men he was watching on the screen.

The whole mixed martial arts craze had originated earlier in the 1990s as a "which fighting style is best?" sort of event. Into "the Octagon" the fighters would go, one discipline fighting another. Brazilian Jiu-Jitsu was just one variety of combat featured on the fight cards, but it was initially the most successful, even when deployed against opponents who were much larger in size. Royce Gracie won the first UFC tournament when he "submitted" three opponents: savateur Gerard Gordeau in 1:44, shootfighter Ken Shamrock (Frank's adopted brother) in 1:49, and boxer Art Jimmerson in 2:18. Gracie subsequently won UFC 2 and UFC 4.

When Gerald entered the Marines in 1997, a future of international travel and highly touted UFC fights was still very much on his mind. In fact, during Basic Training, he hung a photo of Frank Shamrock in his locker. Though Gerald had yet to begin any formal MMA training, fellow Marines saw him as someone already gifted in hand-to-hand combat. Mitch Cox attended a three-day Sniper Indoctrination School with Gerald, and recalls Gerald teaching others in the unit some basic fighting skills. Gerald even led an impromptu training, Cox said, in which he helped fellow Marines practice disarming aggressors, including ones armed with a knife. Soon Gerald joined a Marine Corps regimental wrestling team in Okinawa.

At last, while stationed in California in 1999, Gerald began to train in earnest. Imbued with Marine discipline, he worked with a sense of dedication that he'd never brought to his teenaged wrestling or the track and field he'd dabbled in while trying to get in shape for the Marines. In fact, Gerald told me he was pretty sure he'd never tried that hard at anything in his life, until the Marines taught him how to exceed his own expectations.

Whenever Gerald had weekend leave from his Marine Corps duties, he would drive for hours to Torrance, Calif., the location of the Gracie Academy. He and another Marine, a guy named Rudy, would train all weekend, taking a cheap motel room to share – and sometimes raising the eyebrows of the desk clerks who sometimes asked if the two attractive men wanted the room for the night or by the hour! Then, often taped and bruised from the gym workouts, they would drive back in time to report for duty on Monday morning.

As Gerald began moving away from active involvement in the Marines, he moved to Los Angeles, where he could go from one gym to another to train, often on foot. He trained in Brazilian Jiu-Jitsu with Marcus Vinicious on Robertson Blvd. in Beverly Hills, then he'd walk down Santa Monica Boulevard to Gardner Street, where he would train with Eddie Bravo – the man who first tabbed Gerald "The Finishing Machine," mostly as a means of inspiring the trainee to live up to the name. From Bravo's gym, Gerald could also walk up two streets to Sunset Boulevard and 10 blocks east to Little Armenia to train with the man who would one day train Ronda Rousey, the Olympic medal winner in judo who went on to become the first UFC women's champion. Gokor Chivichyan was a legend in those days, and he made Gerald feel like his son.

On April 21, 2001, less than five years after Gerald watched his first UFC fight on a VHS tape, he stepped into the ring with Aaron Herring for his first professional fight. On that card they need a 170-lb fighter at the last minute and Gerald stepped in on short notice and stepped up a weight class. Gerald had Frank Shamrock in his corner, no less, along with Eddie Bravo. Gerald submitted Herring with an armbar in 2:54, lending credibility to the "Finishing Machine" nickname.

That first fight led to others that year. Gerald lost to Elji Mitsuoka, submitted Mike Meto with an armbar, and submitted Aaron Anderson with a triangle choke (the same move that Royce Gracie used to win UFC 4). Then Gerald TKO'd Noah Shinable, but lost to Charles Bennett. Not bad: Gerald "The Finishing Machine" Strebendt went 4-2 in his first year of professional fighting.

At the end of 2002, Gerald was living in Budapest, Hungary, where he trained with a 150-bout Olympic boxer named Imri Baksai. The guy was a living legend in his native country, especially for coming out of retirement at age 50 to knock out an up-and-coming fighter who had hoped to take down a legend. Gerald was amazed to find that for Baksai, this veteran, storied boxer, training was just a sideline. Baksai made his meager living working at a gas station.

One day, Baksai's gym got a call. Gerald was summoned to London to fight Jean "White Bear" Silva at the Cage Rage Championships. All expenses were paid, including three plane tickets and a hotel near the Piccadilly Circus. Gerald remembers boarding the plane in an Adidas track suit that was specially made for the Hungarian national team, while Baksai turned up in something that would have been fashionable on an American man of the 1930s

– an olive-drab suit with high-heeled boots and a gangster-style fedora. Later, Gerald gave the nearly impoverished Baksai a gift the man could never afford to buy for himself – a pair of $140 boxing gloves from Mexico. But instead of using them, Baksai put them aside for his son's first fight.

Gerald's ascension to the UFC in such a short amount of time took skill, but also considerable luck. He found his first manager through a friend in his sniper platoon whose father happened to be live next door to a guy named Dana White. White, who would eventually become president of the UFC, didn't take Gerald on right away. In fact, he told comedian and UFC commentator Joe Rogan, who was another advocate of Gerald's, that he would sign Gerald to a three-fight contract, but only if Gerald beat Silva in the London event. This was an opportunity Gerald wouldn't let pass. This fight, he vowed, would make him in the UFC. Letting it break him wasn't an option.

(Photo: Gerald Strebendt with Joe Rogan, circa 2002)

In London, Gerald walked out into the ring to meet "White Bear" Silva to LL Cool J's "Mamma Said Knock You Out," which LL exclaims, "Don't call it a comeback!" In his corner were Baksai, Gerald's Muay Thai coach, and a couple of Hungarians who were along for the ride. One was Lajos Vargan, a billionaire who, according to Gerald, owns the building in the background of the Beatles' album cover for "Abbey Road." Over in Silva's corner, meanwhile, was Gerald's hero and MMA inspiration, the one and only Royce Gracie. Gerald pummeled Silva with elbows and knees, and then choked him out at 2:45 in the first round. The raucous York Hall crowd in Bethnal Green fell silent as the fight ended. It was a huge, unexpected upset. Officials went to Silva's corner and demanded his belt, took it from Silva's bag, and gave it to Gerald. When Gerald and his team returned to their rooms after the fight, he and the Hungarians hugged each other and cried. The next morning Gerald took his 1989 Sony Walkman to Hyde Park for a celebratory stroll. He was riding high. He felt unstoppable.

A few months later, Gerald fought what MMA aficionados might say was the biggest fight of his career, against Josh "The Punk" Thomson in UFC 44. Gerald lost, but went on to submit Pat Carr. In 2004, he fought Dave Elliot in early May, fought Jean Silva about two weeks later, and then fought Sean Sherk about three weeks after that. Gerald had but one fight in 2005, and it was against Vitor "Shaolin" Ribeiro at Cage Rage 21. For Gerald it marked the best chance yet to advance his name in the game, as some considered Ribeiro the number-one lightweight in the world.

When asked by a fight publication how he planned to fight Ribeiro, Gerald was very forthcoming with the fact that his size and skill in the ground game could very well determine the outcome of the fight. "The great thing about BJJ [Brazilian Jiu-Jitsu] is it's not a secret anymore, so anyone that's really good knows the styles and strategy when going into a fight like this. If he screws up I'll catch him and take advantage of his mistakes. With the help of guys like Jean-Jacques (Machado) and Eddie Bravo I feel I'll be ready for anything he throws at me. In my last fight against Sherk it was exciting going up against another weight class, but now I'm going to be back at 155 pounds where I'm going to be the strongest guy. I respect Shaolin and his team, but I'm there to have fun, win, and get my paycheck."

In the same interview, Gerald acknowledged having come through some stressful months leading up to the Ribeiro fight. "After the Sherk fight a lot of guys have backed out of fights with me and that's been hard. To have gone through this process of training, cutting the weight, getting ready to fight and not have it happen is very taxing. I've taken time off out in the woods, spent time with my girlfriend, shooting guns, being a country guy and having fun and it's helped a lot. There's no stress, fighting is supposed to be a fun thing for me to do, and for a while there it wasn't like that. I'm just glad I have a really supportive girlfriend and now we could live the moment together and enjoy everything. Before in the UFC I was really nervous, but I'm completely different now. It'll be a lot of fun. Back then I was young, inexperienced and nervous, but I'm more of a man now at 26 and I have a whole new outlook on everything."

Alas, the fight at Wembly Stadium was short. Ribeiro choked out Gerald just one minute and thirteen seconds into the first round. Strebendt didn't fight again until October of 2007, against Will Shutt. His final professional fight was against Lyle Beerbohm, in January of 2008. His professional record was complete at age 28: 9 wins, 7 losses.

All of that could matter, I thought, *but his upcoming courtroom win-loss record matters more.*

CHAPTER 21

ANOTHER MURDER CASE FOR GERALD

U nfortunately, all the research I'd done into Gerald's MMA/UFC days fell short of telling me what I really needed to know: whether Gerald was dangerous, a guy looking for a fight, a trained killer who, not surprisingly, killed. That's what I needed to figure out – whether any of those descriptions applied.

The D.A. will have a field day with that nickname, "The Finishing Machine." I need to be able to show that the name fits Gerald in the cage, not on Bob Straub Parkway.

Of course, we did have in evidence the "I'm a trained killer" statements Gerald allegedly made to people, the ones cited in the Parade of Horribles. They didn't make Gerald look good at all, and that's why Emilia was marshaling a team of investigators to try to either refute or at least add context to the allegations – that is, if we couldn't keep them out of court altogether.

But all of this paled, it seemed to me, next to the fact that Gerald was a key character in a previous murder case. It involved a lover's triangle. Gerald was outside of the triangle, but in close enough proximity to testify against the man who was tried and convicted of the crime. In fact, some close to the case have continued to allege that Gerald was the true killer in the case.

The man killed was named Bryan Richards. Several years after marrying his wife, Angelina, Bryan took out a $1 million life-insurance policy on himself. The beneficiary was Angelina. Several months before the policy became effective, Angelina became friendly with an MMA fighter-turned-reporter named Rafiel Torre. He was a well-known and respected figure in the early years of MMA, but only fought once in the ring. Gradually, people began alleging that Torre was teaching Brazilian Jiu-Jitsu under dubious black-belt credentials. An article outed him as a "martial arts pretender," questioning the legitimacy of the fight and the veracity of his claims as a trainer.

But Angelina apparently believed in him. She and Rafiel were seen together frequently, suggesting an affair, and this was putting a strain on Angelina's marriage to Bryan. It can't have improved matters when Angelina loaned Rafiel $10,000 to open a gym and cosigned his lease.

Then Bryan Richards disappeared. At approximately 11:00 pm on December 21, 2001, Angelina called her sister-in-law saying she didn't know where Bryan was. She reported her husband missing the next morning... and was seen drinking wine with a girlfriend that afternoon, with her missing husband's insurance policy binder in plain sight on the kitchen table. When Angelina was asked what had happened to Bryan's utility truck, she said Torre, her friend and business partner, had it. When Torre then brought the truck back to the house, friends noticed that Bryan's handgun was not in its usual place in the glove compartment.

Angelina then told these friends, including one Gerald Strebendt, that she had remembered something – that Bryan had gone out for firewood. She said maybe they should go look for him at nearby grocery stores. Bryan's body was found by these friends in his other vehicle, a pickup truck, at a nearby Albertson's market just 20 minutes later. He was lying in the bed of the truck, his body covered by wheeled dollies and trash bags.

The insurance agent who sold Bryan his life insurance policy was surprised by how quickly and unemotionally Angelina asked for the death benefit payout – and police later took note that she booked a Mexican vacation with Torre as soon as she got a $50,000 advance on the payout. All the while, Angelina was pointing fingers at several potential killers stemming from past crimes involving Bryan or Bryan's supposed (never proven) drug dealing.

And here's how Gerald figures in the story: He was a student of Torre's and knew Angelina, too. In a deposition, Gerald said he knew about the affair the two of them were having, and that he saw the couple get Bryan drunk so they could sneak out together. He said he saw Angelina give Torre $10,000. Gerald also said that later on Torre told him Bryan was abusive to Angelina, that she just wanted him gone, and that she would pay $10,000 for someone to do it. Gerald quoted Torre as saying to him: "She knows you [Gerald] were a sniper in the Marines and she wants to know if you're interested." Gerald stated that he told Torre he would not kill Bryan.

According to Gerald, Torre called him several times in the weeks after Bryan's body was discovered, wanting to speak to Gerald in person. When the two met, Gerald alleges that Torre admitted to killing Bryan, but in self-defense, after Bryan confronted him at gunpoint about the affair. Torre allegedly told Gerald that he knocked the gun out of Bryan's hands and applied a chokehold from Brazilian Jiu-Jitsu known as *Mata leão* in Portuguese or, literally, "kill lion." Torre said he meant only to render Bryan unconscious, but when he felt something break in the man's neck, he knew he was dead. Torre then got to the reason for the meeting he'd called: he wanted Gerald to provide him an alibi. Gerald maintains he refused, but that he did agree to take and hold Bryan's handgun.

But Gerald says he only kept the gun in his home long enough to contact the authorities, who convinced him to make recorded calls to Angelina. In the first, Gerald told Angelina "the gun that Rafiel gave me has been recovered." Angelina said she didn't know what he was talking about and told him to call Torre. In a second conversation Gerald told Angelina that Torre had admitted to killing Bryan in self-defense, had given Bryan's gun to Gerald, and had told Gerald that Angelina had offered to pay $10,000 for someone to kill Bryan. Angelina responded: "That's ridiculous. I would never say that." When questioned by sheriff's deputies the following day, Angelina admitted that she had spoken to Gerald, but said the only matter discussed was whether Torre was home. When asked how Gerald came to possess Bryan's gun, Angelina said that she did not know.

On December 17, 2003, almost two years after the murder, Torre was arrested and charged with Bryan's murder. The case went to trial in the summer of 2005. Witnesses confirmed much of what Torre told Gerald about a confrontation with Bryan and his gun, followed by a chokehold – but a medical examiner said he found evidence of several minutes of strangulation, resulting in a broken neck. Among those testifying for the prosecution were others from the MMA world: Chris "The Westside Strangler" Brennan, Eddie Bravo, and yes, Gerald Strebendt.

Gerald testified that he told Torre to go to the police and disclose that he had killed Bryan Richards in self-defense, noting that police were bound to find fingerprints and other forensic evidence to implicate him. Gerald testified that Torre told him not to worry – "I was wearing gloves." Gerald further testified that Torre gave him the gun and told him to back up his self-defense claim in the event Torre was arrested. In court, Gerald admitted that he didn't believe the self-defense story, but went along with Torre because he was afraid that Torre would kill him, too. "I thought the best way for me to stay alive was to not cross Rafiel," he testified. Gerald said he came forward to implicate Torre when he learned that Torre was preparing to flee to Thailand to avoid a possible financial judgment in a lawsuit that had been filed against him. Gerald said he didn't want Torre escaping justice.

Meanwhile, Torre blamed it all on Angelina, from planning the death to covering it up. Torre further stated that he couldn't have applied the chokehold that led to Bryan's death because he had injured one of his hands about a week before the confrontation. He said that Angelina confessed to having Bryan murdered, but refused to tell him who she hired.

After Torre's testimony was impeached point by point, this once-respected MMA'er admitted to a series of lies – that he had been a Navy SEAL when he hadn't even completed boot camp, that his Jiu-jitsu credentials were fake... and that he lied to police about his knowledge of Bryan's murder.

The prosecution then asked, "Is it fair to say that your life has been, as one of its marked characteristics, the manipulation and deception of people?"

"Yes," Torre replied.

Torre was convicted of the murder of Bryan Richards and sentenced to life in prison. But, online, the MMA community continued to buzz suspiciously regarding Gerald's involvement. This mixedmartialarts.com forum thread provides some examples:

> So Strebendt helps cover up a murder for 2 years because he was scared but then comes forward when Torre is being sued and may move out of the country. What's the difference? When he came forward the same thing happened that would have happened 2 years before, Torre was put in jail. Was he scared then? Or was he scared that he was going to be implicated by the investigation and left holding the bag? As reprehensible as I find both Torre's and Strebrendt's actions it's a fact of life that deals have to be cut with shitbags to make cases against bigger shitbags. It's very likely that Torre would never have been held responsible for this murder without Strebendt's testimony.

Then:

> Maybe , I said **maybe** (I am just speculating) Gerald was demanding money from Torre to shut his mouth and decided to call the cops after realizing Torre was planning an escape. That would explain the 2 years of silence.

Then:

> Imagine that his testimony was key in making the case. However, I would stop well short of calling him a hero. "Could have felt, rightfully so, things could have been turned around by the police and he could have been wrongly and unfairly implicated." Torre confessed to him, told him about the gloves, gave him the gun and had solicited him to commit the murder two months prior. Waiting two years before telling the truth usually doesn't help your cause if you are worried about being implicated. Whether he wanted it or not he was in it up to his eyeballs. The heat was coming down and Strebendt gave it up to avoid prosecution. That's my take on the matter. Regardless, Torre was a scumbag.

Then:

> Whether or not Strebendt was a Marine is irrelevant, vets/military can be criminals too like anyone else. The fact is, he kept a damn murder [to] himself for 2 years. That, my friends, is being an accomplice (sp?)

to a criminal act that happens to be a murder. Yep, I think… that he broke out a deal with the prosecutor or his ass was going in too.

Rafiel Torre's family refused to accept that Torre murdered Bryan Richards. After Gerald was arrested in the Croft shooting, a letter was forwarded to Deputy D.A. Bob Lane:

> *I am writing on behalf of myself and my other godsons Dr. Ugo Bartell, Mr. Floyd Bartell and Mr. Rafiel Torre. Rafiel is in Corcoran Penal Institution in California for a murder that he didn't commit. We have believed from the start that Gerald Strebendt was either the murderer or knows who actually did the murder. In the trial transcript it was disclosed that there was unidentified DNA found at the crime scene. It was also disclosed that it was not Rafiel's or the widow Angel Richards but Mr. Strebendt was not tested. In his witness testimony he never disclosed that he too was sleeping with Angel Richards. What we would like to have done is a DNA test taken to see if Gerald's DNA was the unidentified DNA found at the crime scene. How do we get that done? Can you request it be done or does someone in California need to request it? If so who do we contact? You do know that Mr. Strebendt graduated from two US Marine Sniper schools. One was the long range sniper school and the other was the regular sniper school. Both schools were First Marine Division schools and a check of his military records should show his scores and may give clues as to why he did not make the Marines a career. I am looking forward to being able to tell the boys that a DNA swab has been taken and that we will know soon who the actual killer was. Thank you for your time.*
>
> *Sincerely Yours,*
>
> *Ms. Barbara Ann Wright*

Torre's son Nico Torre also took to a message board on the San Diego Tribune website and called Gerald a liar. He believed that Gerald had lied to acquire the money he needed to start his gym in Eugene:

> *Ok Gerald. I talked to you recently on your cell phone. I only called to see if it was you, and it was. You may not remember, seeing as I didn't*

reveal my name over the phone. My name is Nico. I'm sure you remember me. I'd like to clear the air a little. My name is Nico Torre (Rafiel Torre's son). I am 18 and live in North Bend, Oregon. Gerald was essentially my mentor at one point in time. I wanted to be exactly like him. I thought he was a great guy. He was funny and spontaneous. He was always making people laugh. My father taught him Brazilian Jiu-jitsu. they trained together particularly often but, as you all know, my father and stepmother (both of whom I love dearly) split up. I believe that was in 2001, possibly 2002. I moved in with my father and Angel Richards. The home life is of no importance. Again, I wanted to be exactly like Gerald when I was a child. What I'm getting at is that children are, more often than not, gullible. I now know that Mr. Strebendt is a liar. I have yet to understand exactly how my father, the accused, was sentenced to life in prison without the possibility of parole.

* * *

A blood sample was found in the truck of Bryan Richards and it belonged to neither Rafiel Torre, or Bryan Richards. You would think that would be an awesome piece of evidence for the case, wouldn't you? You know, Gerald? Randi lives in Coos Bay and Bandon and I now live in North Bend. We all left California because of the lies you told on the stand. We were all driven out of the area because of all of the things you spread about my father. I hope you sleep well at night with your little settlement "Reward" that you know damn well you don't deserve. Does your wife know that you're a liar? Does she know that you said those things to acquire the money that started your school in Eugene? I wonder these things at night when I'm thinking of the entire case. Everybody, I'd like you all to know that I have nothing against Bryan Richards' family. If anything I'm trying to help them more so than anybody else has so far. If they want to be content with their son's death, shouldn't they at the very LEAST know that the RIGHT man is in prison? They're surrounded in their fake world of false pretenses and warped lies they heard from somebody they'd never met before, and that's no way to live. I'm sorry that Bryan is dead, however I am far more broken up at how hellbent the California Judicial System was on putting an innocent man into prison based on one man's story just to close a case that should have taken more time with more care. - Nico

Gerald didn't let the comment stand unanswered but responded in a very compassionate manner that would seem out of character for a short-tempered hothead:

Nico, first of all I want to tell you that I am sorry for what you went through and I always thought you were so cool. You are a good person and I only hope for good things for you. I don't know what to say to you Nico. Your dad asked me to kill Bryan. It's not even disputable... [Your dad] loved you so much he didn't want you to ever think less of him. He wanted me to tell you he loved you more than anybody and that he was a good man. Nico, I am so sorry for what you have gone through. I really hope the best for you. You were a great kid and now that you're a young man I'm sure you have a whole new chapter to your life. I hope you are still the same funny, athletic, intelligent person you were when I knew you. - Gerald Strebendt

Of course, here's the first thing I'd point out to a jury about the Torre murder case: *Gerald wasn't charged; he was a witness.* It should be fair to assume that any decent prosecutor would have filed something against Gerald if he truly thought he was party to the murder or its conspiracy.

The problem was, the Torre case was by no means the extreme aberration in the MMA/UFC community that I wished it was. Gerald's most highly touted opponent, Josh "The Punk" Thomson, was involved in an alcohol-fueled brawl while on a lake cruise in Idaho, and in the melee, he choked one man so badly that he required CPR. Thomson was subsequently charged with felony aggravated assault, serving six months of a three-year sentence before being released for good behavior.

And there was plenty more corroboration to be found for those who assumed MMA/UFC fighters had not just a mean streak, but a criminal bent. Just a simple Google search offered a full page of sordid results, including these three top hits:

Top 15 MMA Athletes That Have a Criminal Record
The 16 Most Notorious Arrests in MMA History
The 10 Most Despicable People in MMA

What potential juror wouldn't tend to assume some guilt by association? How could I prevent all this smoke from clouding the jury's ability to separate the kind of man Gerald was years earlier in the cage, and what kind of man he might be now, years later?

To try to understand Gerald better, I spoke with his friend and former trainer, Eddie Bravo. Bravo is an MMA/UFC celebrity in Los Angeles, Calif., the founder of 10th Planet Jiu-Jitsu mixed martial arts Gym. Bravo is well known for his 2003 win in the Abu Dhabi Submission wrestling championships against Royler Gracie (brother to Royce Gracie)) and for his no-gi style of Jiu-Jitsu which went against the traditional approach to teaching Jiu-Jitsu to students garbed in the traditional two-piece, white garment called a gi. Bravo has released several instructional manuals and DVDs and co-hosts a popular podcast commentary of UFC fights with comedian Joe Rogan.

Bravo said he met Gerald in 2000 during a King of the Cage show. Bravo didn't have his gym at the time, but had been training people in mixed martial arts since 1994. Bravo was developing some techniques that he wanted to teach Gerald, so when Gerald separated from the Marine Corps, he moved to Los Angeles to start the training. Bravo told me that Gerald was his right hand man in opening up 10th Planet and for about two years, worked as one of Bravo's instructors.

Gerald, Bravo said, was a disciplined super athlete. He was "super clean," meaning that he did not drink or use drugs, he maintained an excellent training diet, and he never partied. Bravo sought to develop in Gerald the techniques, power and stamina that would justify the "Finishing Machine" nickname he had given Gerald. Although Gerald's fight career was short and his results mixed, Bravo seems proud of what Gerald achieved – and truly, genuinely sorry for the turn that Gerald's life had taken.

I told Bravo that it was exactly Gerald's hand-to-hand (and foot-to-head) "Finishing Machine"-style technique that would be heavily scrutinized at trial. When I asked Bravo to help me figure out how to counter-attack those who were saying that Gerald shouldn't have needed a rifle to defend himself against Crofut, the fighter-trainer was happy to try to help. I began by sharing with Bravo some of the comments that were popping up on the internet wherever the case was being discussed:

1. Actual Commenter (name withheld): *What's wrong with knocking the guy out or shooting him in the leg?*

2. Actual Commenter (name withheld): *As a UFC fighter he clearly had other options.....he will be found guilty because immediately after the incident he said "I could not see what he had" he didn't ever say he had a gun, knife or anything. The only person with a weapon was Gerald. You can't kill someone because you can't see their hands. You can defend yourself but just like a cop only with reasonable force.. He could of just locked himself in his truck and if the guy broke in with any hard object then he could say he feared he could be greatly injured by the guy and what he was holding. Sorry but Gerald will do time...*

3. Actual Commenter (name withheld): *He was a UFC fighter. What a pussy. Why not just knock the guy out? Job done.*

When Bravo heard the comments, he chuckled. But Bravo told me that, despite Gerald's skills and discipline, he didn't think that martial arts training would be of help to anyone who is being attacked by a man with a gun. "Mixed martial arts is a sport," Bravo told me. "It's an on-the-ground training program that doesn't teach you how to use guns or knives, or how to defend yourself against them." He said that a practitioner's only choices when faced with such lethal weaponry would be to run, tackle or choke the aggressor. In fact, he considered any direct engagement with a suspected armed attacker to be extremely risky. Martial arts should only be considered a last resort, Bravo said, the thing to try when it's the only option left or available. It's a self-defense method, but it isn't considered a technique for disarming someone.

While multiple witnesses with MMA/UFC backgrounds would testify in agreement with Bravo, I knew there were many other witnesses who were prepared to testify to the contrary. Some would say that if Gerald was experienced enough in close-quarters combat to teach others defensive techniques (and he was, of course), he should have been capable of fighting and disarming Crofut that night on Bob Straub Parkway. Mitch Cox, Gerald's Marine Corps friend, was one such potential witness. At the time Cox knew

Gerald, he considered him a "good kid." But given what he saw of Gerald's skills, he told me, it was hard for Cox to believe that Gerald was fully engaged by only one person. He told me, "This kid can fight hand to hand."

There was ample backup for what Cox was saying. All somebody had to do was search for Gerald's name on YouTube to find him effectively kicking, punching and choking people.

Not helpful, not at all.

It was time to talk to weapons people. I contacted George Snodgrass, an experienced knife fighter, self-defense teacher and owner of a local martial arts studio. Snodgrass said he could and would testify that if he felt his life was threatened and he had access to both his superior martial arts skills and a gun, he personally would choose the gun. He would have shot Crofut, just as Gerald had.

But even with this sort of testimony, I felt that Gerald's skills did make him vulnerable in the courtroom. Would he have to testify for me to convince the jury that the gun was his only real choice? Would I have to take the risk of letting him explain to the court why he chose to go for the gun… instead of fighting with his hand or knocking Crofut out with a swift kick to the head? I hoped not. Putting your client on the stand opens him to cross-examination, where anything can happen.

I went to Gerald at the jail and talked through my concerns, warning him about what I thought the prosecution would do with his fighting expertise. Gerald immediately understood the problem and shared my concern.

"Mike, I wish more than anything now that I had just kicked that motherfucker and knocked him out. I wish I had run away. But I didn't… because I thought he was armed! And if I ran, I was going to get shot in the back."

I nodded, knowing that Gerald's comments wouldn't sell with every potential juror.

Gerald continued, "But I'm thinking that if I had beaten the shit out of Crofut instead of shooting him, I'd still be right here. Except that I'd be missing a few things – like the blood draw, showing that Crofut was drunk and high on that medication. What do you think the odds are that he would have been tested right away for substances?"

Pretty slim, I agreed.

"I'd still be sitting right here, and I'd have no defense."

He had a really good point. I hadn't thought of it before.

Within seconds, I found myself punting, asking my client to give me the information I needed to defend him, whether it was exculpatory or not. "Gerald," I said, leaning forward, "people just aren't going to understand why you shot him. Why, honestly, did you shoot him?"

He didn't pause to think. Basically, he blurted.

"I truly thought that this guy was a wack job! I was minding my own business, just driving along up to Riley's house [to borrow DVDs] when he slammed on his brakes in front of me. When he started yelling things like 'you are dead' and that stuff, I grabbed my rifle. I tried to call 911, but my hands just didn't work. I couldn't do it. When I got out of the car, other people drove past. I yelled at them to call 911. I needed help with this guy... to protect both him and myself. But they all just kept driving, they just left us out there. He wasn't acting normal, and I know now that it was the booze and drugs in his system. But all I could see then was this crazy guy, who kept coming at me. I tried to scare him back by chambering a round. The sound was so loud – you know, the 'shank-clunk' of a big gun. After I did that, he darted forward! Nothing about him made sense, Mike. No one was there to do or see anything. Nothing I had tried to do had stopped him. I was in a life or death situation, me or him. I chose me."

CHAPTER 22

THE NATURE OF FEAR

Humans have a knack for detecting the authenticity of fear, anger, and the intent to harm. It's evolutionary biology calling out from thousands of generations back, warning us. Any ancestors that didn't take heed of their instincts when confronted with a dangerous situation didn't reproduce. If they missed the warning signs of someone or something threatening to cause harm, they died.

In modern times however, we've been socially programmed to ignore many of the warning signs we encounter. We've been lulled to assume that we are safe at all times. When survivors of crises and attacks discuss them afterward, they often say "it was unbelievable," or it was "like watching a movie." While we have the imagination to thrust our consciousness into the shoes of a movie actor and experience a film almost as if we were really there, we also have an uncanny ability to assume that conflict and crisis is *unreal* when it is happening to us *for real*.

We think we're safe because, generally, we are. Mankind has never known the safety and comfort we experience today. Americans are rarely hungry or uncomfortable; we're almost always within range of a refrigerator, a restaurant, a coat closet, or a thermostat. When we feel frightened in the dark, we laugh it off as a childhood holdover or we blame the feeling on the movie we saw the night before. We've forgotten, as a species, that darkness was the enemy of our ancestors on the savannah. Darkness was where the predators lurked, with their stealthy night vision and cloaks of camouflaged fur.

Some anthropologists and evolutionary biologists theorize that interrupted sleep and the inability to fall back asleep in the middle of the night is not a disorder but a throwback to more primitive times. Family units and tribes once coped with the looming threat of nighttime by posting a watchman. So I guess you could say that if you wake up suddenly, and almost always at the same time in the middle of the night, it could be because some ancestor of yours had the 3 a.m. watch! Of course, lanterns and then lighting made watchmen obsolete, along with locks to keep us safe as we sleep. But what do we do when something scares us in the dark? Do we laugh it off? Often we do. Scary stuff can be fun, as we know from the long lines we see whenever a new horror flick opens up. But there are times when something happens in the dark, and it takes us right back to our more primal selves.

I love a good scare. I grew up on horror films including *Night of the Living Dead*, *Nightmare on Elm Street*, and *Friday the Thirteenth*. In grade school, I read *Dracula* and *Pet Cemetery* and then graduated on to reading everything Stephen King ever wrote, pretty much. Having heard in more recent years about some silly but wildly popular vampire books, I borrowed the *Twilight* series from Emilia, who continuously delights in telling anyone who will listen that I am "Team Jacob." After I was done with those, she got me started on the paranormal tales in the *True Blood*/Sookie Stackhouse series, *The Southern Vampire Mysteries*.

One night I took a Stackhouse book to the hot tub to unwind. And what happened next would teach me a lot about how we humans react to a perceived threat… in the dark.

It was a moonless February night and the Pacific Chorus frogs were croaking their mating calls from the ditches and the shallow puddles around our farm. I was leaning over the side of the hot tub with my back to our backyard patio. Under a headlamp, I was reading about Sookie, fighting for her life while trapped in the trunk of a car with a hungry vampire.

Suddenly I felt something grab the back of my neck and growl. I screamed and dropped Emilia's book into the 104-degree pool of water. I turned with my hands up and I heard, "Daddy screams like a girl!" My wife and daughter were pointing and laughing.

I laughed along with them and fished out Emilia's book, desperately trying to dry it off with a towel. "You guys are going to get me in trouble for ruining this book! Hop on in." We sat in the darkness and splashed and talked. I was snacking on some crackers that the girls brought out when I heard a terrorizing sound, sort of a growling screech, coming from the hog barn, 50 yards to the southeast. Abigail gasped and my wife said, "What was that?"

"I don't know," I whispered. My irrational mind immediately conjured a paranormal creature of the sort I'd been reading about. But I shook off that notion when I heard the pigs screaming. When we then heard another screeching growl, I jumped up, dripping wet. "Go get the rifle!" Jacy urged. "It's a cougar!"

Hers was a very rational conclusion. A week earlier Jacy saw a cougar and a bobcat, the cougar by the creek and the bobcat in our pasture. Two days earlier Abigail and I were taking a walk down to the creek at dusk when we received a phone call from Georgia, our next-door neighbor. She told us she had been looking out her window when she saw a cougar walking down the hill. I asked Abigail if she still wanted to go for a walk, assuring her I was "probably strong enough to protect [her] from a cougar." But she didn't need my help. She said, "I'm strong enough to shoot a gun." Her firm resolve is innate from a life where she wants for nothing; mine is more learned.

Consequently, cougars weren't new to any of us. I'd also seen one stalk across the pasture toward me while I was weeding in the garden back in 2005. After that, we invested in my kind of cougar repellant: five-inch tusks attached to a 250-pound boar named Samson. Since then I've seen the savaged remains of a raccoon that ventured too close to the boar, and I've watched him eat dead chickens, feet, beak and all. Once, when we were walking through a gate together, he sliced open my jeans and cut my leg. Now we take turns.

Of course, Samson can't be everywhere. A few weeks earlier, Abigail and I found the remains of an epic goose-versus-predator battle. The sole survivor was a gander that lost an eye and came away with other battle scars, too.

Although Jacy tended to blame some large predator for the attack, I attributed it to the plotting of a diabolical raccoon, a theory that the crime-scene feather trail seemed to support. That raccoon apparently killed the non-surviving gander, and, determined to steal the carcass, pulled it through a hole in the fence. "Don't underestimate the masked bandit," I told Jacy. "Never underestimate a raccoon."

Still, when we heard the growls, snarls and screams that night while we were in the hot tub, all the while accompanied by the sounds of pigs frantically screaming and running, and ducks and geese squawking, my mind jumped immediately to "cougar!" It just seemed far beyond what a raccoon was capable of. So I ran inside, threw on some long pants and muck boots, chambered a round in the .45 and grabbed the slug-loaded Remington 12-gauge.

I ran to the gate with a spotlight in my left hand aiming down the side of the shotgun. The hogs were running and making sounds I'd never heard before. Just then, something ran up behind me. Another of my girlish screams escaped me as I turned to meet my attacker – and found Honey, our fierce chocolate lab pup. With some relief, I returned my attention to the chaos still underway.

After two tries, I managed to unlock the gate with my steady hunting hands (which happened to be shaking quite violently). Once inside the dark barn I was greeted with fresh snarls, while hogs ran everywhere and terrified waterfowl loudly flapped their wings. The whole place was noise and movement. The spotlight gave me only glimpses of animals running into the beam and back out again into the darkness outside the barn. I followed. Then something knocked me in the face. My survival instincts kicked in and I let out a war howl (*not* a girl scream this time). I knocked my attacker away without hesitation, only to have it strike me again. It only took another moment for me to realize I was bravely fighting off the branch of a Douglas fir tree.

Scanning the forest, I saw what appeared to be a shiny reflection about 30 meters away. Hoping it was something metal from the fence I scanned back towards it with the spotlight but it was gone – strong circumstantial evidence that it was eye shine from some critter or other.

It was then that I heard a sound in the tree right above my head. "Oh yeah, I forgot," I thought with dread. "Cougars can climb trees and pounce on their prey." I began frantically scanning the dozens of trees all around me, like some paranoid character in a horror film. What I'd heard proved only to be a branch rubbing against a larger limb in the tree above my head. But if it turned aggressive on me, I was ready for it.

And then I heard the blood-curdling, roaring scream up close. I turned my head and saw the sow being attacked. Something was on her back, biting at her neck. She bravely fought back, and Samson, the large tusk-laden boar, charged at the attacker from the flank while I ran at the struggle head-on. Pointing the Remington 12-gauge and clicking off the safety, I took a step back. Then I pointed the barrel towards the ground, clicked the safety back on again and, with just a touch of embarrassment, yelled back to the hot tub, "All clear!"

The younger boar was trying to sneak in a breeding session! It was at that moment that I realized that hog sex could be loud and rough and... didn't require an armed observer. I stowed the weapon, and walked back through the kitchen door, shaking my head. "I feel dirty," I muttered, "and hungry for bacon."

The decisions I made that night in the *faux* cougar attack were a product of my very limited training and equally limited experience. Did I act reasonably or unreasonably in the light of what I knew at the time? The only way to make that determination would be to take into account my background, training, and experience and then examine what I knew at the time of the incident. It works the same way when you're trying to prove a self-defense claim: you look at background, training, experience, and what the defendant knew at the time of the incident.

Now that much of the physical evidence from the scene of the shooting on Bob Straub Parkway was in and evaluated, increasingly I'd be looking at what Gerald Strebendt was thinking that dark night, how his background, training, and experience affected his perceptions and decision-making, and whether it all added up to a legal claim of self-defense.

ASSESSING THE THREAT ON A DARK COUNTRY ROAD

You should know, if you haven't assumed it already, that Gerald was not proud of killing Crofut – not at all. Many times he told me that if he could have pushed pause on the situation, he would have run down the ditch and jumped a fence. Or he would have used his rifle like a baseball bat. He would have done anything but kill Crofut.

But Crofut kept coming at him and Gerald wasn't as sharp as he had been when he was with the Marines and Blackwater. He was unprepared for Crofut's response to seeing a rifle. It wasn't logical, Gerald said, that a man would see a gun and keep advancing. The memory of Brenda Crofut charging up the road toward him and cussing at him until the police arrived, with the rifle still in his hands, haunted Gerald as well. It was either a courageous or an incredibly stupid thing for her to have done, something he might have been capable of when he was in Blackwater, but only if he'd been armed to the teeth.

Gerald felt he had no choice but to shoot, so, yes, he felt justified. He was sad that Crofut lost his life. But Gerald was also angry that Crofut had put him in the position of having to shoot. From everything that Gerald had told me over the months, I knew that he had always gone considerable lengths to avoid having to use his weapon, even in the skirmishes he experienced in Afghanistan with Blackwater.

One of Gerald's proudest moments, in fact, was a time when he did not shoot – even after being ordered to. Gerald was on assignment with the Blackwater guards when the convoy he was riding in seemed threatened. A white SUV had appeared, recklessly weaving in and out of convoy vehicles and gaining rapidly on the car in which Gerald and his team leader were riding. His team leader called out, "Hit 'em, Boot. Hit 'em."

Gerald was carrying an AK-47 Paratrooper rifle with a folding stock. It was outfitted with a telescopic sight with a red laser. As the car pulled closer, Gerald looked more carefully at the driver. The field in his scope was wide enough to see that the driver had a passenger. Rather than shoot as instructed, he called back to the team leader, "Hold on, hold on." The white SUV swerved as it tried to move past Gerald's vehicle, with Gerald tracking it through the scope. To this point the driver hadn't even seen Gerald pointing the rifle at him. As the SUV got up even with the car, Gerald aimed the gun at the driver's face. The cars were so close together on the narrow street, Gerald told me, that he was able to tap the window of the car with the tip of the barrel. Hearing the noise, the SUV driver turned angrily at Gerald and looked down the barrel of the rifle. The driver's face registered panic. He put both of his hands up to show he was unarmed and hit the brakes. The SUV careened off the road and into a small ditch.

Gerald could have killed that SUV driver. He probably should have killed him, according to Blackwater's policies and rules of engagement. Indeed, by not firing, Gerald had risked some lives, including his own. But Gerald was more proud of that moment in his life than most others. "That Afghani man was just in a hurry," he told me.

Yes, maybe like Gerald and Crofut were in a hurry on that night.

From the time that Crofut rammed Gerald's truck with his car, to the moment that Gerald's shot killed Crofut – mere minutes, yet an age – Gerald's jury would be assessing how reasonable or unreasonable it was for Gerald to make the final decision to fire. They would make their judgments by examining every action or inaction, anything that preceded the shot. Given that Crofut was ultimately found to have been unarmed – despite telling Gerald he had a gun and intended to kill him – we needed to be able to convincingly explain Gerald's threat assessment process. And to do that, we needed to show the jury how to scientifically examine, analyze and support not just what Gerald saw, but what his brain told him to do about it.

Perception is everything.

There were certain scientific realities in play on Bob Straub Parkway that night, ones that I believed made Gerald's perceptions and decisions reasonable under the circumstances, especially given his specialized military sniper training and his prior combat experience involving firearms and roadway conflict. The case required a use-of-force analysis and expert testimony to help the jury evaluate how Crofut's actions forced Gerald to react. This sort of analysis is routine in civil lawsuits when a suspect sues a police department for injuries sustained in an arrest. If it's good enough for the government, I figured, it's good enough for someone accused by the government of a crime.

I started from one basic belief: The background, education and skills that Gerald used to assess the credibility of the threat posed by Crofut made him very different from the average citizen facing the same set of circumstances. Gerald had extensive firearms training. He also had extensive physical combat training. He learned the mental discipline that goes with being a Marine sniper. He went to Afghanistan as a Blackwater operator, where he was forced to make decisions on whether to fire his weapon in situations that the typical person will never experience and cannot comprehend. More often than not, Gerald made the decision not to shoot. Again and again he was able to coolly assess a situation and get information that allowed him to decide that firing his weapon was unnecessary.

Until he met David Crofut, that is. And even then, he was anything but trigger-happy. Gerald let the guy chase him 80 feet!

The tricky part for us, as a defense team, had to do with those special skills of Gerald's. Not only did we have to show the jury that he properly assessed the situation on Bob Straub Parkway as one requiring him to defend himself, we also had to show why he properly resorted to a weapon when his skills would seem to have given him other options – like fighting Crofut with his feet or hands, or both. To thread this particular needle in court, we had to find experts with experience in law enforcement, in use-of-force decisions, and in military training. That last part was especially important because being a police officer, especially in a smaller community like ours, bears little resemblance to what it's like to be trained in the Marines to be on daily sniper patrol. And it's literally a world away from what it's like to escort dangerous convoys or hunt down drug traffickers in Afghanistan as a Blackwater security contractor.

I launched a national search to find the right expert. Locating someone with experience in one area of expertise was easy, but finding somebody with the whole package of knowledge and analysis capabilities was tough. After rejecting several possible choices, I settled on Dr. Ron Martinelli, whose areas of expertise were very applicable to the facts in our case. He had been a police officer and a detective. In addition to his law enforcement experience, Dr. Martinelli trained and consulted with military units. He was very familiar with the weapons training administered by the U.S. Marines, and he served as an adjunct instructor to the U.S. Naval Special Warfare Unit with Team 1 SEALs. He also understood our client's MMA training, as he had also been an adjunct professor in hand-to-hand combat. Dr. Martinelli was the only expert we located who gave us the trifecta – expertise in military training as well as hand-to-hand combat and law enforcement perspectives.

Combing through Dr. Martinelli's work, I found that he had been a use-of-force expert witness in a case nearby. It involved a Vietnam War veteran in central Oregon's high desert of Deschutes County who was forced to shoot when a drunk, aggressive man exited his vehicle in the dark and threatened the defendant, saying he had a weapon. It was a very familiar set of facts – right down to the fact that as the aggressor was advancing on the defendant, the defendant was holding a gun, backing away, and talking to 911 on a cell phone. And just as in Gerald's case, the Deschutes County shooting victim proved to be unarmed. Yet, after hearing Dr. Martinelli's testimony, the jury deliberated for less than two hours before acquitting the veteran of all charges related to the shooting.

In that case, Dr. Martinelli explained to the jury the psychophysiology of human behavior during high-stress self-defense situations and life-threatening encounters. I learned from his testimony that Dr. Martinelli had particular expertise in how the human brain evaluates threats, and in how quickly the brain can determine how best to respond. He had been involved in research that evaluated how the brain makes a use-of-force decision when there are environmental factors affecting the decision-making – in particular, darkness. In our case, of course, the environmental factors included not only the darkness, but the headlights shining in our client's eyes.

All in all, I thought that Dr. Martinelli was a huge "get." While other use-of-force and threat assessment experts could regurgitate the particulars of law enforcement and military training that bears upon decisions, this guy had the scientific and academic credentials to help a jury understand not just the rules or the training that underpin a decision to use or not use a weapon, but how these decisions develop within seconds mentally, emotionally, and physiologically.

I also contacted William Brown, Ph.D., an Associate Professor of Sociology in the Department of Criminal Justice at Western Oregon University in Monmouth. He directs the Bunker Project, a program that assists Afghanistan and Iraq veterans with alcohol, drug, post-traumatic stress disorder and legal problems. Dr. Brown is recognized as an expert in the area of the "total institution" of the military and its effect on veterans re-entering the civilian culture. In effect, he is a military culture and indoctrination expert, somebody well-qualified to testify to the post-military behavior of veterans.

I thought Dr. Brown was another great find, and for two reasons.

First, Dr. Brown seemed ideally suited to tell jurors why a reasonable person with Gerald's military training, expertise, and experience as a Marine sniper and Blackwater contractor would react as he did the night of the shooting. He went to Ranger School and did two tours during the Vietnam War. Having served as an infantryman with the 173rd Airborne Brigade, and as platoon leader in B Company 75th Rangers, Dr. Brown definitely knows military culture. I felt that he could back up our defense theory: that on the night of the shooting, Gerald reacted the way the military had trained him to, and – far from being trigger-happy – that Gerald waited much longer to shoot than a typical civilian would have.

Second, Dr. Brown had personal experience and professional expertise with regard to the difficulties of veterans trying to reintegrate into a post-military life. He knows how military training and experience can cause some individuals to respond violently to stimuli, and he has extensively researched veterans in the criminal justice system both nationally and in Oregon. Whether or not Gerald would be eventually diagnosed with Post-Traumatic Stress Disorder (PTSD), Dr. Brown's research could help us address or explain the Parade of Horribles, the prior bad acts evidence the government had gathered against Gerald. That is, if we couldn't keep the Horribles out of court.

Sadly, Dr. Brown's research showed us that Oregon is the number-one state for veteran incarceration. Nineteen percent of all prisoners in the Oregon Department of Corrections system are veterans – and Oregon doesn't even have a military base. This is in sharp contrast to other states that have large military bases like Georgia, South Carolina and Florida, where the rate of veteran incarceration is between 5 and 6 percent. One of Dr. Brown's conclusions was that since Oregon does not have a military base, the state is less prepared to handle military culture and issues. Prosecutors and judges aren't familiar with veterans' issues and are often hostile to them. Now, if you think hostile is too strong a word, consider that our law firm once heard a district attorney in a county to our north say, flat out, that our client was likely to re-offend because he is a military veteran. That sort of ignorance and bias against veterans is common around here, and that's why we knew we would have to educate Gerald's jury about how his military experience was relevant to his thinking process and how he responded to it on the night of the shooting.

On the surface, it might appear that Dr. Martinelli and Dr. Brown had considerable overlap in experience and that they would cover the same ground on the witness stand. But that wasn't true. Each man was our best witness on several different questions or issues. We had a variety of topics we needed expert testimony on, and between the two men, we'd cover the bases – that is, if we could keep the questions and issues straight! To make sure that we didn't have redundant testimony or holes in our theories, we actually created a Venn diagram of our experts, of which Drs. Martinelli and Brown were but two.

Having done all this legwork, we still needed to remind ourselves that none of these experts was guaranteed to make it to the witness stand. We hoped that most or all of them would, and we were confident that if it they did, our odds of winning the case increased significantly. However, we also knew that the government would attempt to exclude the witnesses by poking holes in their qualifications or the foundation of their opinions, and that Judge Debra Vogt would probably bend over backward to assist the prosecution in excluding them – in effect, acting like a second prosecutor, as she has been known to do. There wasn't much we could do about that, except come to court better prepared than the prosecution and the judge put together.

INSIDE THE MIND OF THE SHOOTER

*W*hat did Gerald see on the night of the shooting?
What did Gerald think as the confrontation unfolded?
And, how did Gerald's background affect his thought process and his actions?

These were the key but complicated questions we needed to address at trial to sell our self-defense claim to jurors. Sell? Yes. In a court of law, everybody's selling something. The prosecutor comes in with his wares, and so do I. It's my job as a defense attorney to be the better salesman, the one the jury wants to buy from.

I knew the first question begged for a more complete answer than what we had. By Gerald's account, the headlights were blinding, making David Crofut seem extremely menacing as he followed Gerald 80 feet away from the vehicles. Surrounded by darkness but looking into the lights, Gerald said he couldn't determine whether Crofut had a gun or was reaching into a pocket for one. Of course, even without additional evidence or expert opinion as to what Gerald saw, we still had what Crofut did – he grabbed Gerald's rifle.

The second question – about what Gerald was thinking – went straight to the central issue in a self-defense case: Was our defendant afraid for his life?

Perhaps one of the best ways to determine what someone saw and thought during an incident is to focus on what they said and how they said it. Gerald called 911 before firing his weapon, and this is what he said:

STREBENDT:...*fucking come near me.*

DISPATCHER: *Okay, and what is your name?*

STREBENDT: *Gerald Strebendt.*

DISPATCHER: *Okay, so you were involved in an accident?*

STREBENDT: *Yeah, I've got my firearm out, he hit me on purpose with his vehicle, crashed into my brand-new truck, and now he's over by my truck, and I'm backing away from him. I'm backing away from him. Back away!*

DISPATCHER: *Okay, is he trying to fight you?*

STREBENDT: *Yes, he's coming at me, I've got a loaded weapon on him and he's coming towards me...*

DISPATCHER: *Get in your vehicle and lock the door.*

STREBENDT: *I can't he's – he's at my vehicle, he ran up on my vehicle, he hit me on purpose. He's – get back from me, sir. Get back from me. Ma'am, I can't see his hands. It's dark; I can't see him.*

DISPATCHER: *Gerald.*

STREBENDT: *Get back.*

DISPATCHER: *Stay calm. Gerald.*

DISPATCHER: *Gerald. I'm getting you a new dispatcher.*

(Pause/Inaudible/Static)

STREBENDT: *Send an ambulance right now. Send an ambulance.*

You can read what Gerald said in the excerpt of the call above. You can't judge *how* he said it, however, without listening to the seven-minute tape, which you can do by googling "Gerald Strebendt 911 call" or visiting http://snip.ly/911-call.

Was this the voice of a terrified victim? A road-rager? Or was he a calculating killer trying to cover himself with a slick 911 call... followed by a late-night, C.Y.A. call to his friend Justin Vaccaro, too, perhaps? All were possibilities, and our job as his defense team was to rule out the ones that were harmful to Gerald's case. We tended to feel that the tape of the 911 call, in which Gerald was obviously tense and breathless, would lead any juror to believe that Gerald was feeling fear.

In considering Gerald's state of mind, we also had to look at his background, which is another factor in judging someone's actions in a self-defense case.

Let's start with the fact that Gerald is a Marine. You can say he is a *former* Marine or that he *was* a Marine, but either way, Gerald would be offended. Once a Marine, *always* a Marine. You may be wearing a different uniform or civilian clothes, you may have moved on in life. But you'll always be a Marine because you went to Parris Island, San Diego, or the hills of Quantico. There's no such thing as a former Marine.

Gerald's training and experience as a Marine sniper definitely provided a backdrop to his actions on the night of the shooting. When Gerald's detractors have said that he was and is a trained killer, it is absolutely true. As General John J. Pershing, the victorious Army Commander of U.S. Forces in World War I, said it, "The deadliest weapon in the world is a Marine and his rifle."

Gerald shot David Crofut with a Sig Sauer model SIG 556, 5.56 x 45 mm with a scope. While it was a big, black, metallic, and powerful looking gun that would undoubtedly frighten jurors, we would also want to point out that it looked a lot like the military-style weapon that Gerald had been trained to use during his time in the military. Yes, Sig Sauer AR-15, which was set up for shooting things far away, was a very similar to the military rifle that Gerald was most comfortable with, the M16.

On January 29, 2014, Gerald fired only one shot. The magazine that had been loaded into the rifle held 30 rounds and was characterized as "high capacity," but, notably, no additional shots were fired. Clearly, while he was fearful, Gerald didn't respond by emptying the whole magazine into Crofut.

It's important to note, too, that the Sig Sauer wasn't the only gun Gerald had in his possession that night; he had other choices. In fact, Gerald's Denali truck was a rolling armory. The police located a Colt .22 long rifle pistol in the center console, four Colt .45 magazines loaded with ammunition, two Ruger .22 rifles behind the driver's seat, and buckets of ammunition. The guns and ammo were poorly organized. Bullet casings were strewn all over the car – on and in the center console, in the cup holders, and on the floor. They even spilled out onto the Denali's step-up.

No doubt the presence of all of these weapons would be a hurdle I'd have to clear for the jury. While responsible gun-owners would fault Gerald only for the disorganization and redundancy of what he was carrying in his truck, non-gun-owners would see a "gun nut," somebody possibly out looking for opportunities to use his weapons. Worse, for many potential jurors, Gerald's self-defense claim would be suspect simply because he used not just a rifle, but one that the media calls a "military-style assault rifle." I blame law enforcement for that. In their selectively released statements to the press, SPD worked hard to paint a picture of a trained killer "road-raging" on an unarmed man. And, because there are rampant misconceptions in the U.S. regarding the Second Amendment and related gun laws, that picture is easy to paint.

Many who heard that the shooting involved an AR-15-style weapon immediately raised questions, essentially asking, "Why in the world was he driving around with that rifle in his truck? Was he looking for trouble?" But the Second Amendment doesn't give us "the right to keep and bear sporting goods," i.e., guns for hunting. It gives us the right to bear arms – and that includes both handguns and long guns, subject to the restrictions of state law. Can I drive around with a full-auto .50 caliber machine gun? Yes, in Oregon, I can. It is legal in Oregon to own, possess, and shoot a machine gun. All you need is the federal tax stamp for $200, a willingness to wait about six months to get it, and lots of disposable income to shoot it, because the ammunition isn't cheap and comes out fast. In Oregon, Gerald had every right to carry a "military-style assault rifle" in his truck to defend himself. It could have been a machine gun, if that was his desire. Would the media have portrayed the shooting as being more justified if Gerald had used his handgun instead? Yes, I think so. While each weapon is designed to kill, the government's narrative would have been harder to spin with a concealed handgun and corresponding license… than the scary-looking AR-15.

One day I sat down with Gerald and just asked him the obvious question. "Gerald, why the rifle? I need to understand why you grabbed the Sig Sauer instead of one of the handier pistols."

He didn't pause to consider; his answer was right there immediately. "I was in a panic. I just grabbed what I could find as fast as I could."

Fair enough. But there was a handgun in the center console that was, at least arguably, easier for him to grab. My hunch was that Gerald's choice had more to do with Gerald and less to do with convenience, despite what he was telling me. I suspected that Gerald's decision to take his rifle out after the accident was a product of his training with the Marines. And that's something I set out to investigate.

"Nothing Deadlier than a Marine and His Rifle."

Gerald Strebendt was just 17, you'll recall, when he chose to join the Marines. His mother signed the consent form, and within days of turning 18 and graduating high school, he departed for basic training in San Diego, Calif. When he entered the training center, he found himself surrounded by young men from various states west of the Mississippi. Gerald told me how they jostled and joked, calling each other "devil dog" and "leatherneck" until an impeccably uniformed, heavily muscled Marine ordered them onto the bus that would take them to boot camp.

The first phase of Marine boot camp is intentionally brutal, with the goal of breaking down a recruit. Civilian thoughts and habits were considered detrimental to training, so recruits were prevented from having their own civilian thoughts or following their non-military instincts. The trainers short-circuited normal thought patterns by distracting the recruits with intense physical training, rigid routines, strict discipline, and heavy instruction. The idea of working as a group, as a team, was paramount; recruits were not allowed to think of themselves as individuals. They were even required to use the third-person while speaking, calling themselves "this recruit."

It was right then, during boot camp, that recruits were introduced to their "rifle." This firearm was never referred to as a "gun," and it stayed with the recruit for the entirety of the training. They kept their rifles with them or nearby at almost all times during boot camp, even while sleeping. Gerald learned to think of his rifle as an extension of himself – because that's what the Marines wanted him to think.

After boot camp, Gerald attended the School of Infantry, Survival Evasion Resistance Escape (SERE) School, Scout/Sniper School, Infantry Squad Leader School of the 3rd Marine Division, Company Radio Operations class, and Infantry Squad Leader School of the 1st Marine Division. He was recognized with an Overseas Deployment Ribbon, a Good Conduct Medal, two meritorious promotions, two Marine of the Quarter boards, two NCO of the Quarter boards, and a letter of appreciation from the commanding general.

As a result of all this training, Gerald was qualified on the M16A2 assault rifle, M40-A1 Marine sniper rifle, the M72 SEAL sniper rifle, the M82-A1 SASR (Special Application Scope Rifle) Barrett .50 caliber sniper rifle, and M9 Beretta pistol. He qualified on the exact same rifle range as Kennedy assassin Lee Harvey Oswald did, Camp Pendleton's Edson Range. Both future killers qualified on "B" range as rifle experts in the Marine Corps shooting program.

Hitting a 20x40-inch target at 1,000 yards (10 football fields or over half a mile) became Gerald's obsession. He kept his fingers meticulously groomed for shooting. He sanded down his trigger finger so he could feel the slack get taken up on the trigger pull of his sniper rifle. He would buy $40 fireproof Nomex gloves and immediately cut out the pointer finger off on the right hand. The triggers on the M-40 were what they called "hair" triggers and were set at 2.5 pounds. When Gerald was locked onto a sniper rifle, it became an extension of his body, probably of his entire being. And this marriage of body to gun negated the humanity of his target because looking at man-sized targets at 1,000 yards reduced them to mere specks. Every breath and even every heartbeat had to be timed to pulling the trigger, and when Gerald was shooting, nothing else mattered. There was no feeling, no consideration of consequences. There was only a job to be done: send a lump of metal into a nameless target at a high velocity.

Gerald kept a log book of every bullet he ever fired out of his sniper rifle. The barrels lasted for 7,000 rounds before they had to be replaced, and he had them replaced about once a year.

Gerald was on both the rifle and pistol competition teams in the Marine Corps. His coach was Gunnery Sergeant Nance. "Gunny" taught Gerald to practice shooting his Beretta in his room only one inch from the wall. He was to put a pencil down the barrel, eraser first, and aim at a miniscule speck on the wall and shoot the pencil at it. The firing pin would push into the eraser, the pencil would slide forward from the barrel until it was stopped by the wall, and the lead would put a small dot on the dry wall. The other 4" of the pencil would remain in the barrel because of how close the gun was to the wall. This allowed Gerald to practice many times more than his opponents. His goal was to keep the lead dots together, preferably in one big dot. It was good practice to learn how to avoid jerking the trigger or anticipating the recoil of the weapon.

By the accounts we were able to gather, Gerald was a good Marine, one well respected by those with whom he served. Fellow Marine Mitch Cox was a team leader at the sniper school, and he appointed Gerald to be his assistant team leader. In order to be accepted into the program, an individual needed to have high fitness scores, qualify as excellent with the service rifle, and have high general performance scores. The general performance scores were important, because they related to how well an individual did his job, and how well he conducted himself as a Marine. Mitch was very impressed by Gerald when he met him, because, out of the 20 who began the course, Gerald was the only Marine selected from it.

One of the main objectives of Sniper Indoctrination School, Cox told me, was to train Marine snipers how to deal with high levels of stress under the extreme and extenuating circumstances of their jobs. They were taught various types of self-care aimed at helping them ease their mind after one engagement and staying relaxed and ready for the next. Being a sniper in the Marines, Cox said, is "a thinking man's game." It takes tremendous confidence, patience, and strategic skill—not to mention a willingness to take on heavy responsibility. A sniper that was the rank of E-4 was expected to handle as much responsibility as an E-6 in the infantry, Cox said. He characterized Gerald as "extremely patient" and highly disciplined. It was a technical job, an exacting job, and in Cox's estimation, Gerald was good at it.

Gerald left active military service in 2001, and was honorably discharged by the Marines in 2004. What followed was MMA semi-stardom, and with it, a lasting reputation as something of a high-flyer. While Gerald didn't make a lot of money during his brief stint as a UFC fighter, he made plenty of connections that made life more interesting. He trained with the biggest names in MMA, and met famous boxers, well-known actors, and celebrities like rapper DMX and comedian/UFC host Joe Rogan. Gerald came away from his UFC days able to enthrall a bar crowd for hours with his tales. He could tell you about the time he met British pop singer Robbie Williams while hiking up near the Hollywood sign in Los Angeles and shared his water with Williams' dog; or the time he met Balthazar Getty, of the family that owns the Getty museum in L.A., and swam in Getty's swimming pool; or when he had a 15-minute conversation with Wilmer Valderrama, who played "Fez" from "That 70's Show" while in line at Subway. Gerald had to be explained by someone else in line what "That 70's Show" even was. He had never heard of it or Valderrama.

Gerald could also tell you about Rogan's failed attempt to fix his receding hairline with plugs. He could tell you what it's like to be on a B-movie set with Pamela Anderson and Gary Busey. He could tell you about rooming with a future supermodel.

But on some level, Gerald missed the military. He missed the camaraderie, the excitement, and yes, the weapons. He probably needed the regular paycheck, too. So in 2005, when Gerald was recruited to work with Blackwater USA, tasked with protecting the lives of Blackwater clients alongside other elite former military specialists in Afghanistan, it was a relief for many reasons.

Early in Gerald's case I learned that if you call him a Blackwater merc (short for mercenary), he will quickly tell you that mercenaries are a violation of the Geneva Conventions. "We were 'contractors,'" he corrected me, "protecting dignitaries and those actively fighting a war." Of course, Blackwater "contractors" infamously shot and killed 17 Iraqi "civilians" at Baghdad's Nisour Square in 2007, prompting a criminal prosecution that took place while Gerald was in custody awaiting his murder trial. (They were found guilty.) After that incident, if not well before, the very name "Blackwater" came to spark outrage among Iraqi and American citizens alike, causing the company to rename itself Academi.

Working for Blackwater required Gerald to adjust his skills. While the

Marines had trained Gerald as a sniper who could expertly shoot targets that were far away, Blackwater guards were more often required to shoot targets up close. With Blackwater, Gerald was trained to track individuals from safe place to safe place in an urban environment, using walls, rocks, and vehicles as a shield. There were tricks to this. If it wasn't possible to shoot through the solid engine block of a vehicle, Blackwater guards would drop to the ground and shoot at the concrete under the engine, causing bullets to ricochet into the targets' feet, ankles and shins. Once hit, the attackers would fall onto the ground, vulnerable and exposed to additional shots. Gerald also told me how he learned to shoot through a windshield. Since the curvature of the tempered glass would either make a bullet go up or down from its intended direction, he was taught to aim at the bottom of the glass, near the cowl of the windshield, to hit a target in the chest. He also learned that if the attacker was out in front of the vehicle's windshield, he'd need to aim at the head if he wanted to hit the torso. Gerald was trained to move continually while on duty, even if he was guarding something stationary. It would make him a more challenging target for a long-range sniper to hit.

Firepower was everything when it came to staying alive as a Blackwater guard, Gerald told me. While permits were required to carry automatic weapons and explosives, the company was perfectly willing to be out of compliance if it prevented delays in accepting lucrative contracts. Operatives were more than willing to arm themselves with whatever they couldn't get through official channels, too. They confiscated weapons from targets they had taken down. They purchased items on the down-low from the flourishing black-market arms trade. Gerald told me he frequently had grenades hidden on his person, and carried an AK-47, Beretta Mod 92FS and Glock 17. When I expressed surprise at the grenades, Gerald laughed. "I carried so many grenades that people didn't like to ride with me. They said if I got shot I'd probably explode and take everybody with me." At one point Gerald decided that even his first aid kit was a waste of space. He emptied it of everything but his ratcheting tourniquet and tucked four grenades in the box instead.

Most of the Marines-related information I'd gathered for the purposes of defending Gerald came through a normal records request. I couldn't get anything from Blackwater, so Gerald gave me whatever he had in writing, which wasn't much. But I didn't need a lot of records of any kind to conclude that Gerald was, in fact, deadly with a gun. It was clear to me that once Gerald had decided he was going to fire, it didn't matter what kind of weapon he used. David Crofut was a dead man.

But does experience with a gun, combined with reflexes well-honed by the military and Blackwater make Gerald guilty of murder? That's the $64,000 – or 25 years to life – question.

To gather more information about Gerald, and about snipers, I made a telephone call to Sgt. Major William Skiles. He had trained Gerald to be a sniper, and even though that training was done more than a few years earlier, I found that he remembered Gerald well and had positive things to say about him. What's more, Skiles knew everything that there was to know about snipers and their training, and he seemed willing to take the time to be my expert witness at trial. I told him all that I knew about the situation, to see if he could provide any insights. Near the end of the call, he asked me an interesting question.

"Do you know why Gerald called 911?" he asked.

"For help."

"Yes but why else?"

"I guess the D.A. may claim that he was setting up a self-defense claim. That it was cold and calculated."

"Okay, but why does a lowly grunt call 911? It really sounded to me like Gerald called both for help and for instructions from someone with authority."

"You think so?"

"Sure. He was in military mode. What did he call his weapon on the call? Did you see that?"

I looked over the transcript. "He said, 'I've got my firearm out.' Not a gun, a firearm."

"There you go!" Skiles said. "He needed someone to tell him, shoot or not shoot. In the Marines, a sniper would almost never get the choice to pull the trigger. He'd always have orders."

When Skiles pointed it out, I could totally see it: Gerald needed instructions. As a sniper, he would have had someone tightly controlling his actions at all times to prevent a trained killer from going rogue. Besides, the chain of command must be maintained for any semblance of order in war-time. Skiles would help me educate my jury about Gerald, about his time in the Marines, what military training did to the young men and women of this country, and how it never left them, even years after service.

I also noticed for the first time that on the 911 call, Gerald had called Crofut, 'Sir.' I could suddenly see him, a younger man standing in camo clothing, a young Marine trained to use civility and respectful terms to others even in the face of great stress. When Gerald became a Marine, he was trained with an M16. This was the firearm that he hauled around, and kept close to him at night. In every way that mattered, it was remarkably similar to the Sig Sauer Gerald used to shoot Crofut.

"Hey, what do you think about the fact that Gerald only shot Crofut once?" I asked Skiles. "A police officer would have unloaded his gun into Crofut, right? That's what they are trained to do."

Skiles murmured his agreement, adding, "I'd look at the shot as an attempt to stop the threat, not to kill. It wasn't a rage reaction, and he wasn't trying to eliminate the threat, just stop it. That's how I see it."

Later, I returned to the topic with Gerald himself. Previously he'd told me that he panicked that night on Bob Straub Parkway, and just grabbed what weapon he could. Now I wanted press him on that point. I thought a jury would want more of an explanation than just "I panicked," especially since Gerald had more experience with firearms than much of the population. So, again I asked the "why the rifle?" question. Not atypically, Gerald responded with an analogy.

"Mike, you've told me a million stories about rafting and near death experiences in the rivers," he began. "If you were drowning would you grab a piece of slippery driftwood that was floating by just inches away?"

"Of course."

"Would you grab a piece of driftwood if your raft was within arm's reach?"

"Of course not," I said.

"Mike, I was drowning. I was scared for my life. Fuck the driftwood. I grabbed the boat."

Okay, there it is, I thought. Gerald thought he was going to die, so he reached for the firearm he *knew better* than any other gun that might have been available. There were times in his life when he had kept a hand on his rifle constantly for weeks or even months at a time. With the Marines, it was a subtle sort of brainwashing that made his rifle the most important thing to him, aside from following orders. Of course, in Blackwater, it was just a fact of life. "Always keep your weapon nearby," went the spoken and unspoken rule, "because you're going to need it."

With Gerald's military training and Blackwater experience framing a significant period of his life, it made sense to me that Gerald grabbed his rifle, not the driftwood. He selected the weapon he knew intimately, better than he knew himself. Thus, it was the weapon he took with him to go and meet Crofut in the dark.

CHAPTER 26

CHARACTER AND DESTINY

The events of January 29, 2014 on Bob Straub Parkway were at least partly a product of Gerald's being a Marine and a former Blackwater operative. Of this I was now confident. But it also had its roots in the man that Gerald Strebendt was deep inside, there was no evading it.

Let me start by saying that Gerald is smart, one of the smartest clients I have ever had. He reviewed the discovery, the investigative details, and the science behind everything. He really worked hard to learn what everything meant and how it affected his case. He gave me helpful notes and came up with questions that I had not thought to ask. From his jail cell, he helped direct the case.

Gerald is also highly skilled in dealing with people. He bucked us up when we were down, he complimented us on our skills, and he entertained us, drawing witty sketches of courtroom interactions, accompanied by cartoonish quotes.

Gerald is a natural leader. While he hasn't developed close, loyal friends, he knows how to work a crowd. People follow him. His high-risk status as a former UFC fighter got him placed him in a solitary-confinement wing of the local jail, alongside child sex offenders. It's a place reserved for prisoners who may be at risk of retribution or violence from those out to prove something behind bars. Yet somehow Gerald became the leader of these outcasts, without ever having to make fear or intimidation his tools, giving his fellow inmates life advice and leading them in prayer.

Despite all his attributes, it was clear to me that Gerald was at least somewhat damaged by the poverty and turmoil of his early life. While Gerald considered his childhood generally happy, he didn't seem to disagree when I suggested that his upbringing had taken a toll. There was deprivation, disruption, loss, and plenty of uncertainty in the stories he told about growing up on the Oregon coast.

I'm reluctant to pin anything on Gerald's childhood, because I too came from relatively modest beginnings, with a pipe-fitter father and a mother who was a T-shirt screen printer. But I lived in the safety of a Kansas City suburb near jobs aplenty, while Gerald was raised on the impoverished Oregon coast. I'm also wary of laying too much blame on Gerald's interests in guns and athleticism, because these are my interests, too.

Still, I find I do have a few things to say about the guy.

At the risk of inappropriately taking on the role of psychologist, which is well above my pay grade, I'd have to say I think Gerald's father – or in real terms, the lack of one – was a significant formative influence in Gerald's life. I can't help but believe that Gerald would have been a different man if he had been raised by a consistent male role model who exhibited greater personal integrity. From what Gerald told me, William Strebendt was not at all a good role model. Gerald believes that his father drank too much and remembers his quick, vicious temper. Instead of building up his young son, he seemed to have torn down Gerald at every opportunity – most notably chiding him for his supposed weakness. After William left the home, an alternate father figure, Gerald's mother's boyfriend, Buzz, acted more like Fagin in "Oliver Twist," showing Gerald and his brother Doug how to skirt the law to cheat, steal and get away with things. Finally, there was Steve McMullan, perhaps the most legitimate father figure Gerald ever encountered. The man was nearly killed in his gun shop, probably causing Gerald untold amounts of trauma on the morning when he found Steve's blood in the snow.

But is character really destiny, as Heraclitus the Greek philosopher put it? Many members of the public thought so, and the prosecution surely thought so. I wasn't sure they were wrong – not yet, and not completely.

After his arrest, the local armchair psychologists proclaimed practically in unison that Gerald was a depraved murderer, based on what they knew from initial reporting on the case:

- He was a "trained killer" in the Marines.

- He had been a "cage-fighter."

- He killed Crofut using a "military assault rifle."

- The police thought the incident on Bob Straub Parkway stemmed from "road rage."

Talk about a collection of hot-button issues and phrases, I thought to myself.

Due in part to the judicially muzzled and police-influenced coverage of the case in the press and the continuing chatter on social media, Gerald fairly quickly lost any support he had around him. His ex-wife labeled him a road-rager. James Antsy, whose boys were pals with Gerald when they were children, said Gerald was a killer. The MMA community that Gerald had worked hard to develop since his return to the Willamette Valley did little more than gossip about his arrest, and gradually, move on to other dojos.

All the misinformation, combined with the judge's decision to tape the mouths of the defense and the press, left people free to portray themselves as prescient regarding Gerald's supposed violent nature. "I wasn't surprised" that Gerald shot somebody, people told me and my investigators. (They still come up to me and say it today: "I knew it!") Gerald's so-called friends, and even one notable member of Gerald's own family have said it. We heard late in the case that William Strebendt believed his own son to be guilty of murder. If this was the loose talk running rampant among people who knew Gerald or thought they did, I could only imagine how it might be poisoning the jury pool, with me helpless to prevent it.

Nobody's conclusions were entirely without reason or merit, of course. The Parade of Horribles certainly suggested that Gerald had long walked the ragged edge between lawfulness and unlawfulness. It wasn't difficult to connect the dots between the tumult of his early life, his military and MMA/UFC history, his brushes with the law, and a certain shooting that occurred on a dark country road at the end of January 2014. Gerald had shown himself to be a flawed individual who made flawed choices. It was deplorable but not a shock that people were so ready to assume that Gerald was guilty of murder.

But what was I to make of Gerald's "good callers," the people who were contacting us to sing his praises as a human being? Or, the stories, apparently true, that Gerald told from his own unobserved experiences in life? I couldn't help but conclude that, aside from everything else, and also along with everything else – Gerald was a good guy.

The man definitely had his defenders. For every negative story we heard at Arnold Law, we heard or received two positive ones:

Youth Supporter. One example was Dave King, a local educator for 30 years. Upon retirement he became the half-time vice-principal at Gateway High School in Springfield and, when he contacted us, he had been doing that job for about seven years. King said he met Gerald about the same time he took the halftime position, through a mutual friend. King was interested in joining Gerald's gym, but he thought maybe he was too old to join what appeared to be a "fighting gym" that perhaps was geared to the young and reckless. King was in his fifties at the time. But he visited, and he told us he was pleasantly surprised by the atmosphere he found at Gerald's gym. The workouts were aimed at exercise and discipline, not fighting. He said Gerald was very professional and made King feel welcomed and eventually comfortable enough to join the gym and begin taking classes. "There were people of all ages, genders, and different levels of fitness that participated there," King said. He was especially impressed with how Gerald worked with youngsters, so King arranged to have some of his Gateway students work out with Gerald. Gerald gave the students a discount on fees, arranged for physical education credits to be obtained and encouraged them to be disciplined in school. There were clear expectations for the students, and they were well coached, supervised and motivated, King said.

Encourager. King also told us about a man, Bret Teral, about forty years old, who wanted to belong to Gerald's gym. He was socially and physically disabled, living at home with his mother, and he wasn't up to working out like most of the members, yet he wanted to be a member of the local MMA community. Gerald motivated and encouraged Teral in every way possible, King said, including buying him a training vest to wear and paying Teral to arrange or clean up the gym at night. Teral went on to begin taking Certified Nurse's Assistant classes after being involved at the gym. King said he felt that Gerald was a mentor who gave Teral confidence and a sense of worth and empowerment.

Roadside Mechanic. Another fan of Gerald's big heart was David Bennett, an RV salesman at a dealership north of Eugene. He told me of a time when, due to an engine malfunction, he was forced to pull his rig off the road 15 miles outside of Coos Bay, Oregon, where he had been salmon fishing. Gerald happened by and pulled over to see if he could help. They looked at the truck engine together and decided that the engine needed oil. Gerald drove back to Coos Bay to buy oil and returned with it to Bennett's pickup. When the oil didn't fix the problem, Gerald offered to tow the boat to Bennett's home free of charge. Bennett rode all the way to Eugene with Gerald towing the boat before Gerald drove back home again. That was almost four hours of out-of-the-way driving that Gerald did – just to help another man out.

First Responder. The story of Kevin Ketner, a long-haul trucker based in Winston, Oregon, epitomizes the risks that Gerald sometimes took to help others. Ketner met Gerald in 2013, almost a year before Gerald killed Crofut. Ketner wrecked his semi-truck and tractor trailer near the town of Oakridge southeast of Eugene on Highway 58, a long and winding mountain highway connecting the Willamette Valley to the high desert plateau of central Oregon on the other side of the Cascades. The rear trailer tow tongue had snapped free, causing the trailer to veer off the road, pulling the cab with it. Gerald was driving by and pulled over to assist. "Gerald saved my life," Ketner said. The trucker was thought dead by first responders and was found jammed under the passenger dashboard area. The engine was running at high RPMs and fuel was spraying all over in every direction. With a fire extinguisher in hand and at great risk to himself, Gerald stayed with Ketner in what was left of the truck cab until Ketner was extricated and flown by helicopter for medical treatment. Gerald put this stranger's safety first. When I asked Gerald about this information we received from Ketner and why he risked himself, he said, "He needed help and helping him was the only option."

I-5 Angel. There was another story of Gerald's "highway

humanitarianism" back in 2009. Mackenzie Carr was the Ms. Northwest Professional Rodeo Association Queen that year, and she and her mother, Barb Carr, were hauling Mackenzie's horse back home to the south coast from a rodeo in Yoncalla, Oregon. Not far from Cottage Grove, a town twenty miles south of Eugene, their truck started shaking. They pulled over on the side of Interstate 5 and called AAA to help them with the truck, but they were not sure what to do about the trailer and horse. Out of the blue, Gerald stopped and asked if he could help. Gerald was hauling a utility trailer, but said he would take it to his home in Springfield and then return to hitch up the horse trailer. He also called his wife of the time, Rachel, and with her help, made arrangements to board Mackenzie's horse with his wife's horses until the Carr's could get their truck fixed. Gerald dropped off his trailer, returned, hooked up the trailer, and hauled the horse and trailer to the arena. Then Gerald took the Carr's to a motel next to the shop where their truck had been towed. The next morning Gerald called to ask if the motel had been okay and how they were doing. They tried to offer Gerald money but he refused. Barb and Mackenzie Carr call Gerald "our I-5 Angel."

AAA Alternative. Josh Glendenning, a personal friend of Gerald, had also seen his generosity while driving. He said that he had went fishing and driving around with Gerald many times, often seeing Gerald stop along highways to help people with flat tires, vehicle breakdowns, or emergencies. He said that Gerald would help anyone that needed something done and added, "Gerald is the complete opposite of a road rager."

Mr. Accountable. Gerald also had a history of being willing to 'fess up when he screwed up, even while driving. Paul Guellid stated that in 2005 he was living at 641 W. 5th Street with his parents. At the time he owned a Jeep Cherokee that was parked on the street outside his home. Gerald, his neighbor, came to the door and asked if they knew who owned the Jeep because he had just run into it. Guellid stated that he would not have known who hit the Jeep if Gerald had not come to inquire about it. Gerald offered to pay for fixing it and gave Guellid his insurance information.

Calm and Collected. Another pleasant car-related incident involved Henry Gary who said he rear ended an SUV that Gerald was driving. Gary said he was at fault when the accident occurred while traveling east on South "A" street in Springfield. Apparently Gary failed to stop in time when Gerald's vehicle was sitting at a red light. Gerald got out and checked on Gary's condition, asking if he needed medical assistance. Gary said that Gerald never became angry with him over the collision and didn't conduct himself in a manner that alarmed him. On the contrary: he said that Gerald never raised his voice and was completely civil and polite during the contact.

When I read these reports and spoke to these witnesses, I had a hard time fathoming the side of Gerald that was a potential road rager. There was simply too much evidence that Gerald was a good man. Gerald did too much in the community without the expectation of payment or return just to be swept under the rug as just another "gun nut."

One of the most troubling allegations we heard made against Gerald, dating back to his childhood days living with James Antsy and his boys, was that Gerald had been involved in wantonly killing animals. At Arnold Law, we never believed it, and the following story is just one reason why:

Trained Killer Can't Control Everything. Gerald tells a story about being brought home after a tour with Blackwater. As usual, he returned to the group's training center in Moyock, North Carolina. Blackwater would rent a car for him and whenever he wasn't training, he would drive up and down the coast by himself and blast music. Gerald was taking one of these drives when a cat ran out into the road. He couldn't avoid it; he hit it. Gerald abruptly slammed on the brakes and steered his vehicle into a ditch. There he jumped out and ran back to the cat, which was beyond help and dying. Gerald held it and attempted to comfort it while it was in its death throes, not knowing if it even perceived his presence. He was shocked and horrified at what he had inadvertently done, and interestingly, the incident made him feel extremely powerless.

"There I was, as bold and brash as I ever had been in my life," said Gerald. "I was on top of the world, high flying with celebrities, wearing all my Blackwater gear. I was all ego. For all that I was this guy, this big bad-ass, there was nothing I could do for this cat. I was so ashamed for killing this innocent creature that I sat on the side of the road and sobbed. I remember thinking, 'If Blackwater is so heroic, protecting the innocent from barbarians, why can't I even protect a little cat?'" He buried the animal's body in the weeds at the side of the road.

"I felt like I should have been able to do something," Gerald recalled when he told us the story. He had wanted to fix the problem – like he always tried to fix problems in the stories we heard about Gerald's "good acts."

Listening, I thought to myself, *he's a protector, not a predator.*

While I took these previously private stories about Gerald's goodwill as a testament to his character, in hindsight, I can see that others might divine other motives.

It could be argued, I guess, that Gerald's negative encounters with people – as described in the Parade of Horribles – were caused by the same motives that inspired him to reach out and help others in distress: he wanted to be in control, at the center of the action. I see the argument. But wouldn't this assumption completely trivialize altruism as just another form of selfishness? Sociologists, anthropologists and evolutionary biologists already hypothesize that being nice to others is just a form of survival of the fittest. Our ancestors who were altruistic caused communities to be built and cooperation to be fostered, increasing food production and distribution, and increasing everyone's chance of survival.

That might be something I can use in argument... I need to write that down.

Emilia, ever the practical one, found my line of thinking interesting but not necessarily useful. In one of our regular trial prep meetings, she asked, "What can we do with all of these witnesses? Are they just stuff we use to mitigate sentencing in case we lose on a lesser included Crim Neg Hom?"

I shook my head. "I want them in my pocket to rebut the 'bad acts' evidence," I said. "If Judge Vogt lets in the Parade of Horribles and wants to litigate who Gerald is as a person, she will turn this three-week trial about a shooting into a three-month trial about Gerald. I fully intend to rebut every single one of those bad acts with 10 good acts. I want to show the jury how ridiculous it is to take snapshots of someone's previous encounters and consider them evidence. These "bad acts" have nothing to do with Crofut. They're just a sideshow, a way to distract the jury from the self-defense claim and what really happened that night. If the prosecution wants to play that game – using years-old, isolated incidents to explain someone's current behavior – then we will play that game. But I intend to win it."

THINGS THAT KEEP YOU UP AT NIGHT

As autumn leaves started to turn and we got closer to counting the time to trial in weeks, the stress mounted. Neither Gerald nor I slept much. We both lay awake in our respective beds at night, miles apart, just thinking and rethinking the evidence in the case. Gerald made notes, wrote down questions, and handed the results to me on the random sheets of paper he always used. I did the same thing for myself, on better paper.

It was during my restless nights that I found myself struggling with the smaller, more detailed questions of what really happened between Gerald and Crofut the night of the shooting. I was particularly stuck on the comments made by Bill Powell, the witness who said that he was in front of the two cars before the crash. He told law enforcement investigators that he saw Gerald's truck drive around Crofut, and then stop. Verne Hoyer interviewed him, and then I asked them both to come to my office. I wanted to know exactly what Powell had seen. Gerald had denied cutting off Crofut, and we knew that the ACM data didn't support a crash that resulted from Gerald cutting him off. So what exactly did Powell see, and what might it mean?

Powell said he didn't mind coming down to the office, so Emilia, Verne, and I met with him in a conference room. He told us the same thing he told law enforcement, just about word for word. One small detail, however, changed the entirety of the way the evidence would and could be viewed. As he drew a picture of what he thought he was seeing, he said, "I was in front of [Crofut and Gerald], and I could see two sets of headlights. As I neared the top of the hill, I saw the headlights get in line." He drew the cars getting in line on his diagram. "Then in my rear view mirror, I saw a flash."

"What kind of flash?" I asked. "Like the car in front turned on its high beams or turned its lights off then back on?"

"No," he said, "like a flashlight flips when you point it at the ground then back up. The lights never turned off, and I didn't see the high beams engaged."

"You mean, it looked like his headlights pointed down for a second?"

"Yes, that's what I saw. Maybe there was a dip or something, but I didn't notice it myself when I went through there."

I talked to Powell a bit longer, being careful not to react to what he had said, or even draw much attention to it. I didn't want to risk coloring his testimony with my thoughts. When he rose to leave I thanked him for his time, and closed the door behind him.

"Did you catch that?" I said to Verne and Emilia.

"Catch what?" said Verne. "Sounded just about like he said it to me before, and the detectives before that."

"What he said about what he saw in the rear-view mirror before Gerald's truck went around the Rogue," I said.

"Sure," said Emilia. "His headlights bounced or dipped."

"What causes that?" I asked.

Verne, a former police officer who routinely worked traffic and issued tickets to speeding drivers, said, "Whenever I was sitting in a patrol vehicle on the road, I saw cars do that all the time when the drivers saw me. Usually it was the driver hitting the brakes."

"Exactly," I said, leaning forward in my chair. "Powell saw Crofut slam on his brakes right before Gerald went around him suddenly. Gerald didn't drive around Crofut to cut him off. Crofut slammed on his brakes in the middle of the road, and Gerald was forced to go around him."

"So why did Gerald stop?" Emilia asked. As it had been throughout the case, the question once again was, why Gerald didn't keep going? It was a question we'd have to answer for the jury if we wanted an acquittal.

I didn't know the answer to the question yet, but I was working on it.

Dead Truck

After the crash, Gerald told me that his truck wouldn't start. As much as he may have wanted to drive away, he said, he couldn't get the truck going. I hadn't questioned that reasoning too much. I hadn't wanted to force him into telling me anything new or different. Nor did I want to abuse his trust in me by displaying any distrust of him. But, if Gerald was telling me the truth, could we prove it? We had the observations of law enforcement, the reconstruction report, and our own investigation to start with, but we needed someone knowledgeable about the GMC Denali diesel engine to provide some input. I started calling around to mechanics and GMC pickup dealerships, and finally found Mike Dunks, the diesel mechanic who had actually worked on Gerald's truck prior to the incident on Bob Straub Parkway.

Dunks thought that perhaps the low level of fuel in the tank and the impact of a collision, combined, had pushed a bubble of air up into the fuel line. If it happened, it could have prevented the truck from firing up. Dunks also reminded me that vehicles don't start if they're in gear – and Gerald could well have had the truck in gear at the time of the crash. Nothing there was conclusive, but Dunks was a witness I could call, somebody with plausible opinions to offer.

Next on my checklist, and still related to Gerald's truck: How did the Denali's headlights affect Gerald's ability to see and make judgments the night of the shooting?

Headlights

Gerald told me that he was unable to see what Crofut was pulling out of his pocket – or reaching into his pocket for – in the seconds before Gerald shot him. Crofut was found with cash beside him on the road, more cash in his pocket, and a cell phone that was either in his pocket or had fallen out of his pocket (conflicting reports from law enforcement). As Gerald was retreating from the vehicle, backing up with rifle in hand, he was facing the crash scene, so the headlights would have been in his eyes and brightly backlighting Crofut as he advanced. Given that Crofut had been found unarmed, the visibility conditions under which Gerald fired his rifle in self-defense could end up being the most critical factor in the jury's determination of whether our client was guilty of murder or justified in using deadly force.

I contacted Dr. Marc Green, an expert with specific expertise in visibility conditions and reaction time in use-of-force scenarios. Dr. Green has done extensive research in vision; he is currently an optometry professor and possesses an advanced understanding of basic visual processes. He has also done extensive research on visual processes, visibility conditions, and how they can impact reaction time. He has measured visibility himself thousands of times in his research. He has also consulted in many cases where a law enforcement officer used deadly force on an unarmed person.

When I initially spoke to Dr. Green, he confirmed that the lighting conditions under which Gerald was forced to shoot in self-defense would present difficulty in identifying specific objects. Of course, the question was: Just how bright were the headlights? And how dark was it? Gerald talked about being blinded by the lights, struggling to see Crofut's actions. Would it make a difference if Gerald was standing straight in front of the headlights, as opposed to a bit sideways?

I sent Verne Hoyer to locate Gerald's Denali. After Gerald was arrested, he couldn't make the payments so it was repossessed and sold to another guy in town. Verne found it. The new owner griped when he learned that the truck he bought had been in an accident that had gone undisclosed in the transaction, but he graciously allowed Verne and me to examine the truck. We confirmed the type and brand of headlights, and then, taking advantage of the opportunity, we spent some time checking on other useful details, such as whether the tires could spin while the car was in park, if either tire would spin if only one tire was lifted, etc. Later, Verne brought a truck with similar characteristics to a dark parking lot in Springfield and measured the strength and spread of the headlights in the almost complete darkness. With the data, I planned to prepare demonstrative exhibits from the experiments. It could be useful in cross-examining the State's witnesses.

I moved us onward, to some specific aspects of the government's case against Gerald.

Blood Spatter

Gerald said that before he pulled the trigger, he saw Crofut's hand moving from his hip area or side pocket area toward Gerald. Could we prove it? We had an autopsy report, photos from the autopsy, and photos from the scene. We also had our evidence that the body had been rolled sometime between the shooting and the arrival of authorities at the scene. I called Don Schuessler, our forensic guy, and asked him to request access to Crofut's clothing to examine it for blood spatter patterns. After his review of the evidence, Schuessler was able to confirm that Crofut's right hand was indeed lifted from his side, out in front of his body at the time the bullet blew through his skull. The blood spatter pattern on the back of his hand versus the front of his hand confirmed that the palm of his hand was facing away from the skull explosion.

I was concerned that perhaps Crofut's hand was up in a defensive – "No, don't shoot" – posture. The nightmare scenario would have Crofut standing with his hands and arms outstretched in front of him, with flat palms facing Gerald self-protectively. But Schuessler discounted that possibility, much to my relief. The right sleeve of Crofut's sweatshirt was covered in blood spatter, while the left was not. Further, the right hand was probably in a "cupped" shape, with the middle, 4th and pinkie fingers slightly curled under, due to the concentration of the blood droplets on only some of the fingers, primarily the pointer finger and the area where the pointer and thumb connect.

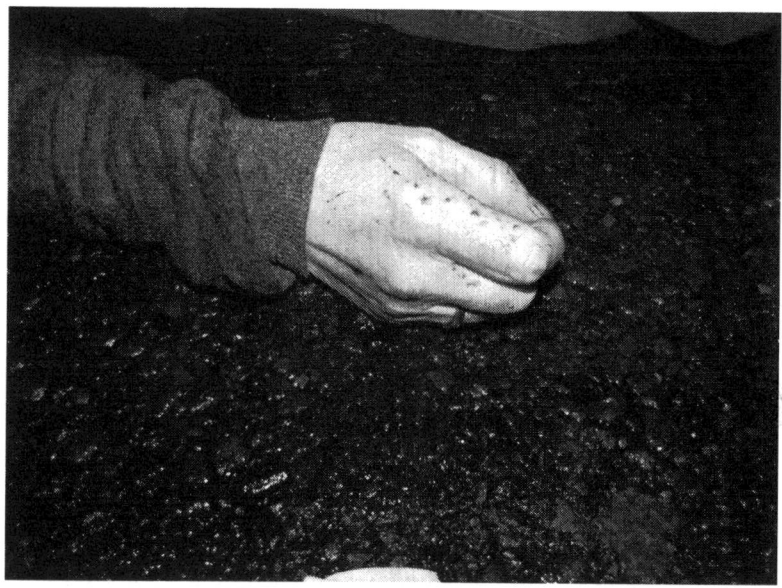

(Photo: Police photo of Crofut's right hand near a wad of cash.)

The spatter seemed to be consistent our long-held speculation that Crofut may have been trying to throw or pass money to Gerald when the shot was fired. Discovery had told us that a wad of cash had been found on the ground near Crofut, and that more money in $100 bills had been found on the console of Gerald's truck. The cash appeared to have been Crofut's video-poker winnings from earlier that evening. Of course, in the dark, with Crofut brightly backlit by headlights, Gerald might not have known that Crofut was pulling out cash; indeed, Gerald said he only saw movement of Crofut's hand around his pocket.

A theory for trial developed in my head as I worked this out: In an explosion of anger, Crofut rammed the back of Gerald's truck. Then once he realized that he had wrecked his wife's work vehicle, and knowing that he had consumed almost a gallon of beer in the last few hours, Crofut desperately wanted to try and settle up with Gerald. Crofut was highly intoxicated, however, and when Gerald refused to parlay, Crofut got angrier and probably desperate.

When reason didn't work, Crofut tried threats. He offered all the money he had on him to Gerald so they could make the problem go away. The only reason I could see Crofut advancing on an armed man in the way he did was if he had been desperate to avoid some other significant penalty — a DUII conviction that could harm his business opportunities, or a DUII crash that, because it involved Brenda's work vehicle, could get his wife fired.

Bullet Fragments

One of the big questions our self-defense case hinged on was how far away from Gerald was Crofut standing when Gerald fired his weapon. We had the ballistics report telling us that Crofut had to have been standing at least seven feet from Gerald, because that's as far as gunpowder residue from the particular weapon traveled, and there was no residue on Crofut. We also had the location of the bullet casing as marked by law enforcement, but our firearms criminalists had advised us not to rely heavily upon that data. Casings are often kicked, either by the involved parties or in the initial response by EMS or law enforcement. Casings tend to bounce and skid, too, we were told, depending on the terrain.

In the hope of locating the bullet itself, Verne contacted a club for local metal detector hobbyists and asked them if they would assist us in scanning the Bob Straub Parkway median. They agreed, and came out *en masse* to search. No bullet was found. Later, during a forensic exam of the clothing by our team, a bullet fragment was collected from Crofut's sweatshirt. This, our expert suggested, meant that the bullet had probably broken apart when it struck Crofut. He didn't think it would ever be found.

Firearm expertise

To further dispense with any bullet or cartridge-related evidence that the State might present against Gerald, I felt I needed an expert in this particular weapon and the manner in which it fires. We had engaged experts to address what happened before the weapon was fired, and what happened after, but we did not yet have an expert to assist us with information about the rifle and the ejection of the shell casing – details that would help us understand whether the casing was likely to have rolled or been moved. Why did it matter? This would help us in our quest to determine where Gerald was standing when the weapon was fired.

In the hope of finding out how far the shell casings flew and in which direction, I called every phone number I could locate for the actual firearm manufacturer and searched the internet for test data. No luck. I left lots of voicemails that were never returned. Next I obtained an exemplar rifle, the same make and model of the firearm used by Gerald, but I knew it wouldn't help me much until I had some way of setting up a useful test-firing situation.

Finally I found and retained Lance Martini of Paradigm Forensic Services, a firearms criminalist. In an initial conference, Mr. Martini pointed out how and in what manner the weapon was sighted at the time of firing (using the scope, using the top of the scope, or using the side of the rifle), all of which would impact the trajectory of the bullet fired. This detail was fairly crucial to our client's case. Gerald said he aimed for center mass without using the scope, yet shot Crofut in the head. I anticipated that the State would argue that he took the time to sight in the shot using the scope, intending to hit Crofut in the head and kill him. I thought that Martini could testify as to how much the path of the bullet was the result of Gerald's manner of aiming, thus providing significant substance to Gerald's version of events. In other words, Martini could explain to the jury just how a person aiming for center mass using the top of their gun could cause the result to be a headshot. He could also advise about the best way to handle the evidence issues involving the shell casing, how to request to examine and test fire the weapon, and the best manner in which to present evidence involving the weapon at trial.

911 Call

The recording of Gerald's 911 call made it fairly clear that Crofut was alive at the beginning of the call. Somewhere during the middle of the call, Gerald pulled the trigger, but the sound of the gunshot couldn't be heard.

Nor could we hear Crofut in the background, although witness accounts had Gerald on the phone while Crofut yelled at him. All along, I'd wondered why Crofut's voice didn't get recorded. Apparently SPD detectives had the same questions, because I received reports in discovery that they had asked the United States Secret Service Forensic Services Division to review the tape. An Imaging and Audio Specialist had processed the audio to enhance the intelligibility of the recording, but she was unable to identify any additional voices or noises.

My interpretation – or at least my operating assumption – was that we couldn't hear the shot because the first dispatcher was in the process of transferring Gerald's call to a second dispatcher when the shot was fired. The transfer seemed to have interrupted the recording, muted it, or made a noise that covered some of the call's audio. Still hoping to gain better clarity on the call, I asked for a tape with the highest possible audio resolution. Then I called Don Ross, an experienced, Grammy-nominated audio engineer who happens to live in the Eugene area. He agreed to give the recording a listen and see if there was anything he could do to enhance it further or separate out particular sounds. We hoped that Ross would help us unravel some of the garbled voices that are heard around the time of the gunshot, and perhaps turn down the sound of the dispatcher to hear the sounds of voices talking simultaneously. If we were lucky, we'd even be able to hear the sound of our client's breaths in and out, providing our self-defense expert some useful evidence regarding the stress that Gerald was under.

As Ross reviewed the audio, I learned a ton about sound – why we hear some sounds and not others, and the limitations of audio technology. He was hindered by the recording's resolution of the data file, but he still managed to identify some sounds on the call that were not the dispatcher or our defendant – a third voice.

Ross explained that some of the same technology that exists to clean up cell phone calls – keep voices crisp and clear – also contribute to us not being able to decipher other voices from the 911 call. But the presence of the third voice on the recording told us something: someone was close enough to the cell phone to be heard on the call when neither Gerald nor the dispatcher was speaking. How close was this someone? We needed to know, because it was likely that the State would argue that Crofut was quite a few feet away from Gerald when Gerald shot him. They would almost certainly use the lack of blood spatter on Gerald's clothes and the lack of gunpowder residue on Crofut's clothes to support their theory that Crofut was not close enough to pose a threat, which would tend to negate our claim of self-defense. Any physical or technological evidence that supported Gerald's version of events was vital, we knew, because it is often more persuasive than memories that are faulty enough to be broken down on cross-examination.

Don Ross and I set up a simple test. We borrowed a Samsung phone, and then laid out an 80-foot tape measure on the street outside Ross's studio. Then we made a call on the cell phone to Ross's studio to record it. With the help of investigators Verne Hoyer and Jeff Dodge, we began our tests.

We started with Verne standing almost toe-to-toe with Jeff, and then, foot by foot, Verne retreated from that position, continuing to talk in a normal voice. At 20 feet from Jeff (representing Gerald), Verne's voice (representing Crofut's) was no longer audible on the call.

In the second test, everything was the same – except this time Verne/Crofut talked very loudly and animatedly. When he was almost yelling, his voice was audible on the recording all the way out to 80 feet.

In tests No. 3 and No. 4, Jeff and Verne both talked at the same time. Each man read the same prepared statement, first in a normal voice, and then animatedly. When both men were talking at the same time, it didn't matter whether they spoke in normal voices or animated ones – we could only get Jeff's (Gerald's) voice onto the recording. On the 911 call, Gerald and the dispatcher basically talked over each other through the entire recording, and the only time any sounds from the third party could be heard was when there was a gap in the conversation.

Where did this leave us? Not exactly where we wanted to be. A good result, useful to the defense, would have been if all of the voices had to be very close to the phone to be heard. Unfortunately for our purposes, the phone picked up more than we were expecting. At normal voice tones, the phone picked up voices past 20 feet. With louder, more animated speech, the phone picked up voices past 80 feet, which is where we stopped testing. When testing with both men speaking, the main voice trumped the background voice, and whenever the main voice wasn't speaking, the background voice filled in the holes. The upshot: the third voice we identified on the 911 call could have been 80 feet from Gerald, or it could have been nose-to-nose with Gerald. While these results certainly didn't enhance our self-defense case, they could be useful in cross-examining anyone who testified for the State about the 911 call and what they might assert could be heard on it.

Digital Forensics

The State's discovery contained several references to 911 calls made by witnesses, including the call from Gerald. Law enforcement used these calls and the information provided by 911 to approximate at least one witness' location at the time the call was made. For example, in the Affidavit executed by Detective George Crolly on behalf of the State in the release proceedings, Detective Crolly stated:

According to Boyles' statements to me and the 911 latitude/longitude information from 911, I could tell that Boyles had just turned off of Bob Straub Parkway onto Mt. Vernon Rd. when she called 911. At 45 miles per hour it would take 23 seconds to drive 1552 feet (crash scene to Mt. Vernon intersection). It is estimated that Boyles left the crash scene at approximately 19:58:32. Boyles' call to 911 was connected 7 seconds prior to the shot being fired.

There was no indication in the affidavit of what qualifications Detective Crolly possesses to arrive at these conclusions, nor was there any indication in the discovery to indicate where the detective retrieved his information. Essentially, the State was employing the "CSI effect" to win credibility.

The "CSI effect" is the impact of science upon juries. We know from our experience with juries at trial that jurors like to see things "proven." They want to see incontrovertible "evidence." Because of the popularity of certain TV shows, science is generally regarded to be the gold standard of evidence. So jurors want to see a photograph, a purple cotton swab, or some kind of positive test. We have to educate our juries that witness testimony is the "evidence" that they will be using to make a decision. In this case, the State offered opinions supported by a dubious analysis to bolster the credibility of the statements of this witness, and could potentially utilize the 911 calls and data to do the same with others at trial. We knew from our research and discussions with our experts that "triangulating" a person's location, using data from cell phones and cell towers, is not a simple science. There are limitations to how closely a person's location can be pinpointed. In this case, Detective Crolly pinpointed a witness's location to seconds from a location or event, without any indication of how he came to this conclusion.

I called Michael Yasumoto of Deadbolt Forensics out of the Portland area. He questioned whether the 911 call center had the ability to utilize the "enhanced 911" technology when Gerald initiated his call. With it, both sides would have very specific information about the location of defendant and the decedent at the time of the call, and/or at the time the shot occurred. Still, Yasumoto told us that the GPS in many cell phones is more accurate than the minimum requirements of the FCC for e-911 (enhanced 911).

With this expert's insight, I planned to make motions against including Detective Crolly's opinions in evidence. I would also use Yasumoto's expertise to counter law enforcement's opinions about cell phones, cell phone towers, cell tower data, use of cell tower data, 911 calls, and e-911.

Brenda Crofut's Blood-Alcohol Content (BAC)

Brenda Crofut's blood alcohol content had not been tested at the scene. While the State considered her a victim and therefore didn't feel the need to know how much she drank that night, we considered it relevant. It would tell us how trustworthy or untrustworthy a jury should regard her observations and interpretations of events that evening. I hired Kenn Meneely of International Forensic Experts to address the issue. Thanks to police reports and interviews with the owner and the bartenders of the Driftwood Bar, where the Crofuts spent their evening, we knew exactly how many drinks Brenda consumed. Using this information and her approximate height and weight, Mr. Meneely stood ready to determine what her likely BAC was at the time of the accident.

We believed Brenda to have been extremely intoxicated, based on the number of drinks she had, on police descriptions of her behavior, and on her slurred, belligerent 911 call. As Mrs. Crofut was a central witness to the events that led up to the shooting, her testimony could be given significant weight by the jury unless we could impeach her on the witness stand. A confirmation of her level of intoxication was necessary to prevent the State from arguing – and the jury assuming – that the inconsistencies in her testimony should be written off as stress or trauma related to being at the scene of the shooting.

Faulty Witness Memories

As I've said before, people's memories are faulty. Research shows that we actually remember only certain things we witness; the brain fills in the rest by logical inference. The result is often at least partly erroneous. We hired Dr. Daniel Reisberg of Reed College in Portland, an expert in memory formation, to review witness statements in discovery. As the car crash and the shooting both occurred at night, visibility alone could have affected the accuracy of the statements that police gathered. In addition, a firearm was involved – another factor that sometimes affects how witnesses perceive events. We hoped Dr. Reisberg would help us spot memory issues and figure out how to handle them in court.

Manic Flip

I retained Dr. Linda Grounds to evaluate the mental health of the shooting victim, David Crofut. From the discovery and our investigator working up in Washington, where Crofut had lived prior to moving to Springfield, we had learned that Crofut had mixed alcohol and a medication to treat depression/anxiety disorders.

We also knew that he had previously been diagnosed with depression, and had a history of aggressive behavior, as evidenced by his ex-wife having obtained a restraining order against him. We were working to locate his previous physical and mental health treatment providers so we could try to obtain his records of treatment. Meanwhile, our Washington investigator was contacting multiple individuals to obtain information about Crofut's behavior – such as whether he exhibited mood disturbances, manic episodes, irritability, elevated or expansive moods, inflated self-esteem, decreased need for sleep, distractibility, etc. Once this investigation was complete, we planned to submit the information we had accumulated to Dr. Grounds so she could try to determine whether Crofut was likely bipolar.

We also knew from our previous consultation with Dr. Robert Julien that certain antidepressants, such as Effexor (without a mood stabilizer), may "flip" a person, in particular a person with bipolar disorder, into a manic episode. A person experiencing a "manic flip" or "manic switch" could experience insomnia, perceptual abnormalities, and psychosis. A manic switch would explain to a skeptical jury why it was that Crofut jumped from his car and advanced on an armed man, grabbing at the gun pointed at him.

As the investigation progressed, the theory I developed was that Crofut was driven by a mix of alcohol, medication, and an undiagnosed mental illness when he rammed Gerald's car, jumped from his car, screamed threats, grabbed the gun pointed at him, and ultimately lunged forward at Gerald. Dr. Grounds could link up this very important piece of our client's defense, if we were able to provide her with the evidence to support the likelihood that Crofut had an undiagnosed mental illness.

CHAPTER 28

THE REENACTMENT

In one of our weekly meetings, I asked Emilia, "Have you ever been in a fight?"

"Not an actual street fight. Just martial arts stuff. I've seen a lot of them though."

"They happen so quickly. They are practically finished before you know they started. It actually takes longer to describe what happened in a fight than the fight actually lasts. I read an article about a scientific study that said that the average street fight lasts three to eight seconds. If it lasts twelve seconds it almost always ends up on the ground."

"Okay," she said. "but what's your point? That Gerald could have ended this in a few seconds? How does that help us?"

"My point is that jurors, or anyone for that matter, have a difficult time putting themselves in someone's shoes during a violent encounter. It's hard to measure time and it's nearly impossible to imagine what someone was going through. We need to transport the jury to that moment with more than words, more than testimony. They need to see it. They need to experience it. They need to experience the incredible darkness in contrast with the blinding headlights. They need to live it as Gerald did. They need to backpedal 80 feet from a threat while calling 911. It's something that you can't easily convey just by telling the story. This is why there are so many fight scenes in the movies, but not many in books. Not lengthy ones, anyway."

"So you're saying that we need a reenactment?" she asked.

"Yes, exactly. Remember what [defense attorney] Mark O'Mara said about the George Zimmerman/Trayvon Martin trial? He said that the animated reenactment really let the jury live it from Zimmerman's perspective rather than just armchair-quarterbacking it. We can't give our jury hindsight. They need insight. Let's put them there."

"Have you thought about calling O'Mara to pick his brain about his case?" Emilia asked. "I've seen him in the news quite a bit since then. Maybe he'd be willing to talk us and tell us who he used to prepare his animation."

I found Mark's contact information through his firm's website and called him. Surprisingly, he was more than happy to drop everything to speak with me. We talked at length about the expert witness who handled the reenactment. The guy used a computerized bodysuit, much like the suits that they use for creating computer-generated images (CGI) for movies and videogames. By computer-tracking body movements via the suit data, O'Mara could demonstrate to the jury exactly what each part of the body would do or was doing at any given moment.

This would be perfect, I thought. I called the expert and got a rough idea on the cost, and wow, talk about sky-high. I was convinced that I'd be getting what I paid for; the only problem being that I couldn't pay for it. And, thanks to Judge Vogt's gag order, I couldn't do anything to raise money to pay for it. So I called up the Oregon Public Defense Services Commission to see if indigent defense funds would be available for this. I spoke to the director, Paul Levy and described to him what I wanted to do and why it was necessary. Paul laughed out loud.

"Mike... no. No way would we fund this. You can get a basic animation from your accident reconstructionist."

"But it won't do it justice," I said, managing to keep the whine out of my voice. "We need to show the actual body movements to properly convey the terror."

"Mike, I've told you before, the state of Oregon doesn't fund the Gold Standard of defense. Arnold Law may want to provide the Gold Standard, but we only fund the 'minimally constitutionally competent' defense. If you want the Gold Standard, somebody else has to pay for it."

That left us to move little stick figures around for the jury's entertainment. Not exactly the portrayal of a terrifying encounter I'd had in mind.

When I told Emilia the bad news, she did a little brainstorming. She asked, "What else could we do? Let's figure this out. What does nobody else do? What can we do for Gerald here?"

"I dunno," I said, "let me think." The first thing to come to mind was videotaping our own reenactment, and at first blush, it didn't seem completely crazy. "We could cordon off a big parking lot at night and stripe ourselves a road, and… just make it happen. We could borrow a Nissan Rogue and a Denali pickup and work through the scenario in slow motion. We could buy a couple of beater cars and crash them together at the appropriate speed and have a time-lapse camera view of a dummy getting hit. Heck, I would volunteer to sit in the truck."

"Um, we will have to vet some of that, but yeah, sounds good to me. I'll make it happen." I knew she would. Emilia's the office fixer. If it can be done, she'll get it done.

Over the course of the next several weeks Emilia and I continued to talk through my vision for a reenactment and what we would need. It was a lot like prepping for trial, and a trial is not unlike producing a theatrical play. The main trial lawyer is the producer, the director, the casting director, and one of the main actors, if not the star – and hopefully someone who the jury recognizes as the protagonist. It's a live production where you can't practice every scene. There are lots of moving parts that must be planned for: exhibits, witnesses served with subpoenas, witnesses showing up at the right time, cross-examination questions written in advance… sometimes the punch list seems endless.

And, yes, there is a script. I write out as many questions as I can think of in advance. I also consider the likely answers and how to respond to any given one. I hardly ever follow the script, because I get on a roll and go where the trial leads me. But the script is there if I need it.

Scripts for plays or television shows go through many edits, sometimes even after the production begins, because that's when you begin to see what doesn't work. And that's where the similarities with a trial end. You only get one chance in court. Some lawyers scoff at the idea of scripting their case, but to me that's either lazy or crazy. What are the odds of coming up with exactly the right way to say something, right there on the fly? Pretty slim, I'd say. And if you listen back to your own closing argument now and then, as I do, you can always find things you could have said better. Even if you don't ever refer to a script you've written, it's there in your head. Just by going through the exercise you've improved your chances of connecting with the jury by using the right ideas and phrasing.

As I got deeper into it, I realized that planning our reenactment was actually more difficult than prepping for trial. That's because the reenactment needed to accomplish several goals at once. First, I wanted to learn from it. I hoped that by putting things into motion visually it would answer my own questions about the case and help me anticipate some questions the jury would want answered – maybe ones I hadn't thought of yet. Ideally, the reenactment would answer so many questions that it would leave the jurors no room to draw their own conclusions or inferences as to what happened. Covering all possible questions is a big job for a defense team, but I knew that the last thing we needed was for a juror to come up with some stumper – something that the panel would either blame me for not answering, or try to answer for themselves. Either possibility could increase the chance of a conviction, so it's always best for the defense to save the jury the trouble of "solving" the case.

The second thing we were trying to accomplish was to create an admissible exhibit for trial. All it would take to get the judge to rule it inadmissible, we knew, was one tiny, erroneous detail – something to allow the prosecution to paint it as "misleading." We had to be 100 percent accurate, 100 percent fair. There'd be no going back and doing it again once the trial started.

I brought Gerald into the conversation about the reenactment, of course, and one of his first questions was the obvious one: "Do you think this will help convince the jury?"

"Gerald, back up. Who are we trying to convince at trial?

"The jury," he said, obviously thinking this was a dumb game.

"Wrong. We aren't trying to convince anyone. That's not our goal. It's great if we do, but that's not our primary mission."

"I don't get it," he said.

"We aren't trying to convince jurors. We are trying to arm the jurors who are already on our side with arguments to convince the other jurors. All I need is one jury member to hang the trial and you're not convicted. But I don't want to hang it, I want an acquittal. To get one, I need help. I need the jurors to be my avatars, speaking my words, articulating my message, and making my arguments. And if I didn't properly anticipate an adverse argument by a bad juror, I need my armed jurors – the ones I've equipped with information – to be so indoctrinated into my theory of the case that they come up with a counterpoint that fits our narrative. They're our deliberation warriors and with our evidence, we train them for battle. That battle doesn't happen in the courtroom, it happens behind closed doors in the jury room. With a good, admissible video reenactment, we can give jurors a wonderful tool with which to convince fence-sitters. They can say, "Look here. This shows X or Y." A piece of visual evidence like this has many uses. That's why it's so important that we do this right."

Emilia and Verne got to work setting up our production. We didn't have the original Denali, but I had just happened to have a big black pickup with similar characteristics. We didn't have the original Rogue, but Patricia convinced a local dealership to loan us a similar SUV. Emilia found us a dry, private indoor space at the Lane County Events Center that we were sure was large enough to handle all the evidence. Indoors and dry was key: About a month earlier, we tried the reenactment outdoors, but it was pouring rain and it looked like we might have to wait well past midnight to get the site dark enough to resemble the scene on Bob Straub Parkway on the night of the shooting. At least the building on the fairgrounds was windowless and would let us kill lights from an electrical panel.

On the evening of our reenactment, there were six of us on hand – me, Emilia, Verne and Patricia (our investigators), and two male friends of Verne's. Jim and Hal were invited because they were about the same height and weight as Gerald and Crofut. Verne had provided them clothing that was very similar to what Gerald and Crofut had been wearing, too.

The room was windowless and mostly featureless, an exhibition space. The word "cavernous" came to mind as Verne and his friends drove in the vehicles and began marking off the measurements we needed to recreate the scene of the shooting. But that's when it hit us – the room was actually too small! While the space was long enough to accommodate the distance from the front of the truck to Crofut's body, it wasn't long enough to include the distance we needed from the back of the Nissan SUV all the way to where we presumed that Gerald had stood. Improvising, we parked the cars just outside of the room, on the loading dock. It wasn't perfect, but it was close enough.

Then Verne began setting out little wooden stands from a giant box.

"What are these for?" I asked, peering into the box.

Verne pulled out a smaller box and handed it to me, as if it would answer my question. "Here," he said, "these are the labels that go with the wooden stands."

In the small box I saw labels with the words "brain" and "skull" and "skin" written on them. Verne planned to put a marker where each piece of evidence was collected, measuring out exactly where it would have been found. As that process began, I swiped one of the wooden stands and handed it to Emilia's eight-month-old son, who was waving his arms and vocalizing from the sling she'd tied onto her back. Then she and I began putting labels on markers. Whenever Verne yelled "Brain!" I would grab a "brain" marker and run it over to him. Then I would hear "Skull!" and do the same thing. When all the collected evidence was in place, we taped the outline of Crofut's body and put an exemplar rifle where it was found. All of this setup took more than two hours. Well before we were done, Emilia's son was sound asleep on her back.

At my invitation, we all began by walking around the scene and sharing our impressions. Patricia was the first to comment. "Wow," she said, "85 feet is a long, long way to follow someone who's armed with a rifle." We chuckled, murmured or whistled low in agreement with her.

"Crofut must have been insane," Emilia added. "He was 100 percent crazy to follow Gerald out there in the dark." I agreed, and I thought a jury would too, if they could somehow see what 85 feet really looked like. I wondered aloud if the judge would let me lay out a tape measure from the bench and down the gallery aisle. I suspected that the tape would go all the way out the door, into the hallway, and maybe as far as the aisle of the courtroom across the hall.

Patricia spoke again, saying, "That gun must have been really powerful, because that shot did a total number on that guy's head." We stood in the center of the debris field with little wooden markers popped up around us like crocuses. The shape of the debris field resembled a very large fan.

Verne agreed. "It was lights out the second the trigger was pulled." He shook his head as he looked around at the sobering scene. "That was it. Boom. Nothing."

After walking the scene, we started to document it by taking photographs. We would use the photos to refresh our recollection, to refresh Gerald's recollection if he wanted to testify, and then, if admitted as evidence, we'd also use them as demonstrative exhibits at trial. Emilia was our photographer, climbing around the vehicles and among the little debris markers, her sleeping son still on her back. Her job included sitting in each seat that was occupied by a driver or passenger that night and taking pictures of the scene from each vantage point.

(Photo: The team discusses what to do next as Emilia takes photos and gives directions.)

What did we learn? Well, the visibility for someone sitting in the passenger seat of the Nissan Rogue SUV was really limited. The Rogue had crashed at such an acute angle in relation to the truck that the bed of the truck would have completely blocked Brenda Crofut from seeing anything at all. She talked about watching David Crofut walk away from her, but it certainly wouldn't have been many steps before he was completely out of sight. Similarly, if Crofut was out in front of the Rogue, waving his arms or stomping around, the Denali and its open door would have blocked just about everything. Brenda could legitimately claim that she hadn't seen her husband stalking around, back and forth in front of the Denali, waving his arms and being aggressive. That's because she couldn't have seen anything until she got out of her seat.

(Photo: What Brenda could or couldn't see from the Nissan Rogue's passenger seat, while Mike looks on.)

The next thing we did was get our actors into costume so that we could retrace their steps and likely actions. We videotaped the various scenarios based on what we had learned from Gerald, from law enforcement, and from the public. We did it in slow motion, multiple times, stopping to reset the players and to try answering anticipated questions. While it was useful to imagine how this part of the incident had happened, nothing ground-breaking was gained.

Then I asked Verne to kill the lights in the room. At first it was very dark, and then we were all very annoyed. For safety, the building had exit signs all over the place, ones that were – as intended – bright and obvious. They were so bright, in fact, that we didn't need the overhead lights to see well in the darkened room. We all hunted through our cars for blankets and jackets we could use to cover the signs. When it was as dark as we could get it, we put our pretend-Crofut and our pretend-Gerald in place. Crofut stood in front of the truck, and Gerald stood several feet back. I asked Verne to turn on the headlights of the truck as Emilia and I stood with the pretend Gerald, facing the lights.

When the headlights clicked on, the brightness of them in such a dark space completely blinded me at first. I had to shield my eyes until they adjusted. Once I could look up, I could see the shadowy figure of our pretend Crofut. He was wearing a hoodie sweatshirt, and he had pulled the hood up onto his head. His figure was so dark that it was almost black. When he moved, shafts of light streamed through from under his arms and between his legs. Unless his hands were extended away from his body, I couldn't see them well. I certainly couldn't see what, if anything, he had in his hands. "Hal," I said. "Reach into your pants pocket."

Hal/Crofut did as instructed. I could see the outline of his elbow popping up and out to the side, but I could not tell what he was doing with his hand. I told him to do it again, adding, "This time reach into your sweatshirt pocket." He did as I asked, and again, all I could really see was the outline of his arm moving. I walked over to Hal and looked at Jim, our Gerald, from what would have been Crofut's vantage point. Jim/Gerald was clearly outlined in the light. He held a cell phone up to his left ear, and the exemplar firearm was in his right hand, against his body, pointed at the ground. It was obvious that there was more than enough light from the headlights pointed at Gerald for Crofut to see what Gerald was carrying. Jim/Gerald looked like an actor, spotlighted on a stage. I walked back to Jim/Gerald and turned back into the light.

Once in position, I asked Hal/Crofut to walk slowly toward me. As he did, more of his features were gradually revealed. He appeared as a frightening figure cloaked in dark shadows when he was more than a few feet from me, but up close I could see more of his hands and his face. I thought about the gun powder residue testing. If Crofut had been up in his Gerald's face, Gerald would have been better able to see Crofut's hands and what he was doing with them. If Crofut was further away, and had told Gerald that he had a gun, Gerald would not have been able to determine what Crofut was doing or reaching for. If Crofut had been within that seven-foot distance when he reached into his pocket, Gerald might not have shot him — at least not in self-defense. He would have been able to see what he didn't learn until after the shooting: that Crofut was unarmed and posed no threat.

When I asked Hal/Crofut to walk back towards the truck, Emilia walked up to me, camera in hand. "It occurs to me," she said, "that Gerald's 911 call may have played a role in the shooting."

"How do you mean?"

"His attention was divided. He was on the phone, trying to talk to the dispatcher. He had this random guy out there in front of him, who he obviously couldn't see all that well. He had the lights shining bright in his face. It makes me think of how many car accidents are caused by cell phone use. Driving is a divided-attention task. Adding a phone to the mix is just too much. It requires too much thought, too much attention. I wonder if Gerald would have been able to pay more attention to Crofut and his hands if he wasn't trying to also talk to the 911 dispatcher."

Verne walked up as Emilia was speaking. He added, "Don't forget the people driving by. He had Crofut to watch, Boyles, Tennefoss-Favre, and all the other cars on the road. There was a lot happening around him in a short amount of time."

Emilia continued, "Maybe Crofut told him what he was doing before he reached into his pocket. Maybe he told Gerald he was going to grab some money, and Gerald was paying more attention to the dispatcher. Maybe that's why he shot him."

We all stood there for a while, letting that thought sink in. "Does that make it murder?" Patricia asked.

"No," I said, "Not murder. But maybe manslaughter, if the jury wanted to compromise. That's 10 years mandatory."

There was a general group shrug and scattered sighs as we all set aside that scenario. I asked Verne to turn on the lights. When our eyes readjusted I motioned to Hal and Jim, and walked them over to the area of the scene where the outline of the body was taped. I asked Jim/Gerald to hold the gun up a bit, towards Hal/Crofut. Then I asked Hal/Crofut to try to grab at the rifle. I could see how the two men could have struggled. If Crofut grabbed the gun, and Gerald pulled it back, it could have pulled Crofut forward. Jim and Hal ran the scenario for us a few times, and Hal really got into it as Crofut, even falling forward onto the hard concrete floor several times – first knees, then chest. We should have brought wrestling mats.

With Hal/Crofut lying on the floor and Jim/Gerald standing with the gun up, Emilia said, "What if they struggled over the gun, and Crofut was falling forward already when the shot was fired? Gerald said he wasn't trying to shoot him in the head. He was aiming at center mass, but hit him in the head. What if Crofut's head was a little lower than normal because he was already falling forward?"

Verne said, "What was his BAC again?"

"Point one five," Emilia replied.

"That's pretty drunk," Verne said. "Think about how a guy that drunk would perform on field sobriety tests. He would struggle to keep his balance. If he was pushed or pulled around, it wouldn't be hard for him to fall."

"I wish we knew how long it was between the time when Crofut touched the gun and when the shot occurred," I said.

Patricia fielded that one with another question, "Gerald didn't say?"

"No, not really. He just remembers everything happening really fast."

"There's a muffled sound on the 911 call right before the dispatcher transferred the call," Emilia remembered. "I wonder if that was the sound of the two guys fighting over the gun. Maybe Gerald jumped back from that and shot him."

"So what about him reaching into his pocket?" Verne asked. "When did he get the money out?"

"I guess they could have scuffled, and Gerald jumped back, and then Crofut moved towards his pocket, then boom," Emilia offered. "But that wouldn't give Crofut time to pull something out of his pocket and start throwing it or handing it to Gerald."

"Maybe he already had the cash in his hand," I speculated. "Maybe the reason his hand was out was that he was falling, and he was going to use his hand to break his fall."

"I don't know where the cash comes in, but the case is better if the gun-grabbing comes right before the shot," Emilia said. "That would be horrific. If I'm the juror, I'm going to acquit him if that's the case."

"But if the gun-grabbin' was a while before?" Verne countered. "Like 30 seconds or a minute more. Then what?"

"Doesn't make it unreasonable to shoot," I pointed out. "The guy had grabbed at the gun before, Gerald could have thought he would try it again."

"I wish we had a witness to the statements that Gerald said Crofut made," Emilia said, just a touch ruefully. "He told Mike that Crofut said he had a gun. If we had some corroboration, it would make this a lot easier."

"We've got what we've got," I said crisply. "Hal? Jim? Again, if you don't mind. With the lights off, please."

Verne flipped off the lights. The rest of us, except Emilia's son, who was still sound asleep on mom's back, watched the scene as it played out before us. Here were Hal and Jim, two grown men with families, jobs, and children, fighting for their lives over a rifle – illuminated only by the single pool of light created by the Denali's headlights. It was chilling to know that no one, save Gerald and Crofut themselves, and the drivers who had caught fleeting glimpses as they glided by in their own vehicles, had seen the confrontation more clearly.

Finally it was time to uncover the exit signs, turn on the overhead lights, and pick up the pieces of our reenactment. While Hal and Jim pulled up tape, I gathered the various wooden stands and their grisly-named labels. While stacking the stands back into Verne's big box, I stood thinking about what all this meant. Putting myself in Gerald's place, I felt more than ever that he had been entitled to fear for his life that night. If I had been in his shoes, standing in front of an aggressive man whom I couldn't really see, one who was threatening me, and one who was continuing to advance on me despite the gun that I now knew could be easily seen in the headlights… well, hell yes, I'd fire.

For the first time I felt that the bad-acts evidence against Gerald wouldn't sink us. If somehow we could get the jury to see that scene as Gerald saw it, if we could get a "jury view" at that spot, at night, so each juror could appreciate the blindingly bright scene Gerald had confronted, the shadowy and menacing figure that Crofut would have seemed, and the void of darkness surrounding it all… I felt we had a very high likelihood of prevailing. And if we couldn't get the judge to bring the jury out there to Bob Straub Parkway, well, our reenactment video would have to do.

I wonder how dark we can get that courtroom?

(Photo: Gerald's perspective while on the phone with 911.)

(Photo: Patricia Jaqua tests the hypothesis that Brenda could roll over the dead weight of a grown man.)

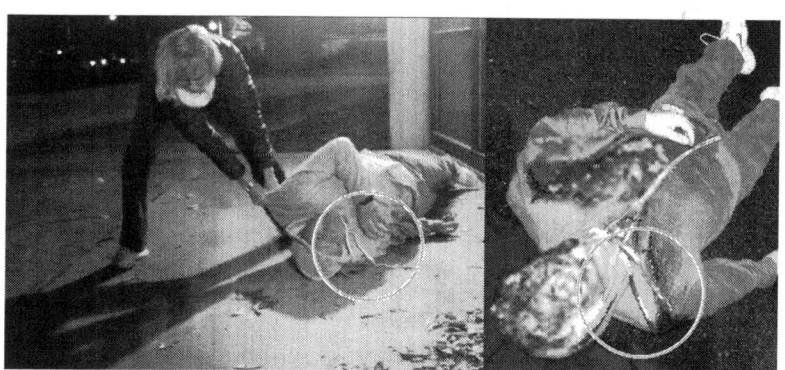

(Photo: Patricia Jaqua also supports the "roll over" hypothesis by recreating the layout of Crofut's hoodie drawstrings.)

CHAPTER 29

A MEETING WITH GERALD IN JAIL

The day after our reenactment, I went to the jail to update Gerald on what we had learned. I had Emilia transfer all of her photos to the office hard drive in the morning, and I printed out a few black and white shots from the exercise for him to see. When he came into the attorney visiting room, I greeted him and we made the usual small talk. Then I showed him the photos.

He picked through them, and then selected one. It was taken from behind "Gerald," showing the back of his body, with him facing the truck. In front of him stands a dark figure, and behind the figure are the bright, white lights of the pickup.

He leaned over the small square table and held the photo with both hands. "This," he said. "This is what it looked like. This is what I remember."

I was pleased. "Alright. We'll work the pictures from this series into our case, maybe opening and closing statements." I tucked the photos into an envelope, which I handed to him. "How are you doing?"

"I'm alright. Mostly. Did you see anything in the news this week about an inmate who died here at the jail? On my floor there was almost another death. Me and the other guys, we heard the sounds of someone gagging or choking. I started yelling for help, and so did the other guys. We yelled and screamed for someone to come. No one came. We yelled for a while more, and finally a deputy walked up. I could still hear the man gagging, obviously not well, but the deputy stopped to chastise all of us for the noise before he went to check on the man. The inmate could have died, but disciplining us was more important."

"That's horrible."

"I know, right? I was pretty upset about the whole thing. The deputies, they threaten to throw you in the hole if you make too much noise, even if it's to try and get medical attention for another inmate. So I filed a complaint against the deputy."

"Did it go anywhere?"

"Not really. But I did get someone's attention. I was taken from my cell down into one of the interview rooms in the hall. I was by myself, sitting all shackled up and stuff. Two sheriff's deputies came in, and they stood over me. It's like they thought they were interrogating me. Me, of all people!"

"What the fuck?" I said. "They know you have an attorney!"

"I'm sitting there with these deputies. All I'm doing is requesting repeatedly to have my lawyer present, and that the session be ended. I said it over and over. The deputies told me that I wasn't entitled to have a lawyer present with me, and that I had to answer their questions."

"Did they ask you about the shooting? What were they trying to get out of you?"

"Honestly, it was like they were trying to bully me into agreeing that the information I put in my complaint against the deputies about the jail's responses to medical needs was false."

"It sounds like they were trying to cover their asses. This is a violation of your right to counsel! I'm getting so sick of this county."

"This just makes me want to get out of here more than ever," Gerald said, adding, "They had me in an interrogation room, which should have had a video camera. I wonder if they recorded it."

"Well I'd recommend that we send a tort claim notice to the county, to put them on notice of what happened and demand a copy of the tape, if they have it. You could have claims for the torts of intentional infliction of emotional distress, in addition to the relevant 1983 claims. They probably won't go anywhere, but if you sent the tort claim notice, it might at least result in some training to help out the next inmate in that situation."

He nodded. "Please, I'd appreciate it if you could do that."

I got ready to leave. "I'm on it. Hang in there, okay? We got this," I said.

"Don't worry about me, Mike. In the Marines, we did these marches in the desert. We'd start at 7 P.M., completely loaded with gear and guns, and hike all night long. They'd push us hard for 50 minutes, then let us rest for 10 minutes. We would do more than 30 miles like that before the sun came up. When we were finished, my toenails came off with my socks." He looked around the attorney visiting room, and gestured to the jail. "This is nothing. I've got this."

When I returned to my office that afternoon, I drafted the tort claim notice and sent it off to the jail, the sheriff's department, and county counsel. Even if the claims never got filed, perhaps someone in the county counsel's office would have a word with the deputies at the jail about interrogating represented individuals in the jail.

A few days later we received a response from the county. The county denied that any wrongdoing was done, stating that the jail was authorized to question Gerald about his complaints against the deputies. I took the response back to Gerald at the jail, and discussed his options with him. When he didn't have additional questions, I decided to avail myself of the opportunity to ask a question.

"Gerald, why is it that you are the center of any drama that happens? It's like, if something is going to happen where you are – well, *there you are*, right in the center of it."

He shrugged. "Just lucky I guess. But you're right. It happens to me a lot."

"Do you think it's because you insert yourself? That you somehow purposefully draw it to you?"

He shrugged. "Could be. I don't really think about it."

"What's the deal with the complaints against the deputies? You don't know any of those guys on your floor. You don't ever see them. Do you even know their names?"

"No," Gerald said. "I don't."

"It's great and all, that you stick your neck out, but why do you do it? Especially for those guys? You are on a floor with sex offenders who are facing more prison time than you. If you even get into a conversation with them, they have all the incentive in the world to make up a story about you admitting to killing Crofut without cause. You need to protect yourself. "

"Maybe they would, maybe they wouldn't." He rubbed his face with one hand, and when he looked at me again, I thought that he looked especially tired, and a lot older than he had when he first came into my office.

Then he looked up with an expression of almost childlike sweetness. "Do you know what we do every night, before bed? All of us? We sit by our doors, and we pray together. We can't see each other, but we do it anyway – same time every day. We all just get down on our knees by the door and pray. Everyone on my row. The guys come and go. A lot of the ones who were here when I started have already been sentenced, so they're gone. The ones still here have nothing. I'm the one constant, so I lead them in prayer."

"Wow," I said. "I had no idea." It was such a frank admission from him that I felt uncomfortable, like I had to break the spell, so I said, "You just make friends everywhere you go, don't you?"

Gerald chuckled. "I wouldn't call them friends," he said. "But they are kind of 'my people' now."

"Maybe for now, but not for long," I countered. "They sure as hell won't be 'your people' for the next 25 years, not if I can help it."

CHAPTER 30
HOW DID GERALD GET HERE?

I've said it before and I'll say it again: From the moment Gerald walked into my office, I liked him. He was confident in an understated, self-deprecating way, yet he had a certain charisma, the kind of magnetic attraction that draws people in. If Gerald was standing in a room of strangers, there is something about him that would make him noticeable to anyone who walked in. It's certainly not because he's a big, visible man (not hardly). It's more because he has a big laugh and a bigger heart. There's just something that – to me, at least – makes the guy worth being around. I truly mourned the fact that the guy was in jail.

Whenever I found my confidence wavering during his case, I would get in the truck to go meet with Gerald. The force of his personality would draw me back to center and keep me positive and focused. And it went both ways, as friendships always do.

Just as he gave me the occasional pep talk, I'd return the favor by giving him one. Ticking off the points on my fingers, I'd remind him of all the positive evidence we had, all the reasons why he should be exonerated at trial. Together we operated from the basic understanding that this case had put each of us in a very rough spot, for differing reasons and purposes. Of course, only he was at he was at risk of going to prison for 25 years to life.

Early on in our attorney-client relationship, I told him the old lawyer's story of an attorney and his client in a murder trial. "This attorney was amazing," I told him. 'His cross-examination was witty but brutal. It was precise and scalpel-like, causing the death of the prosecution's case by a thousand tiny cuts. In his closing the jury nodded and smiled when he spoke of the Constitution, of reasonable doubt and of the facts that undermined the prosecutor's case. During the prosecutor's closing, the jurors rolled their eyes when the prosecutor talked about the client's alleged violent past, perhaps recalling what the defense attorney said moments before about those allegations being nothing but rumor and innuendo. Everything predicted a fast not-guilty verdict. After the judge read the jury its instructions, the jurors filed out to deliberate."

Here I paused for effect.

"Three hours later they came back with the verdict," I continued. "They all walked in with their heads down, making eye contact with no one. Still staring at the floor, the foreman gave the bailiff the verdict form. The judge read it. Everyone gasped, even the prosecutor. The judge read, 'On the sole count of Murder, we, the jury, find the Defendant guilty.' The judge quickly sentenced the defendant to the mandatory minimum and the defendant turned to his attorney, who had just tried the perfect case, and said, 'What now?' The attorney replied remorsefully, "Well, you're going to go take a ride with those deputies, and I'm going to go out for a steak dinner with my wife."

Gerald laughed when I told him that story. "I get it," he said. "No matter what happens, this is my life and you don't live with the consequences."

I was quick to tell him that he was only partly correct. The steak dinner would be a solemn and sad one, I assured him, and I'd have PTSD for weeks as I relived my screw-ups at trial. But in the end, I would learn from my mistakes and do better for the next client. On the day when I had finally put it behind me, though, "you'd still be in prison."

It was meant as a joke and we laughed. But there was a message in the story: It said, "We may be in this together right now, but there's no guarantee we'll walk away from it together at the end." It's just how it is when you're a criminal defense attorney.

Now, and not for the first time, my interactions with Gerald made me think about my own life. We had so much in common – lots of good stuff, but also some of the bad stuff, like a tendency to run our mouths and (at least when we were younger) use our fists to settle disputes. Why was it that we came into this case from such different directions? And how was it that we would likely walk away in different directions, too?

Opportunities and choices. That's what it always comes down to. In another life, could Gerald have been the attorney and me the defendant? That's a very unnerving thought.

For all of Gerald's successes in the Marines, in MMA/UFC, in Blackwater and eventually back in Oregon operating his MMA training center, I had learned by talking to Gerald that there had remained subtle currents of failure and dislocation that left his psyche open and impressionable, just as when he was a child.

Back in his training days in the Marines, Gerald's success as a sniper obscured a basic inability to fit in. Not everyone knew it, but Gerald struggled to assimilate into the culture and rank of the military. Instead of hanging out with his colleagues or his family when he was on leave, he separated himself. He rode the "loser cruiser" from Camp Pendleton to the nearby city of Oceanside, Calif. There he'd go down to the pier with a backpack and a sleeping bag and just disappear. He camped on the streets, on beaches or down in an amphitheater, always in the open and happily sharing his military meals, his MREs, with the homeless. If he wasn't ragamuffin' around like this, he was driving to Los Angeles to spend the weekend training in the skills he'd need if he wanted to fight in the UFC.

Gerald found a home in Blackwater and for a time, he made it his own. It was the living, pulsing counterargument to every time William Strebendt said his son was weak, because this was a place for the elite few and it was a place where Gerald not only survived but thrived. The infamous Blackwater training compound was located in Moyock, North Carolina, at the end of Puddin Ridge Road in the Great Dismal Swamp. It consisted of 2,000 acres of junk land that the ex-Navy SEAL Eric Prince purchased and developed. There was an FBI-staffed driving school (Defensive Driving Institute), an airfield, water for amphibious training, rappelling towers, barracks, and shooting ranges galore. In other words, Blackwater had military facilities that the military would be jealous of. Heck, Blackwater had more Navy SEALs than the Navy did! And the culture was imprinted on every inch of the place. The headquarters building had huge front doors like the head-quarters of Microsoft, but Blackwater's doors had machine-gun barrels for handles.

Just as it was in Gerald's childhood, the rules were there to be at least nudged. Blackwater assignments were thrilling, powerful, frighten-ing, violent, and dangerous. Whether Blackwater guards truly used exces-sive force and firepower is unproven, but stories were told, and war zone rules of engagement are by nature mutable or at least confusing. Certainly the bias was for action; Blackwater operators epitomized shooting first and asking questions later. Gerald's rifle had been his constant compan-ion in the Marines, and if anything, the bond became closer while he was with Blackwater.

Once in Kabul, the continual violence couldn't help but have a pro-found impact on anyone who experienced it. On his first tour, it brought out some good in Gerald. He was charitable to the locals, even providing clean, cold water and Dixie cups to an old man who lived near Blackwater headquarters, which shared a wall with the Indian Embassy. Holding his hand over his heart to express his gratitude at the gift, the old man would then distribute the water to his neighbors and their children.

But trouble was always nearby. If you google the Indian Embassy in Kabul and search for images, you will see a photo of the wreckage left after a suicide bomber rammed the front wall of the Embassy, presumably to ham-mer the Blackwater compound. The same old man can be seen fleeing, with a look of terror on his face.

Gerald's second tour of duty with Blackwater in Afghanistan changed how he perceived the world. He could feel his humanity slipping away, he told me. He felt hate. He despised the way the young Afghani men sneered at him as they drove through the streets, knowing that an IED or an ambush could be awaiting him a block ahead. When under fire, the guards would often shoot in every direction, not knowing where the attack was coming from. They invariably hit random people who had nothing to do with the ambush, as well as animals, food stalls, and buildings. It was typical for pieces of wood, rock, dirt, and even exploded fruits and vegetables to rain down upon them during a firefight. Most of the time, nobody knew exactly what was happening or why. It was nonstop chaos, and it made Gerald Strebendt a different person, as it had so many others.

Gerald has said that, despite all the thousands of shots he had to have fired, he never knew for sure if he actually killed anyone during his Blackwater years. I think he agrees with me, though, that it's highly likely he did. But an operator didn't stick around long enough to find out, not in Kabul. You kept moving, running, and gunning. The only objective that mattered was safe exit from whatever skirmish or battle was going on.

By the time Gerald came home to the U.S., he was no longer small or weak. His world was very black-and-white. He was quick to label the world's users, abusers, and the mentally weak. While he utterly despised bullies, he admired those who used their strength and personal power for what he considered to be honorable purposes. He felt protective of those he perceived to be innocent, and he felt an obligation to provide for those who could not provide for themselves. In his own way, he was an honorable man – not a bully, but a bully of bullies. In fact, his ex-wife Rachel came to call him "a bully." He didn't go out looking for fights, but they frequently found him. He didn't start them; he finished them.

As ever, he was "The Finishing Machine," I thought.

There was no reintegration process when Gerald came home to Oregon for good. Since he had not completed a deployment with the military there were no psych evaluations and no counselors; there was no transition from his Blackwater life to his home life. He lacked the patience he previously possessed. He lashed out without much provocation. His temper rode near the surface at all times.

Gerald fell back on the skills he had learned in his 10 years abroad and opened his training gym. It went well and, financially at least, he began to thrive as a businessman. His personal life, however, did not follow. Gerald made several attempts to reconcile with his father, purchasing him presents and loaning him money. The two argued, and when they became more permanently estranged, his father told people he avoided sitting by the windows when at home. William said he feared that his son might kill him with his sniper rifle.

Like so many vets before him, Gerald struggled with nightmares. He began to drink. He gained some weight. His wife, Rachel, found him to be more confrontational than before, and almost unfailingly aggressive when threatened. Her once happy-go-lucky husband had failed to come home from the war, and the marriage failed. In all the relationships that followed, Gerald admits that he struggled to be present for his partners, to support them in the way they needed when they needed it. For all that Gerald desperately needed – love, affirmation, and companionship – he was unable to provide it to his partners in return.

When I truly had the whole picture, when I could see beyond Gerald's many achievements and look underneath the great stories he told, I understood the Parade of Horribles. Not all, but most, of Gerald's documented acts of aggression occurred after he returned home from his Blackwater assignments. His status as a vet doesn't excuse any of it, but it does explain the aggressive, angry, drunk, paranoid or combative person that Gerald's critics and complainants described.

Like many a vet before and after him, Gerald didn't understand what was happening to him. His former wife, Rachel, didn't understand what was happening to him, either. And there was no one else close enough to him to pick up on the fact that maybe this Strebendt guy wasn't just a bad man; maybe he was a damaged or hurting man. Even Gerald tended to think that *how* he was, was only because of *who* he was.

Instead of getting treatment and counseling, Gerald pushed back and did the opposite of what he should have done. He avoided the memories. He didn't talk about Afghanistan unless drinking heavily. Although he was surrounded by people in the gym and in the MMA community he cultivated, he went out of his way to be alone, craving peace and quiet. People who commented on Facebook about him listening to Enya weren't kidding: he listened to the Gaelic singer's ethereal music while driving, and returned to the coast and the woods often. He drank a lot. He drove a lot. He drank and drove a lot. He had a lift kit and winch installed on his truck so he could make it through the deep snow and keep driving even in the dead of winter. He used the modifications to go up to the Terwilliger Hot Springs at Cougar Reservoir on Christmas and New Year's Eves. Very rarely was anyone up there on holiday nights. He would 4x4 it all the way up to the trailhead by himself and bring a candle to light the cave. He bathed alone in the steamy, warm water while drinking most of a fifth of bottom-shelf vodka.

Of course, I strongly suspected that Gerald had suffered from Post-Traumatic Stress Disorder (PTSD), and that he perhaps still did – who wouldn't? I contacted psychologist Dr. Richard Hulteng to perform a forensic psychological evaluation and determine whether PTSD was a factor in this case. If there was a diagnosis made, it could play a role in Gerald's defense, and if convicted, it could be a mitigating factor in his sentencing.

While Gerald would not have sought out the services of Dr. Hulteng or any similar expert on his own, he was willing to do it to improve his chances in the murder case. Hulteng examined Gerald for about three hours, putting him through the battery of accepted and recommended tests for the disorder. The results were clear and for me, unexpected. Despite all of the classic hallmarks of the disease in everything I'd learned about Gerald Strebendt, the man did not meet the clinical threshold for a diagnosis. No, Dr. Hulteng said, Gerald Strebendt was *not* suffering from PTSD.

I was chagrined. But I think that, at some level, Gerald felt good about the results. It meant he was strong, right?

From what I knew of Gerald, I found the result confusing. I asked Hulteng to explain. He said, "The diagnosis is accurate, assuming your client was truthful during the examination." Could Gerald beat the exam somehow? Had he tried to beat it? Why would he do that?

It's too simple or lazy to say that there's been a straight path from Gerald's earliest life to his indictment on murder charges. Nobody's life is that easy to figure out. Instead, I see one big, vicious circle that closed with Crofut's death and Gerald's arrest. It began with the divorce of Gerald's mother and father. Then it looped through the mistreatment of Gerald's mom, the fact that Gerald and his brother were allowed to avoid responsibilities, the drinking, the childhood law-breaking that became Gerald's adult law-breaking, the false feelings of strength that came from the military and MMA/UFC, finally leading to Gerald's overblown sense of justice and his determination to be the strong arbiter of right and wrong.

When Gerald killed Crofut, some might say – I might – that it was the culmination of a lifetime of education by his screwed-up father and Gerald's own escalating behaviors that were never reined in. Ultimately, Gerald stood on a road in the dark, scared and alone, armed with a rifle against a man who had drunkenly bullied him, just like his father had. Gerald had made it his life's work to be strong in situations of this sort. He'd been on dark roads before, fighting for his life, with only a gun to protect himself. He wasn't a scared child anymore, and his emotions and behaviors had no established limits. Crofut picked the wrong Marine to confront on a dark, country road.

CHAPTER 31

THE FOCUS GROUP

After the reenactment, we were preparing in earnest for trial. We were drilling deep on the self-defense case, of course, but we were also putting considerable time and effort into being ready to meet the bad-acts evidence head-on, if we had to. We thought the bad acts deserved to be ruled inadmissible, and we hoped it would be, but it would be dangerously foolish to base our prep on beliefs, hopes or assumptions.

Overall, we felt good about where the case was and where it was going. But, after a year of living with the facts, it was time to once again be aggressive about confronting any confirmation biases we'd developed along the way. It was time for fresh eyes and ears, ones guided by different sets of beliefs and prejudices. We needed to conduct a focus group – assemble a mock jury and show them the evidence for and against Gerald Strebendt's innocence.

Focus group presentations, mock juries and mock trials are staples in high-stakes civil litigation, but they're generally under-utilized by criminal defendants and their attorneys. It's a time-and-money decision, of course, but I also think that most traditional defense attorneys are pretty nearsighted when it comes to how a case should be handled, often having learned their case routines as an overburdened prosecutor or public defender.

So, while putting together a focus group with the help of a consultant can cost tens of thousands of dollars, I intended to do mine for the cost of sandwiches. And instead of choosing the perfect neutral venue, I'd strip away all the structures and distractions of doing a high-buck event; do it in the office; get to the heart of what a focus group really should be, which is a conversation with outsiders, average folks, about the case.

Of course, we didn't have the luxury of creating some sort of random process to select our jurors. I wasn't disappointed by that; I knew that jury consultants weren't particularly scientific about creating their supposedly "representative" pools, either. Many utilized temp agencies, which meant the resulting pool was over-balanced with the unemployed or underemployed. So our low-cost version of the process had us pulling nine volunteers from among the neighbors, friends, and family of the defense team. One of our investigators brought his significant other. Our brand-new receptionist, with no prior legal experience and no familiarity with the case, came with her husband. We also had a retired public defender, whom I knew mostly because he ate breakfast in the tiny Hult Plaza Café in our building, a throwback of a diner that attracted a gray-haired group of regulars every morning. Even Emilia's grandparents signed on.

The purpose of holding the focus group was two-pronged – to test the evidence and our trial strategy on actual people who could be jurors in the case, *and* to figure out what kind of jurors we wanted on the panel. While both aims are important in a focus group, the foremost is figuring out the jury selection. An essential component of our time with the mock jury included testing out some of our jury-selection questions to see how the incoming answers might correlate with attitudes about the case by the end of the day. After comparing the demographics and the beliefs of the group with their reactions to the evidence, I'd have a better idea what types of jurors I didn't want.

On the chosen day, we seated our mock jury/focus group at tables arranged in an L-shape, facing a screen on which we would show a PowerPoint presentation of the case. But first we asked the group to fill out a short version of our proposed jury questionnaire. We asked both demographic questions and "forced answer" questions – multiple choice questions that don't allow you to say "I don't know."

Why ask these questions? You might think the answer here is "to help us select the jury," but you'd be incorrect. Selecting a jury isn't like choosing a kickball team at recess, working from best to worst. It's more like de-selection. Taking turns, the prosecution and the defense begin winnowing down a larger-than-necessary panel to the nine needed, by "challenging" those they don't think will help their case.

One of my biggest pre-trial worries was ending up with closed-minded people who wouldn't fairly evaluate the evidence. I wanted the open-minded sort. Another type I didn't want was the kind of people who actually come in hoping to be put on the jury. These are true-believers who either want to validate some cause of theirs or to convict a particular individual that they've already formed an opinion about. Of course it would be great to have people on the jury who would be more likely to vote to acquit, but those folks would get stricken from the jury by challenges from the D.A. anyway. So our eventual de-selection efforts would be focused on those who were inclined to convict without being thoughtful about the evidence. We would also work to identify the jury's potential leaders, the ones who might influence the other jurors.

To me, it's much better to have two conviction-minded college kids on my jury than one old, alpha-male leader who is inclined to convict. Nobody would listen to the college kids, so while they might vote to convict, they'd be unlikely to persuade anyone who might be on the fence to do the same. That alpha-male type, however – he poses the threat of influencing not just the fence-sitters, but even the acquittal-minded folks who happen to hate conflict and will do anything to avoid it. I'm good at spotting this guy (or gal; in all my trials, I've only failed to identify the future foreperson of the jury twice.)

How do you find the "right" jurors? Once upon a time you could learn a lot about a potential juror's personality and beliefs simply by asking demographic questions, but now this approach is considered bush league. Sure, you need to know some basics about the person, but it's only a starting point. It's not 1950 anymore. We're now a diverse, complex society. You can't assume anything based on race, employment, salary or neighborhood.

This is why forced-answer questions are more valuable to me. For instance, if I want to know how someone feels about firearms, I'm not going to ask if they strongly approve, approve, disapprove, strongly disapprove or don't care. I'm going to go at it a different way.

For example, I might craft a question that would help me determine whether a person is the type who figures "where there's smoke, there's fire." My own wife is like that. When she sees a client in my office, she wonders what they did, not what they are accused of. Others think a charge is just a piece of paper until the government proves it, detail by detail – and that's the juror I want. So I'm not going to ask, "Do you believe in the presumption of innocence?" Everyone says yes to that. I need to ask something that tells me whether they think smoke necessarily implies fire.

For Gerald's focus group, we asked just two non-demographic, forced-answer questions:

Are MMA fighters violent people? (Violent, Not violent.)

How would you feel if everyone in your neighborhood owned a gun? (Very safe, Safer, Unsafe, Very unsafe.)

The focus group consisted of four women and five men. All but two of them had firearms in the home, though three of those seven gun-owners said they felt less safe knowing that other people in their neighborhood also owned firearms. Three of the nine believed that the mere fact that someone is a cage fighter made them likely to be a violent person in general. Four identified as conservative or Republican and five identified as liberal, progressive, or Democrat. We considered it a group that was fairly representative of Lane County.

Ours was a quiet, nervous-looking group at first. As they waited for us to get started, they mostly sat and stared at the blank screen in front of them. Emilia and I joined them at the table, along with three of our investigators – Verne Hoyer, Patricia Jaqua and Jeff Dodge. I had told the three not to come in, actually. I advised them to spend their Saturday afternoon with family or friends because we couldn't pay them to be there. But wild horses couldn't keep them away, it turned out.

When Verne heard about the focus group, he asked, "Can I come watch?" Verne, I knew, believed in Gerald's innocence as much as I did. He'd already told me he would have pulled the trigger, just as Gerald did, if Verne had been the one facing David Crofut that night. So when I waved him off with "You don't have to do that, it's a Saturday," he only pressed harder. "I've been working this case for more than a year. I want to see what they'll say. Besides, I've never seen a defense attorney do something like this before."

A focus group may have been novel to Verne, but not to me. I'd held one a few years before, when I defended a college student falsely accused of rape. We paid a bunch of law students to be my jury, so I could test out the evidence and my argument on them. I even had my client do a dry run on his testimony. I thought the whole thing went really well, and the students agreed – until it came to my client's testimony. They had believed him innocent until they heard him talk, at which point they became convinced he was guilty. You should know that this client was a perfectly honorable gentleman and he sounded super innocent in informal conversations. But when he "testified," his back went ramrod stiff and he moved like he had a neck brace on. His nerves could not be controlled, which is understandable when you're facing a mandatory minimum sentence of 75 months for rape. But he came off sounding rehearsed, which often reads as untruthful. We got that case dismissed two weeks before trial, making the testimony unnecessary. But the episode gave me great respect for the value of testing out my case on some would-be jurors well in advance of trial.

After they completed the juror questionnaire, our Saturday panel filled out and signed a confidentiality agreement. Then Emilia stepped forward to present small details about our case one by one, after which she'd ask jurors for their thoughts, impressions, and feelings. I didn't get that job because Emilia saw me as incapable of staying even-keeled and unbiased. I thought otherwise, because I know I'm continually playing the devil's advocate in my own mind.

The first slide Emilia showed the focus group/mock jury after introductions and ground rules was a photograph of David and Brenda Crofut. The two sat close together, both smiling pleasantly at the camera. The jury had generally positive impressions of them. They thought that the husband and wife appeared to be a normal, happy couple. I tried not to show my pleasure.

This is a win. We want to humanize the Crofuts quickly so that our jurors develop a confirmation bias against Gerald. Cheerleading for our client isn't the point here. We want to flush out the anti-Gerald points of view.

Next we showed the group a photo of Gerald and his fiancée Kristin, both smiling broadly. While I anticipated that our jurors would notice things that I had not (and I really hoped they would), I was impressed by the things they mentioned:

"I wonder if they're married..."

"...or if they have children."

"The woman has kind of a big nose and, come to think of it, big teeth."

"I think they look drunk."

"Yeah, look at the shiny paint on the wall behind them. They're in a bar."

None of these were observations that I would have made, because I wouldn't have noticed or thought of them, especially this far entrenched in the case. This was a photo I loved. All it showed, to me, was a happy couple. But the focus group noticed things I hadn't seen or considered, revealing to me my confirmation bias. The fresh perspective was enlightening – kind of bracing, too. They did look drunk.

Then we showed them a picture of Gerald on the beach, holding a freshly caught fish and a fishing pole. Once again the jury was quick to hone in on some details.

"He looks fit."

"Looks like a guy who knows his gear."

"Yeah, his wetsuit is black, looks like the expensive type."

"I see a man who enjoys life."

Okay, good, I thought.

The next shot we showed them was a picture of Gerald that we had downloaded from Google Images. It showed him in an MMA fight. He has his left arm wrapped around a man's neck and he's squeezing. While a vein pops on his forehead, Gerald's face is cool and calm, like he could be sitting in his living room. The man getting squeezed looks about halfway conscious in the picture. He is grabbing at the arm desperately, and his mouth is open, like a fish out of water gasping for air.

This photo left the jury speechless for a moment. Some were plainly stunned. Some reacted in ways that told us they were appalled. Emilia's 85-year-old grandpa was one of the first people to speak. He said he supported wrestling as a sport, but he thought UFC was disgusting. It was violent. Abhorrent. MMA had no redeeming factors, he said. Finally finding the phrase he wanted, he concluded, "It's human cockfighting."

Others were less bothered by MMA, mostly the younger men. But all agreed on one thing: Gerald looked cold and calculating. He looked like a man who could kill someone.

So now they've made the jump from MMA to the shooting. That was fast.

The slide show continued with a photo of Gerald, in military camouflage and crew cut, pointing a handgun at an unknown target. A hat shades his eyes. The landscape behind him is brown and dry.

"Nice form."

"Really composed-looking."

"An expert."

But one juror noticed and commented on the fact that the gun had a silencer on it. "I don't think there's any reason to have a silencer unless you intend to use that gun to kill somebody," said Robert.

Just the kind of juror we want to avoid in this case. Condescending. Thinks he's got the whole world figured out, that everybody but him is wrong.

The juror continued. "Just having that [silencer] on there makes me think he's unstable, maybe dangerous."

At that I couldn't help myself, I jumped to my feet. "Silencers are lawful in Oregon," I countered. "They're a form of ear protection, and I would love it if all my country neighbors owned them for target shooting."

There ya go, ya holier-than-thou little prick!

I glanced at Emilia and found her glaring at me. I sat down, took a deep breath and quickly rose again, pretending to need a warm-up on my coffee.

Jumping in like that, I knew, was a stupid, selfish thing to do. Emilia was right to shut me down. Allowing this affront to my delicate sensibilities to get the best of me did nothing for Gerald. The whole purpose of this exercise was to really dial into the dissenters. What this man had to say would probably provide one of the day's best insights. His candor was to be appreciated. It was what we requested of him. He was valuable here. With the coffee cup refilled and the internal lecture complete, I returned to my seat.

Yeah, Mike, sit down and shut up.

Now Emilia was showing a picture of Gerald from his Facebook page, pounding a freshly opened Corona and holding up a handwritten note on yellow paper that said, "Thanks for parking like an Asshole." We assumed that the focus group/mock jury would hate the photo and use it to make negative inferences about Gerald. Surprisingly, their reactions to the photo were benign, variations on "It's just a picture." Perhaps the prevalence of frequent and flippant social media posts have softened up the public to such things?

As time grew shorter, we skipped forward through several slides to audio of the 911 calls. We let them listen several times to Gerald's nearly eight-minute-long 911 call, asking the group to write down their first impressions and list the things that seemed most important. Some thought Gerald sounded calm and polite on the recording, not panicked at all; others thought he sounded frightened. But Emilia's Grandpa Jack thought Gerald sounded like he was "covering his ass." He thought it sounded like a calculated call, one aimed at saying what needed to be said to falsely claim self-defense while planning to kill an unarmed man in cold blood. This impression of his was the one we feared most. It came up often when we round-tabled with Gerald.

The group was very concerned and curious about why the fatal gunshot couldn't be heard on Gerald's 911 call. It really bothered them. Emilia wouldn't explain why it couldn't be heard, so they began to speculate wildly about the cause, and one of the leading guesses came from Robert, my anti-silencer guy. He seemed to key off what Grandpa Jack had said: Could Gerald have shot Crofut before calling 911, and then pretended to be afraid on the phone, so as to set up his defense? It set me to scribbling: *Make sure to call a witness at trial who can explain why the shot can't be heard.*

Moments later, Robert had me scribbling again. Now he was making judgments against Gerald due to his choice of weapon.

"Look at the gun this guy was using. It wasn't a little handgun. With that big rifle, this looks like murder to me. Makes me think of mass murderers, school shooters, people like that."

Of course, somebody like Robert would never be on Gerald's trial jury, not if he could be identified. Someone this opinionated is usually filtered out by one side or the other in *voir dire* (jury "de-selection"). But again I reminded myself that he represented the far end of the spectrum. I ought to be glad he was helping us fashion jury questions. He'd help us identify the less-obvious others who might hold beliefs that are similar, just not as strongly held.

Then it came time to play Brenda Crofut's nearly incoherent 911 call. The jurors thought she sounded drunk and disrespectful. They also honed in on her telling the 911 dispatcher that her husband had told her to stay in the car because the other man had a gun. One juror exclaimed, "Why would anyone have gotten out of the car if they already knew that Gerald had a rifle?" Others agreed, saying Brenda's husband surely was either intoxicated or had a death wish. Unprompted by us, they wanted to know his mental health history.

Throughout the nearly four-hour session, we manipulated the evidence to feed them first the positive information about the parties and then the negative. We set it up so that the jurors would feel compelled to choose one version of Gerald over the other. It would be the upstanding, model-citizen Gerald who helped old ladies and climbed trees to save kittens, versus the cold-blooded "Finishing Machine" killer with a violent temper. At trial, of course, it would be different. The government would go first with the negative portrayal. Then we'd portray the good-guy Gerald, making it our version against the government's.

Grandpa Jack didn't write down a single note during the session. It was impossible to sway him from the position he took early on, which was that Gerald was in the wrong. To him Gerald was a bad guy. We asked our jurors whether it was possible that Gerald could be both of those men, the good guy and the bad guy. Grandpa Jack declared that not only was it possible, it was the likeliest explanation.

"I think he's the kind of man who likes being in the center of things," he explained. "He does good deeds because he needs the attention. He was in MMA because he enjoyed being in the spotlight at the center of the ring. I can believe he did good things in the community, but that doesn't mean he isn't a violent, arrogant man, someone who was completely in the wrong when he shot the guy." Grandpa Jack paused to nod at his own assessment. "He likes the attention. He doesn't care if it's bad."

I thought his was the most insightful comment of the day. It rang true to me. I only wished Gerald had been there to hear it, but that was just the latest and greatest reason I was glad we were videotaping the whole afternoon. He *would* be able to hear it. Maybe he'd even learn from it.

At the end of the four hours we had requested of our focus group/mock jury, we thanked them for their time and handed out their submarine sandwiches. But they refused to leave until they heard the actual facts of the case – the ones that weren't available to the public and hadn't even been revealed to them thus far that day. I was impressed. They really didn't want to go home and salvage some of their weekend? No. They wanted to know what we had in evidence. Going home would have been like reading the whole book but skipping the last and most important chapter, they said.

"Okay, then how about I just do the closing arguments for each side?"

Great idea, they thought. Still finishing their sandwiches, they settled in as if they were going to watch a TV show or a play.

Taking the role of the prosecutor in this murder case, I painstakingly recited the facts and inferences that should lead to a guilty verdict. It was, I said, an intentional murder for no justifiable reason.

Then, as the defense attorney, I revealed the finding of Crofut's DNA on the gun. That was something we hadn't bothered to include in our presentation that day, because we knew it was super helpful to our case – we didn't need to test it. As these individuals processed what I was telling them, jaws began to drop. Somebody gasped audibly. Almost everybody started talking at once.

"No WAY!"

"Why didn't you tell us that?"

"This changes everything."

Then I passionately explained to them, as I would to an actual jury, why Gerald Strebendt was innocent and needed to be found not guilty.

When the votes were taken and tallied before people left, something became very ominously clear to us. With the "bad acts" evidence included in the case, this mock jury would begin its deliberations essentially split as to Gerald's guilt or innocence. But with the bad acts *not* included, everyone – except our new friend, Robert – would vote to acquit Gerald.

It meant that the difference between Gerald walking free or spending the rest of his life in prison could well depend on our success – or failure – in keeping as many of the bad acts out of court as possible.

CHAPTER 32
GERALD'S LETTERS

Gerald's one year anniversary of sitting in jail passed, and he was still awaiting his trial. I was worried about him. Over time, his energy level at our meetings had decreased. He said less, and had fewer case notes for the team. I suspected depression. There was just less fight in him than there had been before. Jail was sucking it out of him.

Not even the opportunity to be proven truthful seemed to take him out of his funk. When I told him it was time to give the polygraph a second try, he basically shrugged in agreement. As I say, the fight was going out of him.

But we did the polygraph nonetheless, and ironically, it closely coincided with the date on which Gerald shot and killed David Crofut some 12 months earlier. Gerald was presented with just three questions:

1. Do you remember hearing the decedent verbally threaten you?
2. Did the decedent say, "You're a fucking dead man?"
3. Did the decedent verbally threaten to hurt or harm you?"

Gerald answered "Yes" to each of the questions. At the conclusion of the test, polygrapher Steven Hebner found that no deception was indicted for any of these answers, and that the pattern of scores indicated that Gerald had truthfully answered each of the questions.

This should have been a rare moment of happiness, of vindication, for both me and Gerald. I'm sure Gerald was pleased; he said so. But his reaction was far from the "Fuck yeah!" I might have heard months earlier. Too much time had passed, too many things had happened, and yet nothing had changed. He was still in jail, still in solitary confinement, and still awaiting a trial that could be yet another year away. "Disheartened" wouldn't have been the wrong word to describe either one of us.

I know that, for me, there was much less elation in this result than I felt when we last did the polygraph, when the results said only that Gerald was *probably* telling the truth. By this late date I was pretty certain that this polygraph would never be a part of his case, and the media would never gain access to it to justify Gerald's actions and restore his reputation. Yes, the polygraph results told us that what happened on Bob Straub Parkway that night could and should be judged separately from the Parade of Horribles. It bolstered our belief not just in Gerald's innocence, but in who he was as a man. Still, the polygraph was unlikely to overcome the whole set of circumstances of his case, the ones that I feared were going to make Gerald legally guilty for something he did not do.

As the months wore on, I visited Gerald as often as I could, weekly if I could manage it. I also sent several of my associates and all of our investigators to him in rotation, just to talk with him and get him out of his cell for awhile. For all of my worries though, Gerald was soldiering on. Even when he was at his lowest, he refused to give up. While his case notes decreased, and his manner was subdued, he still wrote frequent letters and notes about anything he could think of, just to pass the time. His sense of humor carried all of us through the darkest times in the case.

We also saw from his letters that Afghanistan filled his thoughts. However, I found it interesting that I was no longer being told the swashbuckling, cheated-death-by-inches stories I'd heard before. Mostly they were anecdotes tinged with some warmth and humor.

I found Gerald as fascinating as ever. During his time away from Oregon, Gerald really and truly seemed to have done just about everything. Though he and I both knew there was an underside to much of it, we enjoyed talking about his many exploits, often laughed together at his efforts to seem appropriately ashamed of the more eyebrow-raising stories he told. I wondered: what would Gerald's life be like if he was released from jail? Would he continue his raucous, globe-trekking?

It depended on when Gerald was released, probably. If we won his case, it would be soon, and he would still be young enough to do almost anything. If we failed to win, though, Gerald would go to prison for at least 25 years, making him a 61-year-old man before he was even potentially eligible for parole. That is, if he was eligible at all. If we couldn't get him off on the murder charge, Gerald would probably never get re-married, never have the chance to father children, or see grandchildren born. It was sobering to think about.

CHAPTER 33

BAD ACTS HEARING

In the world of criminal defense, there are cases, and then there are cases within cases. That's what the Parade of Horribles was – a set of cases within a case. To make our physical-evidence-based defense work best, we had to get the whole Parade ruled inadmissible and confine Gerald's trial to what happened on Bob Straub Parkway on January 29, 2014. But to get the whole Parade excluded from trial, or even parts of it, we had to work up each alleged incident as a separate case – and there were about a dozen of them. The prosecutor could choose to bring to trial any one of them or none. We had to figure how to fight each alleged incident before a jury – that is, if we couldn't keep the "bad acts" out of court altogether.

That meant every anti-Gerald caller to the Springfield Police Department, every person who told a story to a detective, had to be investigated separately. To get the whole picture of an alleged incident, we might have to chase down not just one person, but two or three. And, inevitably, some of these people were crazy-difficult to find, or almost impossible to pin down for an interview.

In a perfect world with unlimited resources, each "bad act" would be assigned a separate attorney with his or her own investigator. The investigator would review the reports with the attorney, identify a list of witnesses to locate and interview, and together they would develop a defense against the State's "bad acts" evidence, using witnesses and evidence we'd find to refute it.

However, in our very real world of limited resources, we didn't have the manpower or the money to prepare to meet each act as a separate case. Our team of investigators was already chasing down hundreds of individuals – first responders, EMTs, firefighters, tow truck drivers, witnesses who walked by, witnesses who drove by, friends and family of witnesses who made statements to police, people at the Driftwood Bar, good-character witnesses, witnesses with MMA experience, witnesses with military experience, you name it. How could anyone do more?

Virtually all of Arnold Law was Gerald's defense team at this point. We didn't know how we'd add all these sub-investigations to the larger one, but it had to be done. Aside from the whole "unarmed guy shot in the face by an AR-15" thing, the crux of the case, the "bad acts" evidence the State sought to present against Gerald was the most challenging part of the State's case for us. The physical and forensic evidence was still solidly on Gerald's side, and we felt it was ample for getting him exonerated.

But even I could admit that the "bad acts" evidence was incredibly distracting. If I'd had any doubts about that, our experience with the focus group had convinced me; it was imperative that we find a way to keep the jury from hearing it. As much as the Parade of Horribles threatened to become an albatross around our necks, dragging down the preparation of the entire case, it was necessary to investigate each item on the list. We had to do it and do it well, because Gerald's freedom was at stake.

An evidentiary hearing was scheduled to begin January 27, 2015, just two days short of the one-year anniversary of the day after Gerald shot and killed Crofut.

There were several ways we could try to convince the judge that the acts were not admissible – we weren't without cards to play. But the legal focus of the evidentiary hearing required us to prove that *the allegations were not similar enough to the charged conduct* [the shooting], or that *the act didn't actually happen as alleged*. We would end our part of the hearing by arguing that the legal burden had not been met to admit the evidence.

Our investigations had shown us that some of the alleged "bad acts" were easy to refute.

Riley Omlid

Omlid knew Gerald for about a year prior to the shooting. They met through Gerald's gym, where Omlid worked out. We had already learned that, on the night of the shooting, Gerald was planning to stop at Omlid's house to borrow some DVDs before going home to his romantic dinner with Kristin. In police reports, unfortunately, Omlid said Gerald was a potential – if not actual – road rager.

After investigator Verne Hoyer interviewed Riley Omlid, however, it became clear that he stood to offer testimony that was quite inconsistent with what the detectives claimed that he allegedly said. Despite a police report that suggested otherwise, Riley said he didn't know of any of Gerald's supposed fits of rage or anger. He said he never heard Gerald talk about shooting incidents that occurred in his Marine sniper days or during his work with Blackwater. Nor had he heard Gerald talk about being involved in incidents that could be considered road rage. As a matter of fact, Riley said he had ridden in Gerald's vehicle about five times and never saw him overreact to any driving situation. When Verne asked Riley to make some statements that he felt applied to Gerald, one was, "Gerald's not angry at all." Riley also told Verne that when he was initially interviewed, he felt that Springfield detectives were trying to get him to support their theory of the shooting – road rage.

I wasn't worried about Omlid testifying.

Nicholas Johnson

This one was crucial. Why would the prosecutor want to call this guy as a witness? Yes, he had recounted a 2004 road incident involving Gerald, one in which Gerald allegedly followed Johnson in his truck and, in a confrontation, pointed a gun at Johnson. But in that incident, Johnson was the one who was eventually charged with and convicted of reckless driving, recklessly endangering and menacing. We also received Johnson's previous criminal record, which was extensive. We had the testimony of Gerald's passenger who saw the incident and supported Gerald's account of it. Our investigator also located and obtained various letters Johnson wrote to his girlfriend from prison in which he admitted to previous crimes, drug use at the time of the incident, and an anger problem. After we forwarded what we had to the prosecutor, the government decided not to go forward with the Johnson evidence.

It felt good to check one off the list. But others who were prepared to offer "bad acts" evidence remained a threat to our case:

Michael and Jean Cunningham

Cunningham and his wife alleged that Gerald had angrily punched out a side mirror on their SUV in 2013.

The two said they were headed to breakfast at a Dairy Queen in nearby Pleasant Hill, Oregon, when they came upon two vehicles stopped on an access road. One had a busted-out window on the driver's side, and its driver was standing outside the car looking agitated. Gerald was the driver of a pickup stopped across the roadway from the car. Michael Cunningham said that when he tapped his horn to try to get the pickup to move, Gerald "jumped out of the pickup, [and] came rushing back towards my direction as if he was going to rip my head off." As Cunningham drove around Gerald and into the Dairy Queen parking lot, Gerald allegedly hit Cunningham's driver-side mirror with his hand, bending the mirror backward and breaking the glass.

Thanks to Kristin Swenson, Gerald's fiancée, we already knew what had happened that morning at the DQ. Kristin reported that Gerald got a call that morning from Leon Kallai, who was at the DQ and needed help with his vehicle. When Gerald and Kristin arrived, the window glass on Kallai's vehicle was broken, the hood was up, and the whole interior of the car was in disarray. Kallai was shirtless, and standing outside the car looking panicked. Kristin said that Gerald was in the process of crossing the street when Cunningham's SUV pulled up... *and hit Gerald.* Kristin said she saw Gerald fall down from the impact. As the truck drove past honking, Kristin saw Kallai throw something that looked like a tire iron or wrench at the driver's side of the SUV. Gerald called 911 to report the incident, and later that night he went to the emergency room for treatment of a knee injury related to the incident. We had the hospital records to prove it. But we needed Kallai's statement, too.

This allegation was a bear to investigate. Kallai is a veteran who was suffering from serious PTSD. He was hard to find, unreliable, and for these reasons, difficult to interview.

It was a sad story Kallai told, one of an itinerant life shadowed by his time in Afghanistan years earlier. He had met Gerald at the gym, and had confided in him about his PTSD. The night before the DQ incident, Kallai, who was working on a fire crew, had gotten into an altercation with a camp host who didn't like where Kallai and others had parked their cars. Kallai said the camp host rattled the door of a bathroom while Kallai was in it, which he said is something you don't do to a vet with PTSD, especially not when said vet is drunk. Still inebriated and angry, acting on his "primal instincts," Kallai drove toward Eugene sometime after midnight, but ran out of gas in Pleasant Hill. He got mad and threw things when the driver of a delivery truck refused to help him. Kallai got even more upset when he realized he'd locked his keys and his phone in the car and needed to break out the driver's side window to retrieve them. Then he called Gerald, someone he could rely on.

Kallai confirmed Gerald's account of events. He said there was no "move along" tap of the horn from a waiting vehicle; he said Cunningham was honking his horn as he drove between the vehicles. Yes, Kallai said, Gerald was hit by the SUV, which really pissed off Kallai. Yes, Kallai responded by throwing a wrench or something at the SUV – "I was scared for my life" – but he didn't think he connected. Furthermore, he noted that Gerald couldn't have been the one to damage Cunningham's driver-side mirror because he was standing on the passenger side of the SUV as it drove through and knocked Gerald down.

When the SUV was gone, Kallai wanted to angrily follow it, but Gerald basically told him to "chill the fuck out." Then Gerald and Kristin took Kallai back to Springfield with them to calm him down. The Pleasant Hill Police stopped Gerald's vehicle after the altercation, but nothing further occurred. Kallai stated that he was in full PTSD meltdown that morning and that Gerald probably saved his life "because I could have killed someone." He said he was especially glad that Gerald played the peacemaker when the Pleasant Hill cops showed up. "At the time I didn't realize it, but I was pretty confrontational. Like, I was not in a reasonable mind frame, like, at all, at that time. And he's the only reason something stupid didn't happen, you know, in that kind of encounter."

This was a "bad act?" I thought it made Gerald look like a hero.

Tina Ramsdal

The police reports showed this woman alleging that Gerald had made all kinds of puffed-up macho statements to her about his training and background in what we were calling "the cul-de-sac incident." But when we interviewed her, Ramsdal denied making at least some of the statements – such as that Gerald had said "I used to kill people for a living." However, however, Ramsdal stuck to the main gist of the story. She said that Gerald had stopped his vehicle in front of hers, preventing her and a friend from continuing to her home in the cul-de-sac. Gerald demanded to know why the vehicle that Tina was riding in was following him. "I'm your neighbor!" she said. The encounter de-escalated after that point.

What if this evidence made it to trial? The jury could use this story to assume that Gerald made a habit of blocking and engaging drivers. It would be easy for the jury to use this incident to conclude that Gerald was the aggressor on Bob Straub Parkway. It could lend credence to the State's case, which alleged that Gerald had swung his Denali around to the right of Crofut's Rogue, cutting Crofut off and blocking his travel. Of course, the jury could only infer that if they were willing to ignore the ACM data on Crofut's braking and acceleration, and we'd do everything in our power to keep that data in front of them.

The Facebook Post

In the days before the shooting, Gerald posted on his Facebook page a quip about slow drivers:

If you like to drive slow guess what? You should be in the slow lane. If you want to drive greater than the speed limit guess what? You should be in my lane.

If you get this confused somehow guess what? I will strike hard and fast like a cobra should the opportunity present itself.

The post was "liked" by 20 of Gerald's Facebook friends. Several people posted in response, some serious, some in a joking fashion:

- *What if I am a mongoose? I win. We have both seen proof of that*

- *Just one of many complaints I have about idiot drivers in this town :)*

- *No worries I will just honk my horn at you again!! Lol*

- *Oh dear, turn up the Enya and drive home safe?*

- *I may be slow but I'm ahead of you*

Gerald told me that he had made this post in jest. Furthermore, he said the last part of it, the "strike hard and fast like a cobra" comment, was a reference to actor Ben Stiller's 2004 sports-comedy movie, "Dodgeball: A True Underdog Story." In it, Stiller's dodgeball team was called the Globo-Gym Purple Cobras.

The State no doubt intended to paint this as Gerald's manifesto, as evidence of his intent to commit road rage. But if this "bad act" was admitted at trial, we'd argue that it was a joke, and taken in its full context, we thought a jury would agree.

Rachel Chilton

Gerald was married to Chilton for five years, and he was in a relationship with her for two years before that. They divorced in 2012. Chilton had made a broad statement to police during the initial investigation that she had seen Gerald "road raging" as much as three to five times per week throughout their entire relationship. If you do the math, that would have produced somewhere in the range of 1,000-1,800 road rage incidents during the course of their marriage. However, Chilton later backed off on these numbers. She admitted that she had not observed any so-called road rage incidents during the first few years of their relationship, and that there were many months when she didn't ride with Gerald at all. That's because Gerald did two tours with Blackwater in Afghanistan during this period, and when he was home, they drove different vehicles. People who knew them told us that she and Gerald had differing interests and maintained separate schedules – and that this was perhaps the main reason they didn't travel by car together very much. But Rachel continued to claim that she was afraid to ride with him, and that she did everything she could to avoid it.

While Chilton clung to her claims of Gerald's road rage, we managed to get her on the record as having seriously exaggerated her claims. Also, we had a good question we could ask her: If she was so worried about his driving, why did she allow him to drive her loaded horse trailer in 2011, before their divorce? Yes, she had alleged that Gerald had road-raged with a driver that had cut him off that day, but with all the incidents that supposedly led up to that point, why would she have put her horses at risk with Gerald as their driver? There was no evidence of domestic violence or a power disparity in this relationship. Something wasn't adding up here.

Deputy Charles Douglass

Lane County Sheriff's Deputy Charles Douglass claimed that when he pulled over Gerald in a traffic stop, Gerald yelled and screamed at him so aggressively that Douglass quickly wrote the ticket and ended the interaction, fearing that Gerald was going to come out of the truck at him. So concerned was he, in fact, that he made a note in a law enforcement database to warn officers who might encounter Gerald in the future of his hostility. I was able to talk to Deputy Sheriff Jonathan Bock, who was in the car when Douglass made the stop. Bock confirmed that he saw Gerald tailgating and making lane changes without signaling, but he stood at the back of Gerald's vehicle during the stop and couldn't hear any conversation between Gerald and Deputy Douglass. Bock said he thought he would have heard it if there had been yelling by either party.

I thought we could raise some doubt in jurors' minds about this one.

Deputy Derrald Mann

Deputy Derrald Mann stated that after he pulled over a man he considered to have been driving erratically, Gerald pulled up behind the deputy and told him that he had observed the "out-of-control driver," and that Gerald had been "prepared to run the driver off the road" if necessary.

I thought that if this evidence was admitted at trial, we would argue that it was an example of Gerald's "do-gooder" nature. Gerald didn't actually do anything at all, except stop to provide information to the police officer about the driving he observed. You could almost call this a "good act" by someone wishing to be a helpful citizen and support law enforcement efforts. However, Gerald's "take the law into his own hands" attitude and statements were troubling for this case.

Kim Charboneau

This woman told another story of the driver-intervention type. She and her husband pulled up to their house to find Gerald ready to confront them for pulling to the left instead of the right as a firetruck came by. He also said that the Charboneaus had almost hit a "motorcycle cop" and failed to signal their turn 100 feet in advance, according to law. In effect, Gerald had followed them home to give them a refresher course in driving laws. How was this incident in any way similar to what occurred on Bob Straub Parkway? Maybe, if it happened, but did it meet the legal test of being similar to the charged incident? I sure didn't think so.

The Evidentiary Hearing

On the day of the hearing that would take testimony from these witnesses and others, I had the job all to myself. It didn't make sense to have Emilia or anyone else with me; it wasn't worth the meager public defender fee to take somebody else out of the office when it meant less time spent chipping away at our mountain of investigative tasks.

This meant I'd be on my own to do the examinations and cross-examinations of witnesses. I'd do the arguments on a variety of evidentiary and procedural motions – 15 of them, as I recall. While talking I'd wrangle the documents and exhibits. And throughout, I'd be the one explaining to Gerald what was going on and trying to, as always, reassure him that everything was going to be okay.

One heck of an assignment. Like being producer, director, writer and performer rolled into one.

And it wasn't to be just one day of this multi-tasking; by the time we were done it was three days. It was brutal, not just on my nerves and stamina, but to the case. While I felt I got a few good licks in on both witnesses and arguments, there was really no point at which I felt we were prevailing with the judge, in whose hands all the motions and "bad acts" evidence rested.

The only light moment across the three days came right at the beginning, when I saw for the first time the deputy that Lane County had assigned to Gerald for the proceedings. The guy was probably the biggest deputy they had – six-foot-four, barrel chested, with a flat-top haircut. He practically darkened the door when he escorted into the courtroom my increasingly diminutive client, who was shackled in leg irons and handcuffs. No doubt the idea was to prevent this "dangerous" MMA/UFC fighter from getting the upper hand for even a moment, lest he bolt from the courtroom. But Gerald was in anything but fighting form. It was ridiculous, and from the look on the deputy's face when our eyes met, I think he agreed.

We started the hearing with my motion for a change of venue. I called to the witness stand a Reed College professor who testified to the probable poisoning of the jury pool that had occurred when *The Register-Guard* published its August 2014 story on Gerald's case. This was the story made possible by those ineffective redactions of documents *The R-G* had obtained from the appellate court. Dr. Daniel Reisberg said the phrase "road rage" in the headline set the agenda for would-be jurors to be influenced. He added, "I would certainly count that article as strongly suggesting a guilty verdict." He also implied that the judge's gag order made things worse for Gerald's prospects for getting a fair trial, because the order's prohibition of publicity prevented each side from airing its facts equitably from the beginning of the case. I argued that the bell rung by *The R-G* article couldn't be un-rung without moving the trial to another city outside of the newspaper's main distribution area. The State, however, argued it could just pull jurors from a larger-than-usual pool.

Like everything in this hearing, the judge didn't rule from the bench. She intended to write her rulings and findings at a later date.

Then we began the "bad acts" testimony.

Deputy Derrald Mann recounted how Gerald pulled up behind Mann's traffic stop and said he'd been prepared to run the erratic driver off the road. But I got Mann to acknowledge that there was nothing particularly agitated or threatening about Gerald's demeanor at the time.

Deputy Charles Douglass testified that Gerald was very hostile after he was stopped for allegedly driving aggressively and making unsignaled lane changes. He said Gerald called him names and told him to "just write the ticket." On cross-examination, I got Douglass to acknowledge that citizens have a First Amendment right to call people, even sheriff's deputies, "an asshole or a douchebag" if they want to. Later, calling Deputy Jonathan Bock, who was riding with Douglass at the time of the stop, I asked Bock if he'd ever seen Douglass "get rude or responsive when someone's… giving him slights." Said Bock: "I've seen that. Yeah. I mean, he's – he has a lot of passion for the job. He's an emotional guy." I noted that Douglass would be easy to rattle at trial.

Kim Charboneau told how Gerald had followed her and her husband to their home to confront them with driving rules regarding pulling to the right (not left) for firetrucks and how to signal turns legally. She alleged that Gerald told her husband that Gerald lived "close enough to throw a rock through your window." Kim considered lodging a trespass charge against Gerald after the incident and ran his license plate at her place of employment, though I got her to acknowledge that Gerald wasn't trespassing if he hadn't been asked to leave the premises. Oh, and that employment of hers? Small world. Springfield P.D.'s 911 call center. I learned right there in court that Kim had been the operator who took Gerald's 911 call on the night of the shooting. It came first to the county's center, but was then transferred to Springfield P.D. and Kim Charboneau's headset.

After **Tina Wolf (formerly Ramsdal)** testified to the cul-de-sac incident – the one in which Gerald blocked the vehicle she was riding in and accused driver Kevin Shields of following him – I got Shields to acknowledge that the incident didn't contain any threats made by Gerald, just accusations, and that the situation defused pretty quickly.

Michael Cunningham and his wife testified as expected about the Dairy Queen incident in Pleasant Hill. I didn't gain much traction in my cross-examination. But Leon Kallai's testimony proved helpful.

Kallai came into court smelling of alcohol and looking for all the world like he'd been stranded on an island somewhere. To make sure he arrived at the hearing on time, we sent Patricia Jaqua up to Portland to escort him to court in Eugene. Most importantly, Kallai readily acknowledged that he was in a full-blown PTSD episode that morning and that Gerald not only calmed him after the incident with the Cunningham's, he kept Kallai from fighting the police when they stopped them afterward. "He's the only reason something stupid didn't happen," Kallai said of Gerald.

Rachel Chilton, Gerald's ex-wife, told the horse-trailer story. She said a sedan cut off Gerald, after which he "kept pulling up alongside of them and swinging the horse trailer at the car," or pulling in front of the car and slamming on the brakes. "I could hear my pony crashing around in the trailer," she said. By and large Rachel stuck by her assertion that Gerald was frequently aggressive on the road and that she avoided riding with him.

But there was one insightful element of Rachel's testimony: She said Gerald's behavior was different after Blackwater. "I know it got – it certainly was worse after he came home from Afghanistan. Like his whole demeanor was different and worse."

Through witnesses I called to the stand, I tried to refute "bad act" testimony with the accounts of Gerald's "good-act" witnesses, who talked about his careful, safe driving and his willingness to help others on the road. While some of their stories dated from before Afghanistan, Kristin, Gerald's fiancée and the most recent and frequent of Gerald's passengers, said she never saw any reckless or aggressive driving.

During this hearing, I also argued some of the other motions I had filed. I had moved to exclude some specific photos, Gerald's clothing, and the results of law enforcement gathering tire data on Gerald's Denali without a warrant. In each case I argued that proper legal procedures hadn't been adequately followed to allow the evidence to be used at trial.

I also argued to try to keep out of court certain words and phrases – like calling Crofut a "victim," or calling the Sig Sauer a "military assault rifle," or use of the term "road rage." Each, I said, is unfairly prejudicial. In response, Prosecutor Bob Lane said he would try not to use these terms in questions, but he did not think it fair to instruct witnesses "who are already under stress" not to use them.

Undoubtedly the most important moment for our case came on the hearing's last day – which, ironically, was one year to the day after the shooting. Brenda Crofut, wife of the deceased, took the stand for the State. It opened the door for me to take what amounted to an in-court deposition of her, to explore everything she would eventually say during Gerald's trial.

If getting access to her on the stand was my first surprise, the second was her demeanor. She was calm, composed – not exactly matter-of-fact, but certainly not the tearful, grieving widow I might have expected. (From what we'd been able to gather from Facebook, she had moved on with her life with a new boyfriend and some travel.) But there was to be another surprise. In my cross-examination, *she denied everything* – that there was any domestic violence in her marriage to David Crofut, and that he had ever driven fast and threatened to kill them both, despite a Tacoma police report and other investigative reports to the contrary. She also denied that she and David were drunk on the night of the shooting, and testified that her husband had been driving normally before the Denali supposedly cut off the Crofut's Rogue. Brenda said there was no brake-checking on David's part, and no trigger-fast decision by David to ram Gerald's truck. Of course, I had the airbag data – the car's black box data – to call her a liar. I can't say I saw D.A. Lane shrink or recoil at her testimony, but I had to believe it would raise some doubts about the strength of a murder case for any competent attorney.

I left court that day knowing I had three weeks to pull together my final arguments on the most crucial aspect of my defense of Gerald Strebendt – why the "bad acts" evidence should be kept out of court. If the Parade of Horribles was admitted, I wasn't sure that Brenda Crofut's lies would make any difference. I was fairly sure that Gerald would get convicted, just on the basis of the jury's assumption that where there's smoke, there surely has to be fire.

CHAPTER 34

"GO TIME" – ARGUING AGAINST THE "BAD ACTS" EVIDENCE

I seldom do well before a big court appearance. My stress builds up over days and weeks, and by the time the appointed day arrives, I've eaten little and slept less. It's not unusual for me to have been up much of the night and skipped anything that might resemble breakfast, because I don't want it coming back up again. Doctors would call it anxiety, but I think of it as my warm-up, having vomited before my rugby games in college.

On the day we were to argue to keep the "bad acts" evidence out of court, Emilia and I arrived in the office early to go over what we would need to bring with us. We had several banker's boxes of documents, binders, plus technological equipment and cords to haul over to the courthouse. I wanted to have everything with me that I'd had during the testimony itself, which had been held about three weeks earlier, plus all of the transcripts of that evidentiary hearing. It was a lot to be bringing, but I didn't think we needed a vehicle.

After we each filled up a wheeled cart, Emilia and I began pushing and pulling them the six blocks to the courthouse. All the way I was deep in thought, spinning through my argument in my head. Was I tense about what lay ahead? Yes. Was I worried? Absolutely. I felt like it was all on me

– like my performance in the hearing would make or break Gerald's case at trial. If I could keep the "bad acts" evidence out, I felt like we could run the table, and Gerald would walk. If I couldn't keep out some or all of the acts, though, I thought that the chances of an outright win were slim, especially on the lesser, included charges like manslaughter.

Six blocks sounds like a short trip. It is, when you're not steering heavily loaded carts down sidewalks and around mailboxes, light poles and even the occasional sleeping bag of Eugene's homeless population. But I was too busy rehearsing in my head what I'd say and do, to even reconsider taking a vehicle.

Then, just as the courthouse came into view, I lost control of my cart. It fell over, dumping its entire contents onto the pavement and into the path of oncoming cars. The binders had fallen open and paper was starting to blow loose. I stood there, near the entry to the courthouse parking lot, with cars streaming around me. In that moment, all of the stress and worry and obligation just about crushed me. I felt the urge to go down on my knees, maybe even to put my hands on the ground for stability.

The burden I had been living with for a year since Gerald retained me wasn't something I could shoulder anymore, at least not in that moment. The tipped-over cart had crumpled me inside and out. But instead of admitting that I was overwhelmed at having to face this key day in court, I acted as though the spilled cart and the blowing papers and the oncoming car traffic were to blame for my frustration, which threatened to blow up into an adult tantrum.

"Go get the truck!" I snapped at Emilia. "We can't do it like this!" My mind raced with everything that I wasn't willing to say out loud.

We can't save him. I can't save him. I can't do this. I'm going to fail.

Emilia ignored me. Instead, with an eye on traffic, she began calmly picking up the binders and papers to re-assemble the cart. I watched her work, unable to make myself lend a hand. Then she stopped, noticing that I wasn't doing anything to help, and looked me dead in the eye. In a quiet voice that brooked no disagreement, she said, "We are almost to the courthouse. There's no point in going back for the truck. All we have to do is get right over there. We're close. One step at a time. If the cart falls over again, we'll just pick it up again."

With that, she looked away and returned to the task.

She's right, I thought. We *are* almost there. My shoulders felt lighter, and my chest seemed a little less tight. I helped Emilia chase down the last few papers, and when we finished, we pulled the carts without further incident into the courthouse. My moment of weakness had passed. I was ready once again to do battle. I wondered if Emilia knew just how deeply my confidence had failed me in those few moments. I suspected she did. I was grateful that she hadn't chosen to acknowledge it.

Gerald entered the courtroom soon after we did. He wasn't wearing those damned jailhouse greens, but his street clothes weren't much of an improvement. They hung on him. He was a wraith, an almost skeletal substitute for the robust fellow I met in the days after the shooting. As Gerald had feared and complained about to no avail, he had a bad haircut – a really bad haircut. On a better day, I would have chuckled about that – ribbed him about it, too. But Gerald didn't really meet my eyes. He had that thousand-yard stare they talk about. Emilia motioned for him to sit next to her, creating a buffer between Gerald and me. I needed to focus, and Emilia would take care of the client for me.

We had just two motions to argue. The first was the crucially important motion to exclude some or all of the "bad acts" evidence. The second motion was regarding the admissibility of Gerald's polygraph results.

I worked the "bad acts" evidence hard. I pointed out which stories about Gerald hadn't happened the way the witnesses said they did. I noted the ways in which their accounts could be impeached at trial, citing things they had said at the evidentiary hearing. I hammered away at the fact that the acts they described did not resemble the charged incident at all. In fact, to think there was a similarity between the "bad acts" and the shooting, you would have to ignore all of the physical and forensic evidence and assume that Gerald was using his vehicle to taunt David Crofut from the Safeway store to the scene of the shooting. Or, you'd have to think that Gerald had stopped Crofut's car to try to teach him how to signal or pull over for a fire truck. You would have to do what the Springfield Police Department did – you'd have to assume that a guy who was a Marine sniper and an MMA/UFC fighter was automatically the guilty party, just because of his experiences and special skills. In other words, you'd have to attach the label "road rage" to the shooting incident and then look for the evidence to try to support it. You'd have to go to witnesses and ask them, as SPD detectives did, whether they'd ever seen Gerald "road rage" before – never bothering to define what the loaded term meant.

The trouble was, I had very little faith that the judge was really hearing me, or, if she did, that she would rule in our favor – or even rule at all. Part of the reason was legal. There was an appellate case making its way through the courts that would largely determine the future of "bad acts" evidence in Oregon, and I suspected that the judge preferred to wait and rely on that ruling if it didn't take too long coming down. The other reason I had little faith in my ability to convince the judge was… well, just our history as judge and defense attorney. She seemed to think I was always working the angles, always trying to get away with something. And I felt she had it in for me. Maybe neither was true; maybe both were true.

As I argued the defense position, Judge Vogt interrupted me fairly frequently to ask questions. I found it annoying that she kept trying to bring me back to specific facts while ignoring others. But then came a moment that I considered the last straw. She interrupted me to say that I was mischaracterizing the evidence, adding something to the effect that, "I don't think the prosecution has conceded that."

They don't have to concede it! This is argument. You are not the D.A. You are supposed to make up your own mind. This is an adversarial process!

What followed was a conversation that didn't involve me. I was made to watch, standing mute, while the judge and the D.A. speculated on what I was trying to do with my argument. When I got my chance once again to speak, I picked up a transcript of the evidentiary hearing – one we'd placed a rush transcription order to obtain in time for argument – and, well, let's just say I put it down on the table rather emphatically. "I take offense at you saying I've mischaracterized the testimony," I said. "It's all right here." The judge backed off of her mischaracterization comment, but it did little to reduce the tension in the courtroom.

Later, when it was time to argue the second motion, the judge said something like, "Okay, let's move on to the next one." Without thinking, I blurted, "The polygraph?" The judge burned holes through me with her eyes and ordered counsel into her chambers. Emilia stayed behind with Gerald, and spent the time the attorneys were in chambers answering Gerald's questions, trying to reassure him. "Whatever happens we can handle," I heard her telling him as I left the room. "Nobody's gonna die from what happens here."

It didn't take much effort on anybody's part to figure out what the judge was thinking when she took us into chambers. She believed I was trying – *once again*, in her view – to skirt her Trial Management Order, that gag order that sealed all of the details of the case. You see, there was a reporter in the courtroom during our arguments. The judge was no doubt afraid that he'd take the information and run a story on the fact that Gerald Strebendt had taken a polygraph test. The reporter could reasonably assume that I wouldn't be making an issue of it in court if Gerald hadn't passed a polygraph. But the outcome of this arrangement was that all the bad evidence was flaunted to the press, while the good evidence for Gerald was kept secret.

Somehow I got through the day. We all did. I packed up my transcripts and exhibits and when I got back to the office, I took my wife and law partner, Jacy, back to my private office and shut the door. I told her what I told Emilia soon thereafter, when she came knocking at the door.

"I'm done. I quit. I can't do this anymore."

Both Jacy and Emilia were supportive of my leaving the case, if that's what I really wanted to do. I'd been beaten up in court before, I told them, and I was sure I'd be beaten up again. But this case was hard. I was representing an innocent man who, if things kept going the way they had been, was going to get convicted of murder and sent to prison – if not for life, for a very long time. I respected Gerald. I truly liked the guy. And that's what made it so damned hard. He didn't deserve what was happening to him. He deserved better than what I seemed able to do for him.

But I stayed on the case, and for all the reasons I just said. Gerald deserved the best I could give him. I told him I wouldn't quit on him, and I didn't.

There was no ruling from Judge Vogt on the "bad acts" that week or the next week or even over the next couple of months. Eventually, in March, the Oregon Supreme Court issued its opinion on State v. Williams, the appeal case that hinged on the admissibility of "bad acts" evidence.

Unfortunately, the opinion raised more questions than it answered. Neither lawyers nor judges seemed to know how to handle the new case law. Any guiding opinions that might follow were likely to be several months away. Bob Lane quickly filed a motion for additional argument following the Williams opinion. Recognizing that Gerald's case had been postponed again and that these Williams-based arguments could drag things out even longer, we started to think about the possibility of seeking a settlement conference.

CHAPTER 35
GOOGLE YOUR WITNESSES

A defense attorney who has a trial pending doesn't just go to the prosecutor or the judge in the case and ask for an offer to settle for a reduced sentence or a negotiated plea – not if you can help it, anyway. To do that is to give up your bargaining power. It makes you look like you're playing a weak hand. So you try to find another way to get at the issue. In this case, I asked Emilia to bring it up at one of our periodic pre-trial meetings. As usual, she did a great job of nonchalantly saying just the right thing at the right time.

We were having one of our regular pre-trial meetings with the judge and the prosecutor, one of the behind-the-scenes sessions in which we handle scheduling and other issues, when Emilia acted like she just had a light bulb go on over her head. "Hey," she said, lightly, "is this case going to settlement conference?"

Everyone's reaction was to look at me and ask me whether that was something I'd be interested in. Giving a "whatever" shrug, I said, "Sure, I guess so, why not? We're always willing to talk."

By then Gerald's murder trial had been postponed until December of 2015 or January of 2016. We had almost a year to wait, and Gerald would sit in the county jail in solitary that entire time. A settlement conference would give the parties to the case an opportunity to see if the murder charge could be resolved sooner.

If an agreement could be reached on a charge other than murder, we could remove the jeopardy of going to trial – Gerald would know how much time he was going to serve, and it would undoubtedly be less than the 25 years to life sentence he was facing. Of course, the concern was, what if going to trial could get him off completely? Without a ruling on the bad acts, we didn't know for sure where the case stood. But we did decide that a settlement conference was worth aiming for. It was subsequently scheduled for May 7, 2015.

It may not get us anything. But holding a settlement conference gets Gerald a field trip – a day or so out of his cell. And that's not nothing.

Once the settlement conference went on the calendar, it became trial prep on steroids at Arnold Law. The office, already maxed out on the Strebendt case, went into a goal-driven sort of overdrive. While the chances were limited of coming out with a charge and a sentence we could live with, we had to speed up and fine-tune everything we would have presented – and might still present – at a trial. That's how we'd get Gerald the best possible deal, by convincing the judge and the prosecution that we stood to win before a jury. Emilia put out calls to our experts to finalize their reports. Our investigators were told to handle any remaining interviews or document searches and stand ready for last-minute assignments. We finished up our demonstrative exhibits and had them professionally set and printed.

As we prepared for the conference, we had to acknowledge the significant weaknesses in our position. Even though several weeks had passed since the bad acts hearings, we still didn't have a ruling on the bad acts motion from Judge Vogt. That meant we would go into the settlement conference ignorant of what evidence the State would offer against Gerald at trial. Would a few of the acts be excluded, or would we hit the jackpot and manage to keep all of them out? The new Oregon Supreme Court opinion about the admissibility standards for bad act evidence made it impossible for us to predict what would happen. And that made it very difficult to advise our client as to how good or bad his chances would be at trial. All we could tell Gerald for sure was that if the "bad acts" came in and he was convicted, we would have an issue on appeal.

Talk about flying blind.

Of course, things always happen to make matters worse.

One day I was sitting at my computer, prepping a motion, when I heard a knock at my door. It was Bryan, a colleague at the firm. "You should check your email," he said. "I sent you something a couple hours ago and I would have expected you to be running up and down the halls trying to figure out a solution by now."

"A solution?" I asked. "I didn't even know I had a new problem. What is it?"

Bryan said there was a glitch with one of our expert witnesses. It was Dr. Martinelli, the three-in-one expert we were thrilled to find because he could testify on law enforcement, the military and martial arts. Well, it turns out there was a case in Montana at which Martinelli testified – a "stand your ground" case where the defendant was accused of luring a suspected burglar into his home and killing him. The guy had been convicted of the shooting, which could have implications for Gerald's case. But Bryan was more concerned about Martinelli.

"He was apparently brutalized by the prosecution in cross," Bryan told me.

The Montana prosecutor had done her homework. After the defense made a big deal out of Martinelli's education and training, she cornered him on his resume during cross-examination. She got him to admit that his doctorate was actually from an unaccredited distance-learning university that was now defunct. According to Kathryn Haake, a reporter at *The Missoulian*, the prosecutor's knockout blow was this question about his doctorate school. "It was closed because it had virtually no academic standards, correct?" The prosecutor also attacked Dr. Martinelli's claims that he had a "pre-medical background" and had experience "training doctors."

After we all reviewed what we could find about Martinelli and that Montana trial, Emilia walked to my door. "Are we going to kick him or keep him?" she asked.

"I don't know," I said. "I think we lose a ton of credibility if we call him. We would have to *voir dire* about it and possibly bring it up in our opening to soften the blow. That sounds like a lot of effort when he can just be replaced."

"Who do we use?" Emilia asked. "Who could we possibly find who has the total package of what we need?"

"There won't be a total package," I replied. "He was too good to be true. If some Montana prosecutor can tear him up after a Google search, Bob Lane will have a field day with him. Experts like Martinelli may have made a great living before the internet with their impressive credentials, but not anymore. What if we have a real Ph.D. on the jury from an actual, quality university? He will crucify our guy in the jury room."

"Okay, we'll kick him," Emilia said. She headed off to find one expert for use of force in the military, one for martial arts versus an unknown weapon, and one for the physiology of fight-versus-flight. We don't call her the office's "fixer" for nothing. If there was anybody could find us a trio to replace what we thought was our trifecta – and in a real big hurry – it would be Emilia.

CHAPTER 36

GOLDEN BRIDGES

"When you surround an army, leave an outlet free. Do not press a desperate foe too hard." Sun Tzu, The Art of War. (Often described as "Build your opponent a golden bridge to retreat across.")

The day for the settlement conference arrived. Soon we'd know whether all the work we had done was enough to convince the prosecutor to show some favor to Gerald; whether we could convince the judge to convince the prosecutor to show that favor; or, whether it was all going to be a fruitless exercise.

A judicial settlement conference in my jurisdiction is kind of a hybrid, part oral argument, part mediation. The prosecution and the defense present to the judge what they consider to be their strongest, most persuasive evidence – but not in view of one another. The two sides of the case don't even come into the same room. If the judge were to find our evidence compelling, he might try to influence the prosecution to make us a good offer. While we had no interest in having Gerald plead guilty to anything, Gerald had nothing but time on his hands. There was no harm in probing the prosecution a bit, exploring what was possible.

But the tricky part when you're going into a settlement conference is knowing when to show your cards versus holding them close to your vest. Would we let the prosecution see the weaknesses we'd found in their case, or would we keep those cards close so we could use them at trial? The old mantra "never wise up a chump" came to mind for me. I was leaning heavily against showing any cards on this day. But Sun Tzu phrased it more eloquently: "Let your plans be dark and impenetrable as night, and when you move, fall like a thunderbolt."

By now Sun Tzu's *The Art of War* was a well-thumbed manual for both me and my client. (I had given Gerald a copy early in the case to read in his jail cell). More and more Gerald had begun to quote the book as we discussed strategy and tactics.

That's an important distinction, between what's strategic and what's tactical, and Gerald had gotten pretty good at distinguishing one from the other. In fact, he seemed to understand the differences better than a lot of attorneys. Many lawyers know tactics well enough but often lack an overarching strategy for their cases. A strategy is a blueprint to build something, whether it's small or grand, and tactics are the tools you build with. Like most of us, prosecutors and trial lawyers tend to go with the tools – the tactics – they know best. But you don't pick a wood saw when you're building with steel, if I dare be even more metaphorical about it. As much as you might enjoy using your wood saw, it's just not going to do the job.

As an attorney, I try to pick the right tool for the job. I may grab whatever's handy when I'm in the barn – I talked about this earlier – but in my job, I do believe in making my tactics serve my strategy, and not vice-versa. That's why we were headed to a settlement conference. It could be the right tool for the situation.

Gerald and I had already discussed how much more work would be needed to increase the odds of him winning his case, even by a meager five percent. It was a lot of work. And he still had better odds of getting hit by a truck. Gerald made the decision to try for a negotiated plea. In so doing, he quoted Sun Tzu to me. "If your enemy is secure at all points, be prepared for him. If he is in superior strength, evade him. If your opponent is temperamental, seek to irritate him. Pretend to be weak, that he may grow arrogant. If he is taking his ease, give him no rest. If his forces are united, separate them. Attack him where he is unprepared, appear where you are not expected."

I wasn't exactly sure which of those phrases Gerald thought was most applicable to the situation, but I did know that if a settlement was to be reached before trial, the time to negotiate was now. If we didn't, Gerald would be sitting in jail for another ten months awaiting trial. It would be two years, easily, from his arrest to his appearance before a jury. Sure, we still hoped that we could develop some bit of evidence that would cause Bob Lane to see the case as we saw it—a clear case of self-defense. I didn't have high hopes that the case would actually settle, but I knew from experience that I always learned something during the process – something about my case, a new fact, or even something I didn't know about my client. Time is always on a defendant's side, assuming that the defendant can handle all the time spent in the county jail. And lately, I wasn't always sure that Gerald was up to it.

Our settlement conference/mediation session would be handled by Lane County Circuit Court Presiding Judge Karsten Rasmussen. Judge Rasmussen was well known for resolving tough cases. I would say that his main motivation is to benefit his docket, but now and then I'd seen a bit of justice become a byproduct of the process. I could only hope it would be true this time, for Gerald.

On the day the settlement conference was to begin, I invited our investigator, Patricia Jaqua, to join us, partly as a show of force. I always think of that scene in the movie "Erin Brockovich" when Erin's boss throws suit jackets on his assistants to make it look like he had "people." In my case, I didn't have to fake it. Emilia knew the case as well, if not better, than I did and had substantial experience in settlement conferences. Patricia knew the case inside and out as well, and she had also developed a rapport with Gerald. He would need the support of all of us this day.

We reported to Judge Rasmussen's closed courtroom, no press or public allowed. It would be our war room for the duration. Deputy D.A. Bob Lane may have been down the hall in a jury room, or upstairs in his office; we didn't know. We never saw them, nor did we expect to. There are rarely face-to-face conversations in this kind of process. The conference would proceed by "caucusing," meaning that the judge would talk to each side individually and ferry offers back and forth. This allows all parties to speak more freely with the judge, because, ideally, the judge isn't going to reveal what cards each side holds unless they give him permission to do so.

My job, as an effective representative of my client in a settlement conference, is to figure out how to make the judge an ally, if I can. I begin that process with my pre-mediation memo, hoping that if I show him a strong defense case, maybe he'll be persuaded to subtly (or not so subtly) convey the strength of my case to the prosecution. Maybe he won't push us very hard to settle. Maybe he'll even urge the prosecution to offer a deal or – a lot less likely – to drop the charges altogether.

It may seem like a pretty low-key situation, but it's not. A settlement conference may look like a mediation, but it's really a contested hearing. There is gamesmanship and strategy. You never know what cards the other side is holding, and you never know whether what the judge is telling you is coming from him or from the other side. The judge is motivated to get the case settled, so he will work hard to try to reach that goal. Everyone should expect to go home a little sore from the arm-twisting.

Gerald arrived in the courtroom in his jail uniform and sandals. There were no street clothes for him this time. His hands were cuffed in front of him, and he was seated in the jury box 90 degrees from where we were sitting at one of the attorneys' tables. A deputy sheriff came in with Gerald, and he was to be present for the entire conference. Of course, that meant there would be no true confidences today unless we convinced the deputy to step outside. While deputies generally agree to keep these conversations private, they are not ethically obligated to do so like attorneys.

I was reminded once again of the toll that incarceration was taking on Gerald. He had continued to lose weight, if that was possible. The hollows in his face were deep enough to capture shadows. While his demeanor was as pleasant and calm-looking as ever, I could see his stress. Looking out from those eyes was a worn-out Marine, prepared as best he could be, to fight another battle in a long war. As we waited in the judge's courtroom for the day's events to begin, the chitchat felt chipper in a somewhat forced way.

It was Gerald who turned the focus to the business at hand. "How will we know whether to be happy with an offer?" he asked.

"You will never be happy with an offer," I replied. "The sign of a good settlement is when everyone leaves unhappy."

His response was more a tilt of the head than a nod.

Judge Rasmussen began by inviting me and Emilia to his chambers, so we left Gerald in the courtroom with the deputy and Patricia. As soon as were we in seats across from his desk, the judge began poking holes in our case, disparaging our evidence, my arguments, and – it soon became clear – our entire trial strategy. He made some points that I thought were valid, but I knew that this was mostly strategic on his part. It's typical of a settlement judge to belittle your case, try to make your positions feel weak, and then try to exploit that.

We defended our positions fairly energetically, causing the judge to ask, "Is there any purpose of holding a settlement conference?" This told me my letter may have been a little strongly worded.

"Well, Judge, whether Gerald would be willing to agree to plead guilty to anything depends on the offer," I said. "He offered to testify at the grand jury to nip this all in the bud, but the other side wasn't willing to play ball. So now we won't be bidding against ourselves."

I told Judge Rasmussen that we believed, as did Gerald, that our case offered a good chance of acquittal at trial on the murder charge. But we were there to talk, and if the prosecution had an offer for us, we stood willing to evaluate it.

Judge Rasmussen sent us back into the courtroom, and then a few minutes later, he joined us. He was not wearing the black robe that signified the authority of the court. Judges in settlement conferences typically want to create a more informal atmosphere, one aimed at allowing people to speak plainly. However, when the judge opened the door, he came out swinging.

Now, I have been to many settlement conferences. Always, without exception, I've seen judges begin by trying to establish some rapport with the parties, and my sample includes past settlement conferences presided over by Judge Rasmussen. So it was a complete surprise when he didn't begin with his usual opening comments or explanations of the process. His usual statements inviting open communication aimed at arriving at a mutually agreeable resolution of the charges – they were missing, too. He didn't even say good morning.

Instead he set an adversarial tone for the mediation by marching in, turning to the deputy and saying, "What is he doing up, with you all the way over there?" Gerald was standing up and I was standing next to him. The deputy was standing some distance away, by the door. The judge then pointed coldly at Gerald and said, "You. Sit down. Now."

Wow, nothing like dehumanizing one of the parties to mediation before it even gets started.

Gerald replied, "Yes, sir," and sat back down in the jury box.

Here once again was proof of how scared the system was of Gerald's MMA/UFC and Marine credentials. With three doors leading from the courtroom, Gerald's shackles weren't reassuring enough to the judge. He wanted that deputy right at Gerald's side to prevent an armbar or a choke-hold, I guess. At least it wasn't the beefy bruiser this time, the deputy we'd had for the "bad acts" argument.

The judge then sat down across from Gerald and me, with the low wooden wall of the jury box situated between us. A bit awkwardly, he returned to a tone more familiar to me in such a setting, addressing Gerald directly. "You really need to be looking at all the risks," the judge said. "Even though you think your case has some good facts, you need to understand that you are risking 25 years to life. You need to realize that you could get convicted."

He was trying to, very quickly and bluntly, take the wind out of Gerald's sails – maybe mine, too. I recognized it as good mediation strategy on his part. It's what judges do to enhance the possibility of settlement. "The State really believes in their case," the judge continued. "You need to understand that, in reality, of the criminal cases that go to trial, a very high percentage of those cases result in a conviction."

Then, after emphasizing that the State can't afford to bring every case to trial, which is the purpose of seeking a settlement, Judge Rasmussen showed his hand for the first time. "I am not of the opinion that this is an automatic winner [for the prosecution] but there is significant risk to you – and only you."

"Yes, sir, I understand that," Gerald said, respectfully.

"This is a free country," the judge continued, "and you are welcome to discount my opinion. Do as you will with it." But he clearly wanted Gerald to understand that he didn't foresee anything approaching exoneration. "If your idea of a resolution is that you walk out of jail this afternoon, then this is a waste of our time," he said.

With that, Gerald turned to me and asked me if he could speak. I gave my assent. It was, after all, Gerald's settlement conference, Gerald's life. It wasn't on the record; there was no court reporter in the room. While we could choreograph some of the moves and power plays, we couldn't really tell Gerald what he could and couldn't do. We were only there to help him through the process by advising him. Besides, I trusted him to make good tactical decisions. Anything he said would be for the sole purpose of meeting our shared goals.

Gerald's tone was respectful but firm. "I want to thank you for your time, sir. I don't want to be disrespectful of your time, though, so no, I don't think there's any point to this settlement conference. We should probably just get back to work preparing for trial. But thank you for your time."

I wasn't surprised that Gerald saw little merit in moving forward, not after the way the judge opened the conference. But it was pretty obvious to me that the judge was only trying to shake Gerald up, to get him into a malleable position, to scare him into being ready to accept whatever the prosecution might offer. In trying that, he had underestimated Gerald. The judge had lumped him into the "typical defendant" category, probably guilty and definitely desperate. To find out otherwise was no doubt an unpleasant surprise. I'm sure he wasn't accustomed to seeing settlement conferences on the verge of ending before they began.

Judge Rasmussen's demeanor changed immediately as Gerald began to speak. After just a moment's hesitation, though, he went on without really responding to what Gerald had said, essentially ignoring Gerald's request to terminate the mediation. He talked about how cases can be successfully mediated in settlement conferences, and while he spoke, I wrote Gerald a note. "Well played," I scribbled. "Perfect." Gerald acknowledged the note with the slightest of nods, but did not smile or even look at me. He kept his focus on the judge, who soon finished his remarks by saying, "Why don't you talk to your lawyers for a little bit while I go and chat with the other side?"

As soon as the judge was out of the room, everyone began to talk at once. I put my hand up for quiet, and, when I got it, said, "Well, that was interesting."

Patricia agreed, saying, "What is his problem? I've never seen a judge act like that before."

Gerald looked for reassurance. "I did okay?"

"Yes," I replied. "Like I said, perfect. You delivered a strong message that we're not bluffing here. That's important. You respectfully set the tone for the rest of the negotiations."

Patricia was still shaking her head in disbelief over the judge. "He's either in a bad mood or he has a dog in this fight."

While waiting about 20 minutes for the judge to return, we discussed various approaches we could take to steer the other side to its best offer, and then goad them into making it better. We also talked about what we could do if the judge maintained his adversarial tone with us. But the judge didn't even mention his previous statement – or Gerald's – when he came back. He simply invited me and Emilia back to chambers.

We walked into his chambers with him and closed his door. On the wall sat a bust of Harry Truman that the judge had received from his late father. The same bust of my favorite president, from my home state of Missouri, sits on a shelf in my office. For some reason I was reminded of Truman's fairly famous pissing match with General MacArthur after World War II, when the general attempted to sabotage Truman's foreign policy.

MacArthur forgot who his boss was.

Who's a judge's boss? It's supposed to be the law. But under those sober black robes and away from the authority they have in court, judges are just people – people with political interests and personality quirks like everybody else. In Oregon, judges are elected officials and their boss, while it should be Lady Justice, is the electorate, the citizens. That's not always a good thing.

When I turned away from the bookshelf and my thoughts, Judge Rasmussen announced, "I have an offer and it's more than I thought I could get."

I couldn't help but be reminded of a used-car salesman. He pours some coffee in the break room, kills a little time, and then goes back to the would-be buyer saying his manager approved a price reduction and... it's better than he thought it would be!

The judge continued, "Their offer is Manslaughter in the second degree."

I shrugged slightly. "A good start," I said, "but there's no way that's going to fly."

"They've come a long way down from murder."

"They sure have, and that offer says quite a lot," I added. "It says they're afraid to try the case. You don't skip Man-1 and go to Man-2 if you think you have a strong cause. This offer says 'We don't want to try this and eventually we'll offer Crim Neg Hom.'"

"This offer deserves your consideration," the judge replied. "It comes after a lot of work on their part."

Suddenly the situation looked almost bright. I dared to think that maybe the judge had been right earlier, that maybe we would find a way to head off this trial with a plea agreement. My thoughts turned to calculations – how much time would Gerald spend in jail on the various charges that were possible from this negotiation? Or, better put, how little time could he get away with?

Murder, manslaughter in the first degree and manslaughter in the second degree all come with mandatory minimum sentences in Oregon, thanks to a ballot initiative that was passed by voters in 1994. (If you can get enough signatures, you can put almost anything on the ballot in Oregon, and this particular initiative was born of legislative changes that the filers considered to be "weak on crime.") These "mandatory minimums" take judicial discretion off the table. The sentence is the same for everybody, no matter the age, status, or criminal history of the defendant. So we knew that Gerald couldn't hope to avoid significant jail time if he went to trial and got convicted. Not even an agreement between all parties calling for leniency could override those mandatory minimums. So, while we were discussing pleas and convictions on various crimes, what we were really talking about at the settlement conference's negotiating table was the sentence. We could name the crime this or that, but really, unless the plea was to an offense below that of murder or manslaughter, there was no compromising. By law, the sentence was set.

In my head I ran down the sentences; first degree manslaughter carries 120 months, but second degree manslaughter drops the sentence to 75 months. That's a difference of 45 months, or almost four years. It was definitely something my client deserved to consider, especially if the alternative would be 25 years to life after a murder conviction at trial.

For me, as Gerald's attorney, it was an uncomfortably powerful place that I now found myself. I knew that if I brought him the offer excitedly, recommending that he accept it, he would. If I came in angry or even slightly disgusted by the offer, I knew Gerald would reject it. So I had to carefully consider not just where Gerald might stand on this potential plea, but also where I stood. Did I really think we could get a better offer, such as an even lower criminally negligent homicide charge that would let us escape mandatory sentencing guidelines? Pleading to Criminally Negligent Homicide could yield so-called "good-time credit" to reduce time served. It could also make Gerald eligible for various programs that could further reduce the length of his sentence. I reminded myself that Judge Rasmussen came in vowing that Gerald wouldn't be walking out of jail with zero additional time served, but now I wondered if somehow I might convince the judge to help us get there with the prosecution.

After leaving the judge's chambers, I laid it all out for Gerald. "Look," I said, "you aren't going to get them to agree to dismiss the case right now, today. That will only happen, if it ever happens, by pressing it to trial and letting them figure out then how bad their case is… or by us showing them, today, by revealing our evidence, how bad their case is." That, I told him, is like laying out all our cards on the table so they can figure out how to beat us. "We'd lose the element of surprise. We'd risk them figuring out how to repair their case before trial."

I let that sink in for just a moment, and continued. "If you want to settle it today, you need to make some sort of felony offer. I'd recommend you low ball them with Crim Neg Hom, with credit for time served, considered served. You'd walk out of jail next week on probation as a bow hunter." He knew what I meant. With a felony conviction, he wasn't going to be doing anything with guns for the near term and possibly forever.

"Sounds good to me," Gerald said. "Let's make the offer and see. It's like giving your opponent a few easy jabs to see how they react. I'm game."

We took the offer to the judge, who was less than pleased. In fact, the phrase "no way" was part of his response, but left his chambers when we did to contact the D.A. just the same. All we could do in the interim was to eat lunch – or, in Gerald's case, poke at it a bit while caged up at the courthouse. He admitted that he was too nervous to eat.

We returned from lunch to learn that the State was, indeed, offering

Criminally Negligent Homicide. But the State wanted Gerald to serve much more time than he was likely to agree to, and they wanted a lifetime firearms ban. The gun Gerald used to kill David Crofut would be forfeited and destroyed. From Gerald's non-reaction to my bow-hunter comment, I didn't think that part was a significant hurdle.

Judge Rasmussen cleaned off his white board and started doing the math. Outside of Measure 11, the ballot measure that established mandatory minimum sentences, all of the programs and benefits offered in the Department of Corrections might be available to Gerald. If he was sentenced to 60 months, he would get credit for the time he had already served, plus reductions for his good behavior, and perhaps even another reduction if he qualified for an Alternative Incarceration Program (AIP). He estimated that if Gerald agreed to the deal, that he would be a free man in about two years.

As we continued hashing out the details at a round meeting table at the other end of the judge's chambers, I readdressed some of the facts we had ready to bring to trial. I was hoping that I could convince the judge to go back to the prosecution and get a number that was less than 60 months. But, eventually, he confirmed what I had begun to suspect: the judge was picking sides. "Even if you get them to agree," he said, "I won't agree to a shorter sentence."

So much for the neutral mediation. Obviously Rasmussen is worried what the public will think if he agrees to a so-called "light sentence." The public would understand the reasoning behind it, of course, if there hadn't been a gag order preventing us from discussing the facts of the case!

I couldn't help but fume. The public knew only what the police had said – that Gerald was a road rager who gunned Crofut down in cold blood. They knew nothing of Crofut's drunkenness, his ramming of Gerald's truck, his crazed insistence on leaving his car to confront Gerald, who just happened to be holding a high-powered rifle, even as Gerald was telling Crofut to back off. If I'd been allowed to give media interviews, the public would have had a fairer picture of what happened on Bob Straub that night. If they'd heard the 911 call, they'd know what went down. The judge wouldn't have to worry about blowback from his "light" sentence.

What a jaw-dropping statement for a judge to make. It was bad enough to be fighting with the D.A. to get a better deal; now we're fighting with the judge, too? On top of it all, Judge Rasmussen added that he had a couple of stipulations to add to the agreement. He wanted the parties to agree to issue a joint press release, written to his specifications. And he wanted us not to talk about the negotiations or mention any "arm-twisting" that he did or didn't do. We've had two opponents all along. The D.A. and the court.

But instead of saying everything that I was thinking, I only managed to sputter, "So you're a party to the negotiations now?" If he was refusing to approve a sentencing deal, perhaps there was another judge who would, I suggested.

It got fairly dramatic in chambers after that. As the argument began to subside and my focus enlarged enough to see Emilia, I recognized in her someone who felt ready and able to prevent the situation from getting ugly – or, should I say, uglier.

"With all the chest beating that's going on," Emilia said dryly, "maybe we can take it down a notch and get this thing settled."

Emilia doesn't talk as much as most of the associates in our firm. That's mainly because she's by nature a listener. She closely follows not just what's being said, but how it's being said. So, inevitably, when she chooses to jump in, her timing proves to be pretty good. Everything stopped. Everyone turned to her, ready to let her take the reins of the whole situation.

"What?" she sputtered. "Why are all you guys looking at me?"

"Because you're the only rational person in here right now," said the judge.

The day ended amicably. We left without an agreement, but we didn't reject the prosecution's offer. Rather, we pledged to continue talking with the judge about it over the next few weeks and see if we could make any progress.

When Gerald heard about the offer, he didn't react much. He certainly didn't immediately agree that 60 months on criminal negligent homicide was a good option. If anything, he looked ready to reject it. I began to worry that perhaps I had done my job too well. He seemed to think we were unbeatable at trial. I shared some of his confidence, absolutely, but I had to wonder: Had I failed to provide Gerald with enough insight into the potential outcome of a conviction that carried a mandatory minimum sentence? If so, I had to fix that in a hurry. Gerald needed to understand that the judge had maneuvered us into a place where all of his dire comments at the beginning of the settlement conference applied: Without the 60-month agreement, and assuming a conviction on a murder charge at trial, Gerald was facing a 25-year to life sentence.

Of course, Gerald could be acquitted and, I had to admit, going for full exoneration was attractive. But it wasn't my decision, it was Gerald's. Was it worth it for him to roll the dice on the possibility of acquittal? I really felt for him. Before the settlement conference, with no option but to go to trial and hope to be found not guilty, the risk argument didn't carry any weight. Now, that risk analysis might as well weigh a thousand pounds. I mean, our case was good, but with that very dark shadow of a conviction hanging over us, we had to acknowledge that this 60-month deal was worth some serious consideration. Would Gerald really want to bet the rest of his life on our case? Would he really want his fate determined by twelve strangers sitting in judgment of him?

To me, what the prosecution put on the table was a concrete offer to resolve Gerald's case with a guaranteed outcome. The 60-month sentence he would serve after pleading guilty to criminal negligent homicide was as close to putting him in the driver's seat as we could manage. With the plea, Gerald could consider his two years in prison, after reductions were calculated, as just an insurance payment, the cost of guaranteeing he'd be freed in the years – not decades – that followed.

After we left Gerald to his jailers that evening, Emilia, Patricia and I walked downtown to Eugene's First National Taphouse for a drink and some food. To me, it seemed inevitable that Gerald would plead guilty to Criminal Negligent Homicide; he just didn't know it yet. The terms weren't exactly what we wanted, and maybe we'd get them to a better place or maybe we wouldn't, but this was an offer too good to simply reject. With Emilia and Patricia adding grist, we chewed over the possibilities along with our appetizers.

Patricia, our investigator, was particularly taken aback by what she'd seen. She was shocked at how the settlement negotiations had felt, from the very first moment that Judge Rasmussen stepped into the room. "He sure seemed like he was out to protect Judge Vogt and the D.A.," she said. "It shouldn't have been so political."

"What are you talking about?" I scoffed. "This is a political case. Rasmussen is a political animal, elected by voters. The language he speaks is Politics, the same one that elected D.A.'s understand." I took a swig of my beer. "That's your problem, Patricia. The language you speak is justice, and it's a dying language if it ever did exist. Better get used to that."

CHAPTER 37
GETTING TO GUILTY

May 7th, the day of the settlement conference, was a Thursday. On Friday morning I got up early, as I almost always do. I walked around my house in aimless circles, just waiting and watching for the sun to come up. Realizing I was likely to wake my daughter and my wife, I went into the kitchen and started boiling water to make coffee in the French press. Then I grabbed some farm clothes off the laundry room floor, just to put something on. When the water came to a boil, I filled the French press and prepared my mug, adding a spoonful of our farm-raised honey and some store-bought cream. A few minutes later, when brewing was finished, I pushed the plunger, poured my cup and took it outside.

I stood on my back porch on the east side of the house enjoying the warmth of the mug in my hand. It was a spring morning in Oregon, crisp but not terribly cold, and notably, it wasn't raining. When the sun came up I knew it not by seeing it clear the horizon – my farm to the east is too wooded for that – but by the color change on the hills. The tops of the trees turned from a pale pre-dawn gray to the deep, dark green of the forest.

Soon the light in the master bedroom came on, signaling that my wife was awake. Now I could shower and get dressed for work. I drained the coffee mug and bade goodbye to the peaceful stillness of the farm. I dreaded going to the office this day, for I knew what I had to do and I loathed the thought of it. I needed to talk to Gerald about the proposed plea.

This feels pathetic, I thought. *It's like a salesman "getting to yes," except, it's "getting to guilty."*

After my shower, I put on jeans and a fleece pullover instead of the more typical suit. I didn't have any command performances today. A visit to the jail doesn't require a suit, but that wasn't the only reason for the jeans. Given that Emilia wasn't working on Fridays – part of the deal we made when she came back from maternity leave early – I'd gotten myself some Casual Fridays by default. Not that Emilia wasn't always working to some extent; she was. Even with her shortened work week, she remained one of the firm's top billers, mostly by working at home before the kids got up or after their bedtime. But, if I had a choice, I didn't schedule things on that one day a week when Emilia was at home with her children, and I found I liked it. It made for a relaxed end to my work weeks.

Thinking about Emilia's kids, I marveled at how much her baby had grown during this case. When we started working for Gerald Strebendt, her second baby was just a newborn. Now the little one had been weaned and was walking around and talking. That's how long Gerald had been in jail. So much life happens around our clients and out of their reach while they're on "pause" in jail. Of course, life doesn't actually stand still for them; it only seems that way. If anything, aging seems to go on "fast forward" for those who are incarcerated. And a defendant can only watch as his case erases all his past successes and hits "rewind" on any life goals he was working on. If you care at all, it's hard to watch.

I found myself making rationalizations. I didn't really have to be the one to go to the jail today. I could send an investigator to talk to Gerald about the settlement conference and the offer. I could follow up later, get over there when I could. That sounded better than having to face Gerald now, when yesterday was so painfully fresh for both of us. But none of that would work. When I checked my calendar, I saw that I would be out of town all of the next week. I could put Gerald off for a day or two, but not for a week and a half. I would go in to the office to check in, and then I would go see Gerald.

On arrival at the office, my associates foiled my plan for getting to the jail right away. Everyone followed me into my office, refusing to leave until I told the story of what happened at the settlement conference. Thankfully, Patricia was there to do the heavy lifting on the story-telling, because I didn't want to talk about it. Honestly, I didn't feel like a victorious warrior, home from a successful battle. We had earned Gerald a really good offer; that much was true. We had found a way to avoid the risk of his going to trial, and that was an achievement. But it was hard to be pleased about any of it. If I believed Gerald to be guilty, or if the evidence of his innocence had been weak, I would have been happier. But I couldn't see how any additional jail time would be fair to Gerald. That's how much I believed in my client and our case.

Done storytelling, I kicked everyone out of my office so I could spend some time with my assistant, packing our materials and exhibits for next week's out-of-town hearing. I took phone calls from clients. And when I could avoid it no longer, I grabbed all my notes from the day before and walked down the stairs to my truck.

When I arrived at the jail a few blocks away, the deputy on duty at the metal detector was cheery. I'd been there a lot lately, so she knew my name and who I was there to see. Unlike previous visits, where my suit, belt and fancy shoes made it a bit of a project getting through the metal detector, I sailed right on through in my casual clothes. But the succession of metal doors you go through as you enter the jail seemed especially heavy, slow and ponderous on this day. Usually they seemed to clank and hum as they opened, but today each one rumbled as it rolled, like thunder. And for some reason, when they closed behind me, it almost felt like I couldn't trust them to open again.

Doors of justice... closing in. Just like they're closing in on Gerald now. If there's no trial, there can't be an acquittal. Doors closing....

When I got to the attorneys' visiting room, I felt too apprehensive to sit down. I stood there, shifting my weight from left foot to right, waiting for Gerald to be brought to me. It came as a relief when I heard him shuffling down the hallway in his jail shower shoes, though I'm not exactly sure why I felt that way. The tough stuff was still to come. But I guess it felt better knowing we were going to work through this together.

As Gerald entered the small room, I could tell that he was almost as apprehensive as I was. He was as pale as ever, his face seeming not just stretched by weight loss but by strain as well. I saw that he was sweating, and then realized that he wasn't the only one. When Gerald sat down with a sigh, I joined him. If he could sit down, all calm and collected, if he could be a man about facing this music, then I could too, considering this wasn't my life; it was his.

I started with the usual opener. "Manage to get any sleep last night?"

He chuckled a little ruefully. "No, couldn't. Just kept thinking, you know… about the day, about what happened."

"Eat anything?"

"Sure, yeah."

I didn't believe him, but I didn't push it. "Do you have any questions about what happened yesterday?"

"Probably. Probably should be asking a lot of questions, making sure I understand every single thing that happened yesterday. But honestly, man, all I can think about is Kristin."

"Did you guys talk last night?"

"Yeah, I called her, and told her about the day. Told her about the offer."

"What did she say?"

"Not much. Mostly she cried, we cried."

"Sorry, Gerald."

"Mike, I have to know. Will this deal get any better, do you think? Can you somehow get me less time?"

"I don't know. I think we can probably make it a little bit better, by showing them everything we have. Giving them our work product, I mean."

"Okay, but what if they see that and say, 'That's all they got? Let's withdraw the offer?'"

"Not likely to happen but anything is possible, I suppose."

"With my luck, 'possible' means 'probable.'" He made an exasperated sound. "I just want this done."

I nodded sympathetically.

Gerald's face sagged and his eyes fell to the floor. "I can't go to jail for another five years, Mike. She's gonna leave me."

"It's not going to be five years," I said, leaning in. "Everyone is on the same page here – you have credit for the time you've already served, which by now is close to 14 months. Then you should be able to get good-time credits, so long as you don't do anything in prison to fuck up, like fighting."

"So you start with 60 months," I continued. "Then knock off 14. That leaves you with 46. You could get as much as 20 percent of your time knocked off with the good time credit, so that could save you another 12 months. That puts you down to 34 months. Then, if you get into an Alternative Incarceration Program, you could be out even sooner. The stats on the AIP programs show that most people who get into the program knock another 12-13 months off their sentence. I can't guarantee that you'll get into an AIP program, but if you do, you could be out in less than two years. For killing a man. Who was unarmed."

I tapped my pen on the calculations I'd just made on paper. "That's a big compromise for the State."

Gerald nodded. "I always look at the homicide sentences in the news-paper, and I've never seen one this low."

With that, Gerald launched into a story. It was evident to me by that point in our attorney-client relationship and friendship that Gerald tended to process stress and tough decisions by relating the present circumstances to a past life experience. "In the Marines," he explained, "one of my drill instructors said to me, 'Strebendt, it's when you are at your lowest possible point that the Marine Corps will expect the most from you.' I've thought about that a lot. And, well, here I am, at the lowest fucking point in my life. The state, the judge, the D.A., David Crofut, me – all of us – brought me here. And they expect me to be able to make this decision? Now? When I've got no strength, no ability to think? I've got no capacity to really evalu-ate this, Mike. This is a decision that's mine to own for the rest of my life."

I didn't respond. I just waited.

"But I guess the same can be said about the decisions I made that night," Gerald continued. "God, if I only had missed! He would have shit his pants and backed the fuck off. We wouldn't be here today."

Once again Gerald's eyes fell to my calculations on the legal pad. "I don't think she's gonna wait," he said of his fiancée. "If I don't get out of here, I'll lose her."

What could I say? He was probably right. "Look, Gerald, I could tell you all sorts of things, quote sayings to you like: 'If you love something, let it go. If it returns, it's yours; if it doesn't, it wasn't.' But, here's the deal. As much as she has supported you and continues to love you, she's a pretty girl nearing the end of her prime. I'm not trying to be rude or misogynistic here, it's science. Biology. She's in her thirties on borrowed time. Every year she waits to have kids is that much harder for her if things don't work out when you do get out. You are a true gamble to Kristin. And as much as I hate to say it, you will probably be doing her a favor if you let her go live her own life. You can start over when you get out, settle down and have some kids. I don't mean to sound like a prick here, but the reality is, she's not your wife. You don't have kids. She's a non-factor. Make your decision for you."

"Ouch," he replied. "You are as always blunt."

I felt guilty saying this knowing all that Kristin had invested financially, personally, and emotionally into this case, not to mention the same investments made by her loving family. They all supported Gerald when nobody else would, but it was time for me to show Gerald a little bit of tough love.

Gerald couldn't get there, not yet. "What about trial?" he asked. "Why don't we just take this thing to trial? We'll win it, and I'll be out."

"Yes, part of me is chomping at the bit to try this thing. You know that. I would destroy them. Trial is definitely an option for you. Just remember though, your trial date is next year. It's May now, and trial is scheduled for January of 2016." I paused, counting on my fingers. "That's eight months from now. If you were doing a 22- to 24-month stretch on a plea, you'd already be well into it by then. And you wouldn't have to spend the next eight months stuck in here. You can move on to better accommodations, where you can get some sunshine."

"But if we won, I could walk. It'd be over. I wouldn't be a felon; I could still hunt."

That made me chuckle. "Man, you've been there, done that. What more can you achieve by rifle hunting? So you're a bow hunter now; go challenge yourself. Give the fucking deer a chance. A sniper hunting a deer? That's shit. Go sneak up on them Indian style with zero gunpowder. You'll love it."

Gerald laughed along with me.

I continued. "Whenever someone tells me that they're a bow hunter, no rifles for them, I first think, 'He's a felon.'" This brought a new wave of chuckles from Gerald. "Yes, you'll be one of those guys," I said, "but with your training, you'll be a fucking stealthy, deer-killing Ninja. You'll sneak right up on them and slay them. Need protection for self-defense? Go with a pellet gun or a fucking throwing axe. As for the deer, bow season is coming and they'll wait. But Kristin isn't going to wait for two years. There's no way around that."

"I'd like to think she would, but I don't know. Honestly, Mike, I don't know. I think I want to take it to trial."

"You have to remember that you could still get convicted of criminally negligent homicide, or even Man II or Man 1. There's no guarantee that if we take this case to trial on murder and — even if we beat it as I think we would – that we'll run the table on all of the lesser charges as well. Any one of the lesser charges are all prison sentences that would likely end up longer than the 24 months you stand to serve if you take the offer. It stands to reason that if the jury finds you not guilty of murder with the self-defense claim, they should acquit you of the lesser charges, too. How can you be negligent, for example, if you were just defending yourself? But I've seen juries compromise. They'll sometimes do just about anything to get out of the jury room and go home. They could decide to teach you a lesson by convicting you of something, not knowing it's a mandatory prison sentence."

By the time I finished explaining all of it, Gerald had slumped back in his chair, legs splayed out. "What should I do?"

"I'm not recommending anything. I'm telling you the risks and the benefits. I'm giving you the facts, Gerald, and my opinions about the facts. I'm telling you what you need to consider before you reject this offer."

"But we have such a good case. You're really in this, which makes you the perfect person to talk to the jury about it," he said.

"Yeah, but I'm concerned that I'm too close to it, and too close to you," I said. "I'm invested, all the way. I'm worried that I'm not giving you the advice that you need to hear, because I don't want to hear it either." Then I muttered, "Hell, I don't want to even think about it."

"About what?"

"About you pleading guilty to anything! This case is completely fucked up. From beginning to end. It's not right. I don't want you to do it."

"And I don't want to do it."

"I know!" I said shrugging slightly, palms upturned, as if to say, "So where does this leave us?"

Then Gerald said, "Tell me about DOC time," and I knew we were turning a corner. He wanted to know what it would be like in a Department of Corrections prison. "Will it be different than local time?"

"Yes. Absolutely. Assuming you don't do anything stupid while you are in there like fighting." I emphasized this by pausing to raise my eyebrows and give him a warning look. Gerald nodded to let me know he'd heard me loud and clear. "You would be out of solitary," I continued. "You'd get to go outside and do some classes, probably have some sort of job there. All clients say that DOC is way better than local time. The local jail just doesn't have the funds or the space to do the stuff that they can set up out there in eastern Oregon."

"Well that's something I suppose." Then Gerald turned it on me. "What would you do, Mike? If you were in my shoes, what would you do? Would you take the deal?"

"Great question, and one I'm not going to answer. It's your job to tell me what you want to do. The decision is yours, and only yours."

Gerald and I spent the better part of several hours, going back and forth about prison and the plea versus trial. We talked about the case, about the good evidence and the bad. And soon Gerald was once again remembering that day in Afghanistan when he could have fired his weapon and didn't – in fact, defying a direct order to shoot. He recalled seeing that red dot of the laser sight right on the chest of a man driving a white SUV that had been approaching Gerald's convoy in a way that appeared threatening. But he turned out to be just a guy in a hurry – somebody not thinking of the consequences of zigzagging around cars filled with heavily armed Blackwater mercs. Despite his stupidity, the Afghani lived, because Gerald hadn't squeezed that trigger. But Crofut died for his stupidity and, while Gerald was comfortable with the decision he'd made based on the facts on the ground that night on Bob Straub Parkway, he couldn't help but regret it... and continue thinking how it could have ended differently. With two men still standing.

Unprompted by me, Gerald also spent some of our several hours together that day taking stock of his life. He thought he had a good childhood, or a good-enough one. But he was ashamed of the way he had lived most of his adult life. Lacking any guidance or criticism from people of good character, he had become what he despised: an arrogant bully. He totally bought into the fame of his short time as an MMA celebrity. He rode high on his name and his skills. He got indignant when people didn't acknowledge who he was at MMA events. He mouthed off to cops. It was true, he acknowledged, that he could kill a man with a gun, a knife, or even his bare hands. He used to think that made him a winner. But his life was a failure in all the ways that mattered, he told me. Sitting in jail, he had none of the things that he valued. He had no support. He had no security. He had lost his gym and his home. If he pleaded guilty, he and his fiancée most likely would end their engagement. He couldn't look forward to much. Many of his friends in the MMA world didn't want anything more to do with him. His students had moved on. Gerald was alone and could only foresee more of the same.

"I did everything wrong," he told me. "I'm a damned fool."

There was really nothing I could say to make him feel better. To me, his self-assessment seemed, sadly, on the nose. He didn't deserve to be in jail for defending himself. But yes, everything in his life had somehow led him here. He hadn't done anything to prevent it.

As the afternoon came to a close, I could tell that the guards were going to kick me out soon for the inmate count and dinner hour. I hit the button to let the deputies know I was ready to go.

"Gerald, I am going to head out. You really need to eat."

"I will, Mike, I will," he said, as unconvincingly as ever. Then he said, spontaneously, "You know, I don't think it matters when I get out. Even if it were today, I think Kristin would probably still leave."

"Why do you say that?"

"Because I've been in here for more than a year, and she's been out there, trying to hold it together. I think part of her has already started to move on, like you said. She's been living her life without me all this time. I haven't been able to do anything to help her."

"What are you saying? What do you want to do?"

He looked at me right in the face, and said, "Do everything you can do to make it better. Even 36 months would be better than 60."

"What if we can't make it better?"

"Then I'll do it. I'll plead guilty."

"And you're… all sure?" I asked.

"I'm not fucking sure of anything right now, Mike. How long have I been in here? They arrested me March 7th in 2014. It's May now, a year later, and I've hardly seen the sun. I've been sitting in a concrete box, in solitary. I've got no one to talk to. Nothing to do. They feed you shit food, and you shit it out where everyone can see you do it. They've set me up to be demoralized and desperate to leave this place. Well, it's worked. I'd rather plead guilty and do a few years than risk spending the rest of my life, or even another year until my trial, in a shithole like this. Living like a dog in a kennel. Yes, Mike, I'll plead guilty. And then I'll leave this godforsaken place and be better after prison than before I was arrested."

He paused to chuckle. "It will be like a 'boot camp for personal growth.'" He laughed some more and then said, "Make it happen."

On that we shook hands.

I left him in the attorneys' visiting room alone, and the deputy closed and locked the door to escort me out. I made it through the heavy, clanking and rumbling doors of the jail and out to my truck. But once inside it, I began to cry. I had made it through the whole meeting with Gerald without losing it, but now frustration and grief swept over me in waves. The details weren't final, but I knew that he was going to accept something close to the deal on the table and plead guilty. I might be able to make it a little better for him, but not much. Gerald was going to go to prison.

I have failed. That's all there is to it. There should have been something more I could have done.

I started up the truck, pointing it toward I-5 and home. As I drove I replayed the case in my head, rethinking some of our tactics and trying to figure out what we'd missed, what I had done wrong, what evidence we could have produced to bring about a better deal.

Eventually I had to pull over. I couldn't focus, couldn't drive; I was in tears again. I had committed myself to Gerald, to seeing this case through to the end. But it hadn't been enough. I'd gone out on that battlefield with him, but I hadn't been able to shield him, because the case wasn't good enough to get the charges dismissed or I wasn't good enough. My investigators had failed. My associates had failed. My expert witnesses had failed. I had failed. We had all failed. I grieved for Gerald – for his choice in pulling the trigger that night, for his lost year in the county jail, and for the fact that, despite all of our efforts, he was going to be behind bars for quite a while yet.

This isn't justice. There is no justice system, I thought. Justice isn't for the ignorant masses. Justice is for poets and philosophers to talk about. The "injustice system" is simply a dispute resolution system. Gerald resolved a dispute with his gun and the government and Gerald resolved their dispute with words. I guess it worked as designed.

I was angry at the prosecutors for taking the case this far. I was angry at the judges, too, for their rulings, their hostility to my client and our defense, and the apparent agendas underlying it all. And I was angry because I felt so inadequate. Shouldn't I have been able to get the system to see what I knew to be true? That Gerald had been confronted by a drunk, enraged man who had just rammed Gerald's truck? That David Crofut threatened to kill Gerald? That Crofut had chased Gerald and tried to grab his gun?

I pounded the steering wheel. *Justified. I would have shot the guy. Hell, my wife would have shot the guy, and probably sooner than I would have.*

Once again I found myself crying in the cab of my truck alone, this time on the side of the highway. Not one of my finest moments. But who would know? After just 'another day at the office,' trading years of someone's life like baseball cards, I felt entitled to a moment.

Within a minute or two I was composed enough to drive. I made it home and let my wife take care of me for the rest of the weekend. I avoided all connection to the outside world, focusing on my family and my farm.

Since next week would take me out of town on another case, and the following week was my vacation, I decided to turn the case over to Emilia to manage. I told her to use whatever office resources she needed to get Gerald a better deal and support him in my absence, keeping me apprised, of course. I knew that, in metaphorical terms, Gerald was my dog and I should be the one to put him down. But it was too hard. I couldn't do it. I wouldn't do it – and my resolve was as firm as when, after shooting my cocker spaniel, Liberty, I said I'd never put down my own dog again. I left it to Emilia and the rest of the team to pull that particular trigger, because I was spent. I'd had enough. I'd go to court with Gerald when the time came, but it was someone else's turn to work out the final details.

As I began driving to central Oregon that Monday morning, Emilia went to see Gerald to confirm with him the current status of the offer and that he understood it. Then she contacted the less-experienced prosecutor who was working with Bob Lane, to try to come to an agreement about the number of months Gerald was to serve. With the judge's assistance, she was eventually able to secure a small reduction, from 60 months down to 58.

I learned from Emilia that when she told Gerald the news, he paraphrased Moe Green from *The Godfather* by saying, "Ha. You don't buy me out! I buy you out."

Would Gerald have liked a bigger reduction in the sentence? Of course. But at least this marked the beginning of the end of his nightmare. So it wasn't happiness that had him smiling and making quips with Emilia, it was relief.

Over the next few days Emilia and others from Arnold Law contacted the Department of Corrections to confirm the details of the Alternative Incarceration Program and how "good time" is calculated. Emilia also talked to Judge Rasmussen several times, both on the phone and in person. Finally, she went to see Gerald. Reading off her handwritten notes on a yellow legal pad, she reviewed the offer with him one last time.

"We can counter or accept," she told Gerald. "What do you want to do?"

While she waited, he stared at her for several long seconds. "What do you mean?"

"I mean, do you want to do this, as you see it here," Emilia said, gesturing to the paper.

"Yes," he said, as if he'd already asked and answered this question too many times. "I'll do it. I already agreed. Two months [off of 60 months] is two months. I'll take it."

With that, Emilia had him handwrite a note on the yellow paper to confirm his acceptance of the offer.

Then Emilia went about winding down the case. She called Judge Rasmussen to confirm that Gerald had accepted the last counter-offer. She called the office and told my assistant to contact our whole team of lawyers, investigators, and the experts we had working for us across the country. The case had settled, she told everyone, so all work should cease immediately. Then Emilia called me.

"It's done," she said. "We have a few details to confirm for the text of the judgment, but it's over. I called off the dogs."

After having spent a few days working out some of the anger, frustration and self-pity I'd felt on Friday, I felt relieved at the news. The hard part – the hardest part – was over and Emilia had gotten us there. I was grateful for that.

"Well, the future is in Gerald's hands now – not mine, and not a jury's," I said to Emilia. "I look forward to seeing what he does with it."

CHAPTER 38
PERCEPTION IS REALITY

"Perception is reality." This is what 17th Sergeant Major of the Marine Corps, Michael Barrett once told Gerald, as Gerald was standing tall in front of him to answer for something he may or may not have done. Back then, Barrett was First Sergeant from Third Battalion Fourth Marines. He told Gerald that he was going to pay for what he perceived that Gerald had done, whether or not Gerald had actually done it. He said to Gerald, "You say you didn't do it. You may in fact be innocent. But it looks like you did it, so you did it. Perception is reality."

Yes, perception had become reality for Gerald Strebendt.

Gerald had agreed to enter a plea to criminally negligent homicide. Regardless of whether he was innocent by law, he had killed an unarmed man with a powerful rifle. The number and vehemence of the complaints against Gerald for his past misdeeds had put his case over the top. With the background of all the bad acts evidence, a self-defense shooting had come to look more like a case of overkill – at least to the government and the internet keyboard choir. There was a risk of losing at trial, so perception was going to have to be Gerald's reality now. He had to live with it – to live through it, too – and he was prepared to do so. His sergeant would almost certainly approve.

What happened to Gerald made me think hard about my life:

- the times I ran my mouth

- the fact that I never threw the first punch but certainly invited it

- the drinking in my rugby days, and everything that went with that

- my assertive driving – which I call efficient, but others may consider aggressive

- the periods of suspended driving privileges, due to too many tickets

- my full-throttle legal pleadings and correspondence, which I hope I've mostly gotten over

Have I ever threatened violence? Yes, when I believed it was appropriate, maybe to protect my wife or my friends, but also – maybe, possibly, sometimes – simply because I felt "the equities," the basic fairness/unfairness of the situation, warranted it.

I know that there are people out there who do not like me. I've always had a short, quick, explosive temper that I can usually control, but not always. As a child in my first real fist fight, I scared the heck out the 13-year-old who thought he was going to beat me up, by going crazy, swinging at him with these giant, flailing haymakers. After it was over I didn't remember anything about it. I completely saw red during the fight and it obliterated everything conscious. But I know that I didn't hit that kid a single time. Instead, I destroyed my fists all over the metal vent on the gym lockers that I had backed him up into, and left marks and dents everywhere. That part I didn't have to remember. It was there for all to see.

In short, I've never gone looking for trouble, but I've always been ready for it. And maybe that readiness has helped me find it. Fatherhood, turning 40, and the personal defeats in life that teach us things the hard way… they've all made me mellower. But the regrets and life lessons remain, and I like to think they help me relate to clients.

Seeing what happened to Gerald has really made me think twice about carrying my handgun. He had the right to be armed, just as I have the right. But if I were ever to use my weapon in self-defense, I know I'd likely be exactly where Gerald is today. Every single person that I had ever cursed at, threatened, menaced, mouthed off to… all of them would be calling the local police to report my behavior. There would be no shortage of bad acts to be attributed to Mike Arnold. And what could I say? I mean, other than yes, I did curse at him, threaten to knock his teeth out, call him some profane names, etc., etc., but he was asking for it. I can't even ballpark the number of confrontational situations I've faced.

Sometimes I think it's better to leave any self-defense shooting to my wife, Jacy, who is a much better shot than me anyway. When we used to hunt for whitetail deer together in Missouri, she did the killing and I did the carrying. While some of the adverse parties in her divorce cases have threatened her due to child-custody issues, she at least doesn't have a track record of aggressive confrontations to color her actions, should she need to defend herself. Well, except for that 14-point record Missouri Big Buck/ Boon and Crocket whitetail she shot her first day of deer season at age 12. But dead whitetails tell no tales. People do, and if folks wouldn't have much to say about Jacy, they'd have plenty to say about me.

Take a lesson, Mike. Take a good, long look at Gerald Strebendt and learn something.

Days passed. The State was pressuring us to wrap up the case with a sentencing hearing, but I was out of town, and there was no way that Emilia was going to let things go to court until every "i" was dotted and "t" crossed in the paperwork. We had to make sure all the wording was in place to ensure that Gerald had access to the Alternative Incarceration Program, without which he'd serve a lot more time than we envisioned. But, at last, the details were handled and the court set the sentencing for May 21.

Judge Rasmussen called me to his office on May 20, the day before sentencing. He wanted to talk about the so-called joint press release, he said. That was something that had been proposed during the settlement conference, but it was never agreed to. Upon hearing from him, I had our press guy prepare a draft for me to send to the judge – with the understanding that the judge would merge his version with ours. But when I received the advance version by email, it contained absolutely none of the language we had provided. Instead, the proposed news release mostly served to paint Gerald in the most negative light. It focused on Gerald's purported mental health issues, which seemed to be the excuse the State and the judge had come up with to explain the light sentence for shooting an unarmed man. They refused to revise it, and the meeting with the judge was intended to pressure me to go with their make-the-judge-and-D.A.-look-good-at-the-expense-of-the-truth press release.

In his chambers, I told Judge Rasmussen: "I'm not signing that because it's not true. I'm not signing my name to a brokered lie to make the D.A. look good."

I didn't know it at the time, but the judge had probably written it – which may have explained why he defended it so vigorously. After a little back-and-forth with me, he said, "How about we change the wording to 'mental condition' instead of 'mental issues,'" he said. "That way it could mean anything. It could mean Mr. Strebendt's state of mind at the time of the shooting." When I looked at him blankly, he added, "Fear."

"That's bullshit and you know it," I said. "No one is going to think that. Leave me out of it."

I told the judge that in any media interviews I might do after the sentencing, I planned only to say general things about respecting Gerald's right to take control of his case and his future. I was not going to participate in any sort of joint statement.

"Gerald needs to agree to this statement," the Judge said, pressing again. "It's in his best interest. People will think he had PTSD and will be more forgiving of what happened. It'll help him to assimilate after prison."

"Are you kidding me? That's more bullshit. The public needs to know he was justified in the shooting and he took the deal to reduce the risk to himself, not that he was some kind of crazy. I'm out. You all are on your own."

Previously the judge had told me that it was the D.A. demanding the joint press release, but after this meeting, it was clear that Judge Rasmussen was very much involved, and that he was probably trying to control the narrative in a way that would cast him in the best possible light. If that's not human nature, it's definitely the legal system doing its best to cover its posterior. Clearly, he (and probably the D.A.) didn't want to look "soft on crime" by cutting what some would consider a pretty sweet deal. But never again would I tacitly assume that any judge's goal is going to be strictly the pursuit of justice, and I've begun issuing a caveat to any client considering entering into a settlement conference: While justice is ostensibly the goal in any proceeding, there are political goals as well.

[Not surprisingly, there would come a day when a client of ours asked for "the same judge that gave Strebendt such a good deal." We issued our caveat almost as a warning, but the client wanted what he wanted. The negotiations that followed ended when this same judge told us that the D.A. wouldn't budge on the number of counts our client needed to plead to. Later on, the deputy D.A. notified us in writing that it was the judge, not the D.A., who wouldn't accept the deal. We were floored, but not surprised.]

By the time we got to May 21, there wasn't much left to do or say – not to Gerald, not to one another, and not to the judge or the prosecutor. All that remained was the judicial theater, which included Brenda Crofut making noise about wanting to speak during the sentencing. The parties had agreed that there would be no big statements or grandstanding by anyone; we all wanted the hearing to go quickly, without making a lot of news. We especially wanted the Crofut family to stay quiet to avoid additional undeserved attacks on Gerald, who had endured enough. The judge and prosecutors probably wanted to avoid being beaten about the head by the family and in the press, too. The end result: Brenda Crofut would not speak. She would, however, present a letter to the judge in open court.

Gerald came in, dressed in a button-down shirt and dress pants. He also had real shoes on. He wasn't allowed a tie or a belt, but his hands were free. I shook his hand, hugged him, and together we stood for the hearing to begin. We stayed standing as the judge asked Gerald questions about the agreement, and the details of the sentence. With a quiet but firm voice, Gerald stood at attention with his hands behind his back and answered. Did he understand the agreement? "Yes, sir." Was that his signature? "Yes, sir." When asked for his plea, Gerald gave it. "Guilty," he said.

I thought to myself that even though Gerald had killed a man, spent a year in the county jail awaiting trial, and would spend at least another year in jail after this day, he had been, relatively speaking, lucky. If Crofut had not been drunk and high on Effexor, if Crofut's DNA had not been on the gun, if witnesses hadn't seen Crofut stomping around the road waving his arms aggressively, Gerald would not have gotten the deal he did. If Gerald had not trained my associate attorney at his gym, he wouldn't even have come to my office, and to me, that too possibly meant he wouldn't have gotten the deal he did.

So many ifs. And, for Gerald, I suppose, so many "if onlys."

Yes, I had to admit, it could have been so much worse. How does a man come through life with so many people ready to make accusations against him, even untrue ones? It was something I was trying to answer. I wondered if Gerald was trying to answer it, too.

The remainder of sentencing went quickly. We stood, then we sat, then stood, then sat – in this respect, court is a lot like going to mass on Sunday. When the judge asked if Brenda Crofut had anything to say, Bob Lane handed the judge a letter written by her. The judge glanced at it for maybe three seconds; he clearly did not read it.

Then the judge thanked her and pronounced the sentence.

Gerald looked forward, his face stoic.

The cameras in the jury box pointed at us and clicked quietly.

Then it was over. Gerald sat and waited for the courtroom to empty, at which point he'd be taken into custody again.

Unexpectedly, the judge's judicial assistant came out and asked *The Register-Guard*'s reporter, Jack Moran, to come in to meet with the judge. Taken aback, the reporter agreed.

This was a clear departure from normal judicial-journalist relations. But what did I expect in a case that was such a total departure from justice? Backroom deals? Why not? But at least the Fourth Estate had an ethical and responsible reporter walking back there.

With Moran gone, we had the courtroom to ourselves. We all hugged Gerald and shook hands. The cuffs were put on him and he was chained up. The deputies escorted him from the courtroom, and we watched him go out as the doors closed.

That afternoon each side held their respective press conferences. Lane County's elected D.A. Alex Gardner had this to say about the resolution: "Each of them contributed to this going the way it did. But ultimately, the greater package of choices was in Strebendt's control. He's the one who ultimately pulled the trigger and caused the death. And that's why he's criminally responsible for homicide."

At the press conference Bob Lane chose to highlight a different problem in the case. He was concerned that if Gerald was acquitted he would be able to walk into the Springfield Police Department and walk out a few minutes later with the very gun that killed Crofut.

I had very little to say, as it was Gerald's decision which was much more complex and nuanced than a soundbite would allow. "This is a pretty sad day for everyone involved in the case," I told reporters. "But we respect his decision to basically take control of his life and settle this case."

The next morning, I met Gerald at the jail. He was livid. "Did you see that bullshit that Alex Gardner told the press? They lied!"

Gerald was referring to news reports on the lengthy press conference that the D.A. did after the sentencing. In it, he was clearly trying to walk that very fine line between "It would have been hard to win this at trial" and "We didn't screw up by charging him with murder." I've got some sympathy for that, though not a lot. It's a tough one, politically speaking. No matter what you say, some segment of the population is going to be angry.

Apparently the newspaper didn't get whatever secret message the judge tried to deliver to Jack Moran in chambers. The newspaper article noted that it was very uncommon for a murder case to settle down to an accidental homicide charge, which is usually reserved for fatal traffic accidents. The bylined reporter, not Moran, pointed out that murder charges, when pled out, typically drop to manslaughter with either six or ten years of prison. But Gerald didn't even get the mandatory minimum of five years that state law typically calls for in criminally negligent homicide cases involving a firearm. Thanks to our research with the DOC, we were able to walk our way around that minimum through the terms of the settlement agreement we reached with the State and the judge.

Gerald's beef with the D.A. was how he emphasized the mental health assessment as part of Gerald's plea agreement and his "mental condition" relating to "rules of engagement" that only apply in combat. Gerald said "They are trying to say this was PTSD without saying it was PTSD. They know that's misleading. They know I passed the psych eval!"

"Now you see why everyone wanted to muzzle me," I replied. "Do you think I would have let these mistruths stand? They also selectively released an affidavit that bad mouths you. They could have released the 911 call but they released a fucking biased affidavit. Lying by omission. It's the way politicians work. The judge is a politician. The D.A. is too."

"What can you do about it?" he asked.

"Nothing. I tapped out. I'm done. Go to prison and worry about this later. You have the rest of your life to set the record straight. D.A.'s and judges have short memories. There will be plenty of time to tell your story later. Maybe you can write a book or something. I mean, "Dateline NBC" wanted the story so maybe it's a good story."

Gerald wanted to call the reporter right then and "set the record straight." I told him to cool off and suggested he write a prepared statement first. I said, "I never call a reporter or send an email when I'm still angry. I write what I want to say and then wait for an hour, then edit."

"So, should I call the reporter?"

"Look, Gerald. Here are my press rules about when to talk to a reporter and what to say. First, does it help the client? You have to know in the end if it's the client's best interests and that you aren't just talking to see your name in the paper or to make yourself feel good. Column inches aren't your goal. Your goal is your client's goal. You need to think about what you want to accomplish – what's your strategic goal – or if you should just let sleeping dogs lie and move on."

"Second, is it the truth?" I continued. "You need to make 100 percent sure you are confident in the facts or opinions that you're giving. The third one is related to the second and the first. Will you always be able to stand by what you said? Will you ever have to retract it? Once you say something it's there forever, so make sure a year from now or five years from now you are okay having said it. And finally, does the client consent?"

We went through the goals and the facts and ultimately, he decided he wanted to talk. We wrote down some bullet points, and later he ended up calling *The Register-Guard* reporter from the jail and talking to him at length about the case. It was his chance to finally thumb his nose at the gag order and set the record straight. He talked to the reporter, Jack Moran, on a recorded line, discussing his lack of "mental health" issues and what really happened the night of the shooting. Moran ended the conversation with these questions:

MORAN: *"Why did you take the deal, Mr. Strebendt?"*

GERALD: *"It's basic math. It's not a 58-month sentence, Jack. They gave me a 17-month sentence. I have to be in jail until the end of this trial anyway, and they pushed the date back to the end of February. This is seventeen more months then I would have had to do anyway, with a 100 percent guarantee of freedom at the end. It's insurance. It's 17-month insurance so I don't have to run the risk of anything happening at a trial or of a jury getting it wrong. They can throw all the lesser included offenses, all the way down to basically me yelling at somebody, me assaulting someone at the lowest level. They could throw this all at me. So, it's a 17-month sentence that they promised me and we agreed to.*

"Mr. Arnold said, 'You will beat this. We will beat this, [but] seventeen months is not worth the risk of 25 to life.' I agree that it's just not worth the gamble. I'll do 17 months."

MORAN: *"I guess we are just going to cover everything. What about all [the allegations of road rage] that Rachel talked about. I know that some of that is true."*

GERALD: *"I got to go. They're pulling me out. Um. Don't yell at your neighbors for driving too fast. They'll come back to haunt you. Yeah. I got a new kitten and my neighbors were driving like maniacs so I said, 'Slow down, there's cats and kids.' In 2011 I got mad at a motorist. Don't ever get mad at anybody. They'll come out of the woodwork if you ever have to defend yourself. I'm getting thrown back into my cell, Jack. I gotta go."*

MORAN: *"Okay. Thanks for the call."*

GERALD: *"Bye."*

CHAPTER 39

RECKONING AND REDEMPTION

After the plea hearing, Arnold Law did its best to make sure Gerald didn't feel abandoned. One or more of us visited him daily. But that visitation continued for less than a week, because Gerald wasn't long for Lane County after the sentencing. Soon he was gone, off to somewhere that for security reasons we weren't allowed to know. That was okay – we were happy to see him headed to an environment where he'd no longer be in solitary confinement, as he had been for most of his time in the county jail. Under the supervision of the Oregon Department of Corrections, he would be able to be around other people (for better or worse), and gain access to other amenities and programs that county jails don't provide.

Predictably, *The Register-Guard*'s news story on Gerald rekindled the embers of the case. The internet buzzed about the outcome. Some decried the plea as unjust to Gerald, or unjust to Crofut and his family. People who were not at the center of the case and privy to the key facts of the evidence questioned what had happened and why. Many criticized the actions of the District Attorney's Office – but the complainers were of two minds about the sentence. Some decried the shortness of it. Others, however, thought the D.A. shouldn't have brought the case in the first place.

Even seventeen months later, this incident, this case, is still very much alive to the family of David Crofut. Joanna Martinez, Brenda's daughter, told me, "That man got away with murder and killed my father out of self-ishness and pure anger." Would a trial – the ultimate dispute resolution tool – had given her peace after an independent jury of twelve weighed in which side's narrative was the more plausible? We will never know.

The news is always full of stories about the failures of the justice system, both locally and nationally. Children are taken from parents and placed into abusive homes by the government departments charged with protecting them. Unarmed mentally ill and people of color are shot by poorly trained or trigger-happy police officers. The country's leading politicians cross legal and ethical lines and aren't held accountable. The inconsistent application of laws that should be black and white results in a lot of unsatisfying gray, unfortunately. Gerald's case was yet another example of how flawed individuals, of whom Gerald definitely was one, both influence and suffer from the deficiencies of our legal justice system.

Eventually, after about a month, we learned about Gerald's new digs. After spending some time in a transfer station north of Eugene, he was sent over to eastern Oregon, to the largest prison in the state, the Snake River Correctional Institution (SRCI). Following a period of transition, Gerald found himself in the prison's minimum security unit. The max unit of SRCI was across the street, a looming, ominous beast surrounded by razor wire. In an ironic twist, Jason Dizick, the man who slit the throat of Gerald's childhood father figure, Steve McMullan, was doing 65 years over in that hulk of a building. Gerald told us he was glad that he wasn't in the max facility, as Dizick was perhaps one of the few people in the world Gerald would risk his freedom to harm. Retribution is a dish that's hard to turn down if it's set right in front of you.

In a letter Gerald mailed soon after his arrival, he told me that from the get-go he was something of a celebrity at SRCI. He asked us for copies of his indictment and the Final Judgment, so he could prove what charge he had been convicted of and the length of his sentence. Many inmates didn't believe that he actually shot a man in the head and only received what was, in their eyes, a "slap on the wrist."

I couldn't see the prison sentence as a "slap on the wrist," not when it had been meted out to an innocent man. The shooting was justified. It was wrong for Gerald to be incarcerated, and not even his minimum security situation was going to make me feel any better about it.

Apparently, though, I was supposed to feel great about it. As I walked the streets of Eugene, from my office to the courthouse and back, I regularly ran into lawyers who chatted me up, praising the work I did and the "great deal" that I got for Gerald. I nodded and smiled, and tried to say the right things. But inside, the praise fed my guilt, which was rooted in the unshakable feeling that I had failed my client.

It did help that Gerald seemed pretty upbeat about prison, at least as compared to jail. For the first time in more than a year, he wasn't spending all his time alone. And even if the other guys were there for doing bad things (rape, assault, drugs), at least he wasn't in solitary anymore. He reported that he was finally able to exercise and get outside, which was allowing him to replace his ghostly pallor with a healthy tan. Thanks to his regular access to weights and the track, he was putting on weight – real muscle weight, not flab. Since we couldn't visit him anymore, we waited apprehensively but hopefully for each update on how he was doing. Gerald could call us if he had the credit to do so, but calling him was harder. We had to call the prison to schedule the call, which sometimes took several days to arrange.

Through these limited communications, Gerald acknowledged that there had been a lot of posturing and chest-thumping required to earn his place in the facility. I warned him against too much of that, fearing it might result in conflicts that could impact his "good time." It was no secret that Gerald *could* fight, and I was concerned that he *would* fight. Whether he knew it or not, he might be even *looking for the opportunity* to fight. Fighting was Gerald's response to almost every challenge, every push, every stressor in life. I worried that people would test him, and that he would rise to their challenge. Again and again I told him, *avoid anything that could lead to a fight.*

Fighting was only part of my worry, though. It wasn't long before I got some hints that Gerald was battling some significant depression – and who wouldn't be? I mean, the man was in prison, cut off from his life, his friends, and his family. He had a lot to grieve – the loss of his freedom, the loss of his business and financial security, and the loss of the everyday lives we all lead "outside."

As we all had suspected, Gerald and his fiancée, Kristin, had ended their engagement. She stood by him and supported him for 15 months during the pendency of the case. She had talked with him and cried with him almost every day that he had access to a phone. She put her money into the case. She convinced her mother to put money into the case. She held onto the hope that Gerald would be coming home. But, no longer. Gerald's guilty plea ended his case, and the resulting prison term closed off the avenue that he and Kristin had hoped to travel back to a normal life together. She said goodbye. And as she left, she took with her Gerald's main reason to hope and persevere. Without that anchor, Gerald was adrift and looking for new moorings.

Emilia and I tried to comfort him as best we could. At first we sent Gerald something more than weekly – a letter, something related to his case, or something we thought he'd enjoy. Once, for example, I sent him a book about archery and bow-hunting, since he wasn't going to be able to own firearms anymore. At a loss for words of my own to comfort him, and knowing what a big reader he is, I also sent him books about traveling, philosophy, and science.

My actions were driven, I'm sure, by wanting to somehow connect Gerald to the outside world. Who else would be in touch with him? I didn't know if he had anyone but me and the others at Arnold Law. I wanted him to feel that at least we cared. In newsy letters I told him that I had met with Detective Crolly and the property clerk at SPD to obtain the property that had been seized from him during the case. Detective Crolly had told me to say hello to him and spoke pleasantly of Gerald and his prior dealings with him. I also told him that I had run into Bret Teral from Gerald's old gym, who sent his regards. But I didn't tell Gerald that Teral had confessed that, as highly as he regarded Gerald, when he learned about the shooting, he "wasn't surprised."

I also told Gerald that I had read one of his letters to my daughter, Abigail, and that I had signed her up for Brazilian Jiu-Jitsu lessons at McKenzie Martial Arts in west Eugene. She, however, had additional aims. "Gerald is going to give me personal lessons when he gets out of prison," she assured me. Abigail knew who Gerald was. She had been privy to work conversations throughout the case and she knew why her dad was working so late so often. I told her that if she wanted to train with Gerald, she'd be waiting until 2017 for the opportunity. If anything, it seemed to make her want to work harder. I proudly reported to Gerald on Abigail's first Jiu-Jitsu tournament, and on her fierce determination on the mats. When the girl with the best skills in Abigail's training class mounted her, Abigail got her to tap out simply by squeezing as hard as she could. I had to laugh at that. All heart, not much technique – just like her dad?

Abigail's interest in martial arts didn't come entirely from Gerald, I should note. She and I "play fight" a lot at home. I had to train her to say "play fight," because she used to tell people that she and Daddy were "fighting last night" and he used a (insert scary-sounding MMA term) on her. That's the sort of thing that can result in a call to Child Protective Services. But Abigail was every bit the aggressor as we tussled. She looked forward to the day that she could learn and use a guillotine chokehold on me, she said. Once she caused me to tap out with an arm bar. Ouch. We both learned that it doesn't take much weight to hyper-extend an elbow.

(Photos: Abigail, facing the camera, grapples with Eleanor at McKenzie Martial Arts, Eugene, Oregon.)

On one occasion, Gerald wrote us specifically to tell us about the prison guards. He said the guards all knew him and had been preparing for his arrival, and that they had treated him respectfully from the first day. While they couldn't figure out how to pronounce his last name, they treated him like a human being. He had been told by more than one guard that they respected what he did against Crofut, and they didn't believe that he should have had to go to prison for it. Amazingly, these guards were going out of their way to ease his time there. He received the best work assignment he could have in the DOC – the garden. The guards would load Gerald up in a van and drive him outside the prison walls to the plot of land where inmates grew vegetables for the prison meals during the spring, summer, and fall. As Gerald weeded, dug and harvested, he drank in the view with his eyes, using it to sustain him when back inside the walls.

Quickly, Gerald became trusted as few inmates ever are. The prison guards began to drop him off and leave him to work unsupervised. At any moment, Gerald could have walked away. With his training, he could have easily escaped to the wilderness to endure some pretty rough conditions if he had to. But he stayed, and apparently he worked hard and well. Occasionally the guards forgot that Gerald was even out there. On a couple of occasions, when it became clear that no one was coming to retrieve him at the end of the day, Gerald actually had to walk back to the prison and pound on the doors to get back inside.

In fire season, Gerald received another relatively plum assignment – working on an inmate team that assisted local wildland firefighting crews. The work entailed digging fire breaks and mopping up hot spots. It was another job that put Gerald totally in his element. He was outside, in the woods, doing something challenging and physical.

In the second summer of Gerald's time in prison, he was assigned to SRCI's contract program to plant thousands of sagebrush plants on Bureau of Land Management (BLM) lands. The purpose of the program was to improve the habitat of the Greater Sage Grouse, a species that is totally dependent on these scrubby bushes. Gerald was individually selected to take care of the young plants in the program's greenhouse, which had been suffering some neglect under another inmate's watch. With that appointment, Gerald spent the next year sowing seeds, watering and otherwise caring for the growing sprouts that became his responsibility.

A side note about that job, one that I find both touching and revealing of who Gerald really is: Whenever he could get away with it, Gerald snuck food out of the prison – not for himself, but for the birds, rabbits, and mice that frequented the greenhouse. Gerald claimed he did it to distract the critters from nibbling on the vulnerable plants, but if that was his aim, he could have used traps and bird netting to solve the problem. Once the kind of man who bought ice cream for a dog on a hot day, Gerald was now the kind of man who fed birds and animals instead of killing them or keeping them away. I took a lot of reassurance from that.

The prison can hold Gerald, but it can't change him, not deep, down inside.

Still, it gradually became clear that Gerald was hoping that prison *would* change him – at least in the ways he would want to be changed. Around the time that Gerald was assigned to the sagebrush program, he began writing long letters to me about his life. Receiving the introspective letters made me think that his time spent outside, in the gardens, woods, and greenhouse, was doing wonders for the wounds in his soul. He wrote on whatever paper he came across—napkins, in the margins of documents, on pages torn from magazines. He even wrote me a letter on the back of a pamphlet for suicide prevention.

Did he choose that paper on purpose? Did he want us to know he's aware of his depression and is taking steps to combat it?

When these letters started to come, I began to feel a new kind of responsibility to the man. I didn't know who else he was talking to, but I felt like it was important that he talk to someone, anyone, about what had happened to him and what he was going through. I told him many times that I thought he should seek counseling to help him through all of the traumas of his life. While he never confirmed doing that, he did mention that he had enrolled in a theology course, and also some parenting classes. He didn't have a lot of other options for filling his time, he explained, and he felt like these particular classes would give him something useful for his life, even if he didn't ever marry and have children.

From Gerald's letters, I learned things that caused me concern. He talked about the various factions in the jail (such as the skinheads and the Mexicans) and how each had lobbied for him to "join" them. A man of Gerald's skill and notoriety would be a valuable asset to any group or gang,

I knew, but aligning could be a very bad idea. I was relieved to read that he hadn't "joined" with anyone. And, perhaps unsurprisingly given his reputation, they had accepted his decision to go his own way.

I could see that part of what Gerald was sorting through while in prison was his own personality and its defects. While many of the bad acts alleged during his case were false or grossly exaggerated, Gerald admitted in his letters and calls that there was often at least some truth to the character of the allegations, if not the actual substance of them. Maybe he didn't do exactly what was said, but maybe his actions and attitudes involving other people had made it easy for them to build stories around his words or demeanor. In one letter, he recounted with a mixture of humor and "aha" recognition a conversation he had with his bunkmate. Gerald had complained that he felt like the "road rage" label attached to his case was misapplied. His bunkmate responded by laughing heartily. "Strebendt," he said, "you road rage all 'round here, and you ain't got no car!"

In bits and pieces, Gerald told us of his many life regrets. He told of a confrontation with a woman in a bar that he felt embarrassed about. He had chastised her for spending money on beer when he could see by her Oregon Trail card that she was on food stamps. While other patrons looked on uncomfortably, Gerald engaged her in a loud, belittling argument about her lifestyle; namely, of taking advantage of government support instead of taking responsibility for herself. His comments so inflamed the room that another patron got up to join Gerald in haranguing the woman. There was no purpose to his comments, Gerald acknowledged. He didn't achieve anything, he didn't change anything. All he did was shame someone he had never met before and would never see again. Now, with nothing but time to engage in self-examination, Gerald was mortified by his behavior. He wished he could provide an explanation for it, he said. But he couldn't.

Another story Gerald told in his letters was more recent. Some of the fighters he was training were to compete at a venue in Portland, so Gerald drove up there accompanied by a female friend. They drank vodka mixed with cranberry juice all the way to the venue. When he pulled up in his shiny black pickup truck and got out, he heard people who were waiting in line whispering his name: "That's Gerald Strebendt! He fought in the

UFC!" Gerald was puffed with pride as he was accorded VIP treatment. He was also, however, drunk, and his behavior proved it.

The first fight of the night was one of his female fighters, and she got knocked out. In flagrant violation of the rules, Gerald ran up the stairs to the cage door, demanding to be let in to care for her. He had words with the security guard who, following the rules, would not let anyone who wasn't a doctor inside. Gerald's response? *"Don't you know who I am?"*

The argument continued until someone in the ring finally gave him permission to go in. While Gerald tended to his fighter, the provoked security guard called for backup and the assembled team met him at the gate as he exited. Gerald could see what was coming, and he fairly licked his chops waiting for someone to put a hand on him so he could fight. When one of the guards grabbed his wrist, he thought, "It's on." But before he could do anything, the three experienced bouncers (former law enforcement) flipped him onto his head and broke his wrist. It was like a scripted-for-television moment. He never got a chance to even try to land a single punch or kick. He lay there on the floor, held down by the guards, struggling uselessly as 3,000 people who knew his name and former fame watched. All the while Gerald was drunkenly shouting, "Don't you know who I am? I'm Gerald Strebendt!" When he finally surrendered, the guards got him on his feet and escorted him to the door as the whole arena watched. Out on the sidewalk he was forced to endure a behavior lecture – in full view and earshot of those who had previously noticed and admired him.

Then Gerald reached way back, to something that happened well before most of his UFC career and Blackwater. He had returned to his mother's home in Coos Bay, Oregon, before an upcoming MMA bout, a bout that included several future UFC fighters (Jeremy Horn, Antonio McKee, and Antonio Banuelos). On December 7, 2001, he called 911 to report that he had just beaten the crap out of a sex offender who had entered his home uninvited. Coos Bay police officers arrived at the scene to find Jesse Hayes lying on the floor of the garage, covered in blood.

Gerald told the officers that he had seen Hayes walking near a local grocery store, and recognized him as someone that Gerald had seen arrested for failing to register as a sex offender. Gerald had been present when Hayes was taken into custody, he said, because he was on a ride-along with police from the adjacent town of North Bend at the time. How did Hayes end up at Gerald's house? The fact that Gerald was writing to us about it told us that, whatever the scenario, Gerald was now feeling guilty about it.

Police reports of the incident show Gerald saying he talked to Hayes outside the store, but the two parted, and sometime later Gerald found the guy in his garage, demanding money. Gerald said that when he refused to pay Hayes, the two fought and Gerald called 911. But what police saw seemed strangely at odds with the idea that Gerald was attacked by Hayes. The officers who responded to the scene found Gerald very animated, licking the blood off his cut knuckles and repeatedly shaking and rotating his neck and shoulders. Hayes was much smaller than Gerald, only 5'1" and 140 pounds, and police found Gerald's statements inconsistent. They also noted some statements made by Gerald that smacked of vigilantism: "This is for all the people that have been victimized"; "This guy is a predator. He's not the victim"; and "I would do it again." Gerald also refused to take a polygraph.

Hayes told a different story, one that Gerald was now admitting was largely true. Hayes said that he had recognized Gerald on the street and approached him. He said that Gerald suddenly told him he owed Hayes $20 and invited Hayes to his home for payment. Hayes didn't think Gerald owed him anything, but hey, free money. When Hayes entered the residence to get the money, however, Gerald took off his sweatshirt, dropped a ten-dollar bill on the ground, and started punching him. Despite what the police considered obvious evidence that Gerald lured Hayes into his house to impose his own brand of vigilante justice, the case went to trial and Gerald was acquitted by a jury after only a few minutes of deliberation. One of the jurors asked in open court if they could award damages to Gerald, probably because Hayes went off script during his direct examination and told the jury all kinds of unsavory things about himself and his criminal history.

Now, almost 15 years later, Gerald was 'fessing up to having lured the homeless man to his garage to hurt him because Hayes preyed upon children. Even if Hayes was the worst, lowest form of humanity, doing this had still been wrong, Gerald acknowledged. It risked his future, and not just in the MMA. He could have been – *should* have been – convicted. But Gerald would never have the chance to make reparations to Hayes, as Hayes was murdered in 2013. His lifeless body was discovered outside of a warehouse, covered in trash, beaten and strangled.

In one of my letters to Gerald during this period of his introspection, I wrote, "Why are you in jail?" His response nearly knocked me back in my chair:

"Because I have been a scoundrel and an asshole for years and Allah, Karma, and God have finally caught up with me."

With that single, self-aware sentence, Gerald confirmed what I had believed about him for quite a while: The guy had lived for many years at the edge of the law, always toeing the line, never getting caught. He pricked the pride of many and left soreness in his wake. These people did not forget him. When the media caught wind of the shooting, these individuals made the decision to contact law enforcement about their run-ins with Gerald. Investigative work that would have taken the authorities weeks of phone calls, letters, and drive time was boiled down to just days. In this way, we can say that the prosecution's decision to pursue criminal charges against Gerald Strebendt for the shooting death of David Crofut was part and parcel of the digital age and the ease with which people can participate in not just the conversation about a crime, but also its prosecution. It's as easy as hammering a few choice words into a keyboard, or having seen something online, dropping a dime to add your two-cents' worth.

For each of Gerald's bad acts, there were good ones to cite. In the years before Gerald killed Crofut, he had:

- stopped and disarmed a drunken motorcyclist who had a handgun

- called for help when a neighbor's house was on fire

- notified the police when it sounded like his neighbors needed help during a domestic dispute

- and taught self-defense techniques to police departments in Lane and Linn counties.

Without the online posts and phone calls attesting to despicable incidents and disparaging his character, Gerald may have skated through the shooting incident as he had skated through everything else. But the calls and statements were made, and they were made by people who had been given reason over the years – by Gerald himself – to assume the worst about Gerald Strebendt. It didn't help his cause that shootings of unarmed individuals, especially by police, had put shootings, and especially those committed with so-called assault weapons, under a national microscope.

Yes, I would have to say that Gerald was a casualty of our digital, always-on age and its ability to whip up frenzy quickly. But Gerald was also a casualty of himself, and now, in prison, Gerald was starting to get that. I was happy for him. I knew that the only road past this horror was through it, and it necessarily included the soul-searching he was so obviously now doing.

Talking about his past mistakes led to Gerald to take the next step and attempt some reconciliations. Unfortunately, some of the people Gerald wronged were gone, like Hayes, his beating victim, or unknown, like the woman drinking beer on food stamps. Others rejected Gerald's overtures. Perhaps most poignantly, Gerald tried and failed at making things right with his own father. Once, well before the shooting, Gerald had offered his hand to William, his dad, and said he was sorry for everything that had gone on between them. The handshake was rejected. From prison, Gerald tried again, this time writing a letter. He told his father that he loved him and asked for his forgiveness. The letter went unanswered.

In November, six months into his sentence, Gerald wrote:

My dreams are getting better but they still have the power to bring me to my knees. I will conquer them. Did you know that during the Indian wars of the 1800s, quite a few people were shot with arrows and they left the arrowheads inside to save them? Eventually, even after ten or more years, people managed to expel parts of the arrowhead and shaft that remained. It took the human body years and years but eventually they'd get a boil-like sore and a 10-year-old obsidian arrowhead would squeeze out. I wonder if trauma is like that? I don't see why it wouldn't be. I will overcome these things. I just know I will.

Lately I have been going over the times in my life where I had decisions to make and I went left instead of right. I'm admitting to myself where I've been wrong. God-damn, it's a painful self-reflection. I don't have enough paper to give you all the examples but I can freely admit them all. I'm left wondering if I've ever made the right choice. I've just always been so foolish. I think I've had the average dose of laziness and combined that with the liability of a poor education. Combine that with more than the average dose of fear and you have quite the dangerous fool.

I swear, I will shed this old skin and rise again. I meditate on it every day and I see so many areas for improvement. I'm just thankful that I have had an opportunity to learn how to be honest with myself. If I ever have children, I would teach them that the most important thing he needed to conquer in the world was love. I would teach them how to make a sundial to navigate by day and how to locate Polaris by going off the handle of the Little Dipper to navigate by night. I would teach my boys how to treat women right. I would teach my girls to fight.

It's not too late to be the man I want to be.

I know that Emilia, and everyone at Arnold Law, joins me in saying… we hope he's right.

(Photo: Gerald Strebendt, age 37, and "Patch" at the Snake River Correctional Institution, 2016.)

NEW FIGHTS, NEW OPPONENTS

G erald Strebendt killed David Crofut on January 29, 2014. He was arrested March 7, 2014. He pleaded guilty more than a year later, on May 21, 2015. A year after that, in June of 2016, he was approved for participation in an Alternative Incarceration Program. This was good news to me and Emilia, because it stood to minimize his time served. Still, the earliest date that he could be released from behind bars is sometime in 2017 – and that's providing he successfully completes the program. Without programs, he'll return to the community in early 2018.

If Gerald fails to get into his early release program, he will spend almost four years in jail for shooting and killing a man in self-defense.

What will he come home to? Gerald's fiancée at the time of the shooting, Kristin, has moved on. His gym and its patrons are gone. But at least one professional possibility awaits him, a return to the ring. In 2016, while writing this book, I spoke to a MMA fight promoter who said that he wants to set up a pro fight for Gerald when he gets out of prison. When I told Gerald about it, he said he was game. "Prison is an elite training camp," he quipped. "We have Olympic weights, a track, and a regulation football field. I'm stronger than I have ever been. I'm deadlifting 410 lbs. We can't spar in here but I'm sparring in my mind, rolling (a term of art for practicing submissions in BJJ) in my mind, practicing techniques in my mind.

Let's see if I still have it in me, that is, the new me: the felon who now meditates and gardens."

I believe he does have it in him, so long as he can stave off depression. In our continuing contact with him, mostly by phone and mail, he tells me he is reading authors like Nietzsche, Homer, and Thoreau. (He read "Walden" three times). He was also listening to one particular song, over and over: "Seven Years Old," by Lukas Graham. It's a song about coming of age, the passage of time, and of coming to terms with life as one has lived it.

Picturing Gerald in his cell, listening to this song and reckoning with how life had put him in so many bizarre situations leading up to this one horrible turn of events, I can only feel sad. He was innocent of the crime, but with his plea, he was found legally culpable anyway. And, arguably, his plea was the culmination of the life he led and the stories and insinuations that arose from that life in the wake of the shooting. People called him "The Finishing Machine," for God's sake. There were two stories of almost heroic kindness for every one that made him out to be an angry guy looking for a fight, and not all of the bad-acts stories were true. But enough of them were, and it made a difference.

As for me? In some ways, life is back to how it was before Gerald became my client. I still have my farm, and the struggle continues to balance the tugs of my loves – my wife Jacy, our daughter Abigail, and now a son, Alexander – against the needs of our law practice. Free time is still spent in the barn or on the tractor – which is a tool as good for clearing the mind as it is for clearing brush.

In other ways, life has changed forever. In my law practice, complex criminal cases have continued to find me. As Gerald's case ended, I was retained to defend another man charged with murder – this time it was a Hood River County case that involved an alleged cliff killing for insurance money. Not long after that, I was retained by Ammon Bundy after he was arrested during the armed occupation of the Malheur National Wildlife Refuge in eastern Oregon. For a few weeks, there wasn't a higher profile criminal case in the United States.

Looking back, I can see how I yearned for the experience and the opportunity that comes from advocating for a cause you truly believe in. It's why we become lawyers, isn't it? To take on a behemoth adversary – the government – for an innocent client, to fight against seemingly unbeatable odds… I wanted that highly public platform to prove myself, my mettle, my worth. Yes, I absolutely wanted the legal world to notice me and my skills, but mostly I wanted to prove these things to myself. In certain key ways, I succeeded. The responses of my legal colleagues were overwhelmingly positive and even laudatory when the details of Gerald's sentence were revealed. I'd gotten him "the deal of the century," some said, clapping me on the back.

While I appreciated the kudos, I wondered what colleagues would think of me if they knew all the details. To outsiders like those who were singing my praises, Gerald was a road-raging hothead who shot an unarmed man after a car crash. But the insiders knew what the evidence showed: that victim David Crofut, who was extremely drunk and likely the true road rager that night, brought his own death upon himself. To me, the fact that Gerald was doing any jail time at all beyond time served was a personal loss. I felt it deeply.

Coming to know Gerald Strebendt through this case has made me a different man in significant ways. No longer do I enjoy representing an innocent man charged of a heinous crime. In some ways, in fact, I dread the ringing of the office phone, and the new case it might bring me. Defending an innocent man charged with murder is one of the hardest things I do. The pressure I put on myself, my family, and my co-workers almost breaks me (and them, of course). It's much easier to sleep at night when you're defending someone who is guilty. Here's why: If you fail and your client is convicted, at least you can send them off to prison with the knowledge that they did wrong, and probably deserved their punishment.

But this case continues to provide me sleepless nights. Before Gerald I had been a lawyer for more than 13 years, and I was no stranger to the flaws in our justice system. I knew, from experience almost on a daily basis, that the roles of victim and defendant in any given case can be mutable and prone to rapid change. Indeed, the mantra in some prosecutors' offices is "Today's victim is tomorrow's defendant." But never before had I wanted so badly for justice to prevail for a defendant/victim. Gerald's "Parade of Horribles" was as bad, as damning, as any I could ever imagine. Yet the guy was, both on the street that night and by the legal definition of self-defense, innocent. And the fact that the system couldn't sufficiently separate Gerald from his bad acts to acquit him – well, it broke my heart.

The Crofut family is also deeply disappointed in the case's outcome, of course. David's Crofut's stepdaughter Joanna Martinez put it this way: "People need to see that what happened that night could have happened differently and that Gerald was wrong for what he did. My father was unarmed and did not deserve to lose his life over a minor traffic incident that they were both wrong for. Gerald knew what his intentions were when he got out of that truck armed and ready to fire. This was not the first encounter Gerald had similar to this. My father simply was in the wrong place at the wrong time and lost his life to a mentally unstable man who severely needed help. We did not get justice for Dave or my family and I think Gerald got away with murder and got sentenced very lightly for his actions. He will soon be released to live his life as he does and I fear for the community because he is unpredictable and angry and we will forever be without Dave."

Over the last year-plus since the plea agreement, I have come to recognize that, to a large extent, I am Gerald Strebendt. Similar age and working class background. Same aggressive type of personality. Same tendency toward quick bursts of anger. But for a few choices in life, the tables could have been turned — Gerald could have been the one warming himself in front of his wood stove that night, while reading about a roadside shooting involving me. All that really separates the two of us are the significant choices we have made in life. Not just the split-second decision to pull a trigger or not, but the thousands of big and small choices that offer us course correction opportunities and bring us to where we are today.

It's undeniably true that each of us is little more than the sum total of the limitless choices — and the circumstances – we encounter. Ever wish you could go back and change just one thing? What if Gerald had been able to somehow stop Jason Dizick from slitting the throat of Steve McMullan, the best father figure Gerald ever had? Would that have changed the course of Gerald's life? Or, what if he had chosen to quietly retire from the military instead of joining Blackwater? Would either of these life revisions been enough to save David Crofut, and with him, Gerald? Or is there something about Gerald, the man, that made some sort of deadly conflict inevitable?

There are no easy answers in life, especially when it comes how to address or avoid violence when it crosses our path. All we have are our wits and our life experiences to help us choose wisely. For Gerald's sake, I hope this sad and fateful journey from Bob Straub Parkway through sentencing is the life experience that finally helps the Finishing Machine choose a better way of living.

I know of one person who is betting against Gerald, and that's Joanna Martinez. She wrote:

> *I hope every day of his life he sees Dave's face and I pray one day he has enough guts to stand out and say he was wrong for what he did. He has never apologized for his actions to my family and that to me shows his true character. He is an angry man who needs to seek help or he will eventually take another life, without a doubt.*

It's that last sentence that gives me pause. It describes the possibility that I dread the most – that freedom from incarceration brings nothing good or even better to Gerald's life.

My hope is that Gerald's old way of life, marked by drinking, aggression, chest-thumping and posturing, is over. I hope that the choices he makes when he retakes control of his life will propel him far beyond dark roads and deadly opponents. Maybe it's time for a new nickname. Gerald "The Finishing Machine" Strebendt is finished. That guy exists no more. I wonder what sort of man will take his place.

ABOUT THE AUTHORS

Mike Arnold is a trial attorney in Eugene, Oregon. He grew up in Parkville, Missouri, and moved to Oregon to attend law school. He tells stories for a living, delivering a narrative through facts and evidence to juries around the state. Often, these courtroom stories end with a **jury's two-word verdict**. Mike also enjoys telling stories to his daughter. These tend to be more complicated tales that reveal, to Abigail's dismay, that someone in the family is actually an alien or a robot.

Mike gained notoriety as an attorney when he stood on the courthouse steps as **Ammon Bundy's attorney** and told the remaining occupiers of the Malheur Wildlife Refuge to «please stand down.» In the aftermath of the standoff he was credited with assisting in the negotiation of a **peaceful resolution** for the four remaining holdouts of the Oregon occupation.

Another of Mike's murder cases was featured on a **CBS "48 Hours"** **episode** entitled «Trail of Tears.» Mike is also the host of a legal podcast called "Law Is War with Mike Arnold," which includes episodes with analysis of the Ammon Bundy (Oregon Standoff) verdict, murder of Nancy Cooper, trial objections, jury selection, jury nullification, etc. (**Purchase** a Gerald "The Finishing Machine" Strebendt **t-shirt** to help support him in his MMA comeback.)

Ep. 6: Was He Framed For Murder?
The True Crime Story of Nancy Cooper

Emilia Gardner is an Oregon attorney. Reading was her first love, and there were no bounds to what genre of book she could and would curl up with and enjoy. A love of writing soon followed, but it would never take the place of consuming the words on the page written by others. Emilia is a straightforward woman and attorney, and her communication style is evident in her writing: simple, to the point, and effective.

OTHER BOOKS BY THE AUTHORS:

VersusPublishing.com - MikeArnold.com